THE
SECOND
SUMMER
OF LOVE

HOW DANCE MUSIC
TOOK OVER THE WORLD

ALON SHULMAN

THE
SECOND
SUMMER
OF LOVE

HOW DANCE MUSIC
TOOK OVER THE WORLD

ALON SHULMAN

JOHN BLAKE

Published by John Blake Publishing,
The Plaza,
535 Kings Road,
Chelsea Harbour,
London SW10 0SZ

www.johnblakebooks.com

www.facebook.com/johnblakebooks
twitter.com/jblakebooks

First published in hardback in 2019

Hardback ISBN: 978 1 78946 075 9
Trade Paperback ISBN: 978 1 78946 090 2

British Library Cataloguing-in-Publication Data:

A catalogue record for this book is available from the British Library.

Design by www.envydesign.co.uk

Printed and bound in Great Britain by Clays Ltd, Elcograf S.p.A.

1 3 5 7 9 10 8 6 4 2

Every reasonable effort has been made to trace copyright-holders of material
reproduced in this book, but if any have been inadvertently overlooked the
publishers would be glad to hear from them.

John Blake Publishing is an imprint of Bonnier Books UK
www.bonnierbooks.co.uk

This book is dedicated to my wonderful wife Samantha and our children Felix, Lara and Serena.

Thank you, my lovelies, for making each and every day a Summer of Love for me.

Love One, Love All.

CONTENTS

In the beginning there was Jack
And Jack had a groove
And from this groove came the grooves of all grooves
And while one day viciously throwing down on his box
Jack boldly declared, 'Let there be house,'
And house music was born

'My House' by Rhythm Controll
featuring Chuck Roberts

INTRODUCTION

OUR GUIDES

I am very fortunate to have incredible direct access to some of the most important and influential people who were present at the birth of acid house and/or involved in the global spread of electronic music and club culture. This first-class cast of characters have shared their personal insights and experiences with me, and therefore with you, that give us a truly first-hand account of the scene. The scene as seen through their eyes. The eyes that were the lookouts for an entire generation. The Watchmen, if you will.

Cultural history can never just be about dates and facts. Sure, the people, the places and the events are essential to the story, but to fully understand what went on and where it left us you need to get into the very essence of the feelings and emotions of the people who were there. A spreadsheet listing the raves alongside dates and attendance figures means nothing. Firstly, the nature of the illicit events and the spontaneous appearance of them means that they often went unrecorded. To be fair, people weren't there to record history, they were there to dance, and each of them would then drift away until the next time. As Keyser Söze said, '... convincing the world he didn't exist. And like that – poof – he's gone.' You can't understand the scale of the experience and the raw energy of a free 2,000-person unlicensed rave in the middle of a forest if you are comparing it with a festival crowd of 200,000 who've each paid the big bucks to be there. Without knowing what our guides were thinking and why they were thinking it you couldn't begin to understand how dance music took such a hold on society.

Some of our guides on this journey were so essential to the story of dance music as we know it that without their drive and determination the whole genre could have fizzled out. These legendary people had a vision and a single-mindedness to deliver on something so new that even the 'coolest of the cool' at the time didn't know what was going on. Of course, by this point, unless you were The Fonz, you'd have been delusional to think you were the 'coolest of the cool' – even the word 'cool' wasn't cool. No one was cool and at the same time everyone was cool. Cool?

Individually and collectively, what these people fought for and created has helped to shape nearly every aspect of contemporary life. Much of what we do today and the way we do it owes something to the doors they kicked in, the boundaries they shoulder-barged and the hurdles they knocked over. Having knocked stuff down they then built new stuff back up. Their initial inspirations and what they helped create is here forever. They were and are part of something so special that it broke down cultural, racial and political divides and smashed the pieces so completely that they could never be put back up. They, along with thousands upon thousands – no, millions upon millions – of you have turned global youth culture into a powerful unified nation: 'One Nation Under a Groove' – feet don't fail me now.

So, without further ado, I'd like to welcome you aboard and introduce you to the guides who will join you on this journey. 'Enjoy This Trip!'

ALFREDO – The Alchemist

BRANDON BLOCK – The Jester

CARL COX – The King

CARL LOBEN – The Commentator

CYMON ECKEL – The Voice

DANNY RAMPLING – The Pioneer

DAVE SWINDELLS – The Observer

FATBOY SLIM – The Funk Soul Brother

GRAEME PARK – The Northern Crusader

IRVINE WELSH – The Wordsmith

JAMIE CATTO – The Cosmic Healer

JAY STRONGMAN – Daddy Cool

JON PLEASED WIMMIN – Mr Blonde

MARK MOORE – The Superfly Guy

MIKE & CLAIRE MANUMISSION – The Free Spirits

MOBY – The Thinker

MR C – The Geezer

NANCY NOISE – The Balearic Queen

NICK HALKES – The Insider

NICKY HOLLOWAY – The Ringmaster

PAUL OAKENFOLD – The Guvnor

PETE HELLER – Mr Big Love

RUSTY EGAN – The Instigator

TERRY FARLEY – The Rock

TINTIN CHAMBERS – The Optimist

TREVOR FUNG – The Catalyst

Get a flavour of what our guides are about in Appendix A.

SETTING THE SCENE

We're going to look at the meteoric rise of dance music. So what? Good point, why should we care? After all, there have been many musical movements that led on to many other musical movements. So many bands that paved the way for other bands. Without blues you probably wouldn't have had rock 'n' roll, jazz plus soul equals funk, Bros minus the bass player equals Bros, AC/DC minus Bon Scott plus Brian Johnson equals AC/DC, Queen minus Freddie Mercury does not equal Queen, Prince plus sampling minus Hendrix equals Bruno Mars … so what's so special about dance music? The answer, my learned friends, is refreshingly simple: dance music minus or plus anything is still dance music and the more you take away or add the bigger and better it gets. Really? Yes, dance music has evolved continuously since its inception and all the elements that make it what it is today can be found at a moment in time, a moment that we now refer to as the Second Summer of Love.

The Second Summer of Love was powered by acid house,

the greatest musical revolution since rock 'n' roll. Acid house seemed to come out of nowhere. One minute you'd be grooving in your brogues and shoulder pads at an upmarket nightspot or getting down like Mr Brown in your clobber that made you look like a cross between a Victorian street urchin and an audience member of Soul Train, then from nowhere you'd suddenly pop up in a basement in the back of beyond sporting dungarees and a super-sized T-shirt and look at the people dressed just as you were a week or two earlier and think, 'Man, these people just don't get it.' Within a few months you'd see thousands of people dressed just like you had been with their dungarees and oversized T-shirts, waving their hands madly like something resembling a cross between an air-traffic controller and a nudist running through a swarm of bees. You'd look at these wide-eyed Bedlamites and think, 'Man, these people just don't get it.'

Eventually, one day you'd be in a club bustin' a move or two, throwing some shapes and wearing that latest something or other, when you'd notice someone staring at you and your crew and you'd suddenly realise what they were thinking: 'Man, these people just don't get it.' Hopefully, you wouldn't care and keep on dancing. The scene was growing at such a rate that no one could keep up and this was before the emergence of the internet, when suddenly everyone would need everything now, now, now! Acid house, and the dance music that followed on from it, would go on to have such an impact that its shock waves are still being felt three decades on.

The Second Summer of Love began in England in 1988 following an exciting summer in 1987 which set the conditions needed for the explosion of '88. For most it was just one summer (that stretched from January to September-ish), but its repercussions and vibrations carried on throughout 1989 and

1990 and arguably into the mid-90s, well into 1994 when its echo finally subsided. By this point dance music was everywhere, a global phenomenon that couldn't be labelled a fad, a craze or even really labelled at all. It transcended race, class, sexuality and cultural divides and created a new way of looking at the world and at each other. Its influence is immense and continues to shape every aspect of daily life.

* * *

Dance music is not just about music, it is about a culture that sprang up with the help of the underground of Detroit and Chicago. Try as it might, it couldn't seem to break through with enough force to allow it to flourish unaided. It would take a more gentle and organic approach to get there, and acid house and the culture around it would be that catalyst which, over the summer of 1988, inadvertently went on to create something that would change youth culture forever. The Second Summer of Love was a youth movement with music pumping through its veins but with a new outlook and world view at its heart. It crossed the Atlantic, and that's when it all happened. It went from a simmering cauldron in the UK that was starting to bubble up to something global that just boiled over. Cups of tea all round. Milk and two sugars?

What could possibly have happened to create something so far-reaching?

To find out, I suppose the best place to start is at the beginning.

IN THE BEGINNING

House. The place where we live. A simple word with a universally recognised meaning. Or so we thought. By the end of the 80s house was so much more to a whole generation. It was a type of music, a lifestyle, a culture and a phenomenon that would go on to take the world by storm and shape global youth culture.

House quickly became the umbrella term for dance music, the sound of the clubs, which quickly spread via parties and radio to the mainstream. It spawned what we now know as electronic music and its many first-cousins including techno, EDM, trance, big beat, drum 'n' bass, deep house, jungle, trip hop, garage, hardcore, gabba, acid house, grime, acid jazz, ambient and breakbeat. No family party would be complete without the eccentric relative, the life and soul of the party throwing shapes on the dancefloor, smiling and sweating, full of joy and love, not caring what they look like or what you think of them, but just enjoying the moment. Nice to see you, Uncle Acid House.

Dance music has conquered the world. It is everywhere. It has spawned a massive global industry that incorporates artists, clubs, albums, soundtracks, fashion, retail, sport, brands, plus politics, advertising, movies, TV, clubs, all generating tens of billions of dollars every year. It has even spawned this book. It has remained the foremost youth movement of the last three decades and continues to grow and evolve.

And it all started with house.

'Oh, no it didn't!' I can imagine the shouts of disapproval and agitated people leaping out of their chairs with that statement as I write. And they'd be right. So let me rephrase:

It DIDN'T all start with house. Gasp!

But surely it had to start somewhere, and for that matter what is 'it'? Already I can see problems ahead. Everyone has an idea of what 'it' is but explaining it (or should I say explaining what 'it' is) could become one of those endless threads on social media that goes nowhere. Sometimes a concept can't be defined and sometimes, like one of those team-building trust exercises when you fall backwards and hope that Doreen from Accounts will be there to catch you, you need to just jump in with a bit of blind faith. Take funk. We all think we know what it is, but knowing that it is more than just a type of music makes it as difficult to quantify as it is to recognise. Hearing James Brown and seeing him 'Get On The Good Foot' is definitely funky, but it takes the genius that is Bootsy Collins, a sentient being who radiates pure funk, to give it a definition that makes no sense at all and yet couldn't make more sense. Funk is all about The One. Ya dig? Thank you, Bootsy.

For our purposes, 'it' is a culture born out of a state of mind and based around a shared love of music coupled to a sense of freedom that not only spawned multiple genres of new music but also created new ways and places to listen to them – and by listen we don't just mean hear but we really mean experience the music with like-minded people of all nationalities, races and sexual persuasions from every conceivable type of background. Something was created that quickly broke down divides and barriers and had a planet following and believing a unifying message – something that vote-hungry politicians and leaders strive for now but will never achieve. Perhaps they should look, listen and learn how this all came about.

There are lots of claimants to the originator's crown. Following some of the threads on social media with people putting their cases forward can make you see that some people are so personally vested in the lifestyle and the scene that you can see there is some validity to what they say. It is easier to point out where things *didn't* start than to pinpoint the moment when they did. I wouldn't want to throw my hat in the ring and fuel these endless back and forth discussions, but I think we can all agree that, as important as Jeremy Healy and Boy George have been to club culture (no pun intended – seriously), their July 1989 outing from E-Zee Possee featuring MC Kinky, 'Everything Starts with an E', was not the beginning of anything.

You can't start talking about the Second Summer of Love and the acid house explosion without looking at the First, where you'd imagine the seeds would have been sown. Then there are the pioneering electronic artists that helped pave the way, as well as the DJs who introduced the wider world to acid house and created club culture. Locations also feature heavily, with key places like Detroit, Manchester, London, Ibiza and Chicago as well as clubs like the Paradise Garage, Warehouse, Spectrum and Shoom. We've also got technological contenders like the 1200, 808, 909 and 303. Sound is important too, from the squelchy to the boom-boom. Plus we've also got to discount the charlatans and pretenders as well as the hard-done-by and disillusioned.

The Second Summer of Love itself takes place at different times for different people. We seem to like labels and '1988' is one that has been regularly stamped as the date when we all apparently came together on a big dancefloor filled with love and immediately started grooving away to new sounds while exploring new possibilities. Of course, those experiencing 1988 were enjoying the influence of those whose Summer of Love was in fact 1987. The majority had their moment in 1989 and 1990 when the scene became more widespread and more easily accessible.

It was a life-changing voyage of discovery for a generation and has continued to inspire and influence generations of 'explorers' on their own journey. With the online world making everything so much more accessible, anyone can be the first to discover 'new' things which of course are not new to those that already experience them. A bit like Columbus jumping for joy when he became the first person to see his New World, which must have been a baffling sight to the locals who had been living there quite happily for thousands of years.

We think of summer as a few months when the sun hopefully shines and we are more carefree than usual before real life drops back in. This has led to a misconception that the Second Summer of Love ran for a few months in 1988. That is not the case. After lots of research and interviews with those at the forefront of what was going on, this book covers the Second Summer of Love from its first seeds in the mid-80s to it sprouting in the latter half of 1987 and on to its heyday throughout 1988 *and*

1989, followed by its warm glow until the early 90s by when enough seeds had been sown to turn the dance music tree into a massive orchard, with each tree bearing fruit (of varying quality it must be said) and with the whole world seemingly liking those apples.

> **TINTIN CHAMBERS:** Acid house, the Spirit of Ibiza, I think is something different to one person than to another. There was magic to be had in the music, in the atmosphere and as the scene developed (I think there would have been just a thousand people into this when I joined) in the camaraderie of understanding you were part of something special, something different that was pure and unknown.

The key is in the title. 'Second Summer of Love'. Not the first, but the runner-up, a moment of influence that was itself influenced. This is a very British moment, and not because it came in second. It is heavily propelled by incredible musicians, producers, DJs and venues in the USA and pushed forward by a moment on the Balearic island of Ibiza when the stars seemed to align. That's not saying that house and acid house records didn't originate in the States and that the Balearic style didn't come from Ibiza. I'm also not implying that a bunch of British banditos stole these things and put their Union Jacked label on them. The conditions were spot on to bring a wide range of influences together within the reach of a uniquely talented and forward-thinking bunch of people at exactly the moment when they were looking to create something new, and a public was waiting to be shown a new direction. Like Dr Frankenstein, they worked hard, connected the dots and joined all the pieces together in time for the lightning storm to strike just at the exact instant as they pulled the lever. They were about to unleash a monster. 'It's alive!'

The story of acid house, the Second Summer of Love and dance music is a story about inspiration and evolution. We need to examine the influences, the influencers and the influenced while looking forwards and backwards (and in some cases sideways). It is a story that has no end and, while it has a beginning, that is not likely to be the start of the whole story or even the start of your story.

Imagine you are Christopher Columbus and heading into the unknown. It is only really unknown to you, but nevertheless you don't know what you will find or where you will find it. Suddenly you see the Promised Land – it is all you imagined and more, and quickly you immerse yourself in everything this New World has to offer. You don't care who planted the tree whose fruit you are eating, you just know that it is delicious and that you want more. It hasn't occurred to you that you're discovering something that has already been discovered. It didn't need you to witness it to exist, it already existed. As you head on deeper into the unknown, discovering new sights and sounds, you probably give little thought to the original inhabitants left standing on the shore, waving you off on your journey. They were the ones who planted the trees, cut the paths and built the bridges. They learned their craft from legends and became legends themselves. You may not even know who they are, but they continue to shape the world around you. In the middle of the group is a man with a huge smile, both hands raised in the air as he wishes you well. He seems larger than life and you wave back as you turn and head off. He can't know you and you definitely don't know him but you have a sneaking suspicion that somehow this stranger is on the journey with you. You might even remember to try and find out who he is. And possibly one day you'll find out how very influential he is and that his name was Frankie Knuckles.

THE JOURNEY

BY PAUL OAKENFOLD

When I went off to celebrate my birthday in Ibiza on that fateful trip I had no idea that my life was about to change and the impact that the holiday would continue to have. My party happened a couple of days after I first experienced the magic of dancing under the stars at Amnesia and one of my friends said, 'I hope all your dreams come true.' Sitting down now as a DJ and a producer, and reflecting on an entire dance music-based industry and global cultural force that I am a proud part of, I can honestly say that my hopes and dreams, which were never this big, have more than come true.

I'd always loved music. I grew up with it in the house, my dad was in a skiffle group and by the time I met Trevor Fung, by chance on a coach, I was a bedroom DJ. I told Trevor that I wanted to get into music and he was surprised when I told him I was a chef but didn't try to persuade me to stick to the day job. We became firm friends, he actually went on to give me my first professional gig and we remain very good friends to this day. In fact it was because Trevor was running a bar in Ibiza that summer that we went there for my birthday, and it he who introduced us to Amnesia where we witnessed Alfredo sharing his Balearic message.

That story helps me sum up what the dance music club culture is all about – friendship. It creates moments where new friends are established and old friendships are strengthened, and introduces an entire generation to each other with a unifying calling card. It is a creative world that allows everyone to add their own stamp on the experience. We move as one. From the DJs and live acts to the clubbers via the designers, promoters, producers and club characters, there is no uniform and no 'right way' to be, you can be yourself and enjoy whatever part of the experience takes your fancy. It is all about living life to the full and having fun. DJs don't go out to work, they go out to play, and that sense of enjoyment is what helps lift the crowd and take them on the journey with the DJ.

Being interviewed for this book made me realise just how lucky we are. Not just the DJs, but all of us who get to enjoy this incredible creative landscape that now exists. Sounds very grand, but mixing the paints at the beginning was a lot of fun, and looking at some of the mad adventures and near misses that happened in the early years of acid house and across the years that make up our Summer of Love I'm amazed we ended up where we did. Maybe it's because so many people embraced the scene and fell in love with the culture so quickly that it took off the way that it did, and it's because of the sheer quality coupled with the sense of freedom that it seemed to instantly become such a dominant force. Maybe with a slow burn it would have fizzled out. I don't think that would or could have happened, but you never know!

When I look at how quickly dance music grew I am amazed that such an unstructured thing could take hold so firmly – and continues to deliver so much quality. Looking back now and hearing how much great music is produced in every corner of the world, it is clear that when we started our scene and launched the first Balearic and acid house club nights like Spectrum and Future we already had the blueprint of a sound and a culture to follow that had been developed in cities like Chicago, New York and Detroit, with DJs like Larry Levan, Juan Atkins, Frankie Knuckles, Marshall Jefferson, Derrick May, Ron Hardy and Tony Humphries. These guys also had a musical blueprint that allowed them to incorporate their influences from disco producers like Giorgio Moroder to the amazingly futuristic Kraftwerk into their sound. From the start it was all about the music, but in an inclusive way. Not being in the know was no barrier to getting involved – we were all learning on the job. The music we danced to made us happy and we even had our own emblem – the yellow smiley.

What I always find amazing is the timing. The music, the DJs, the audience, the venues, they all came together at the same time backed up by a huge outpouring of creativity. The political climate was pretty gloomy and young people were looking for something new – and we had it! This wasn't like some big brand launching an overpriced perfume to those that could afford it with some cynical attempt to reach out to the 'yoof'. We sprayed everyone and anyone who came near and the beauty is we all owned it and wanted everyone to experience it. Things happened quickly, with the growing crowds wanting more and more and not just on the weekends. Weekday clubbing wasn't for everyone, but we wanted to play and the people wanted to come. Most people would party all weekend and go to work all week, just living for the weekend, when they could let go and be part of whichever dance tribe they wanted to join. Some of us felt that we had entered our own paradise and couldn't go back to the daily grind – we looked for new ways to forge careers that went hand in hand with our new state of mind.

With so much in place and a big regular crowd of happy clubbers, it didn't take long for everyone to call '88 the Second Summer of Love. We were riding the wave of the year before and by the time the wave hit the public as a whole it had turned into a tsunami sweeping everyone along for the ride. Every night had something going on and what was really great was that the crowd let us DJs experiment. You could drop a classical piece into your set and people cheered – we were creating our own identity and our own sound. We brought the American DJs over here and they in turn took us over there. We partied in clubs, bars, fields, hangars, warehouses and everywhere else, seven days a week, and then there were the albums, the singles, the visuals, the sound systems, the lighting, the flyers, the posters, the clothing. We even had our own look and our own language. Without realising it we'd created an industry.

Fast-forward to today and the dance and electronic music scene is at the forefront of many aspects of everyone's day-to-day life, even if they don't realise it. It influences high street fashion, language, big brands, computer games, film and television and is found in every strata of commercial, personal and cultural life. It contributes billions to economies all around the world, employs hundreds of thousands of people and entertains many millions of people every day. As for me, I am still riding the wave and haven't stopped since getting off the plane from that first Ibizan summer. As a producer and remixer my studio is always at full capacity, I get to remix major artists and release new artists on my label, and as a DJ I am fortunate to be able to experience amazing audiences around the world and to play unique sets at special locations that I could never have imagined being at, including the FIFA World Cup, the Great Wall of China, Stonehenge and on Mount Everest.

Dance music really has conquered the world and we're a better place for it. From humble beginnings and with plenty of hurdles to get over, it is now an unstoppable force that will be with us forever. The whole scene just grows and grows and with the rise of social media we can share great moments with like-minded people all over the world in real time. Just like at that first night at Amnesia, strangers become friends, friends become great friends, and great friends become friends for ever.

The greatest thing about the culture that drives the scene is that we all keep discovering or are introduced to new sounds, new technologies and new concepts that expand our understanding of what we are capable of achieving, which keeps us on our toes, keeps the whole scene fresh and relevant, and nurtures the next generation of artists and new musical subgenres. And it makes a lot of people very happy, which can only be a good thing.

Keep smiling and keep dancing!

Peace and love,

Paul Oakenfold
Los Angeles, 2019

A MOMENT IN TIME

Let's imagine that it is some point in 3,000 BC, probably a Thursday, on what is currently known as Salisbury Plain in Wiltshire, England. Although the concept of dates, place names and countries has yet to be thought of, if you were beamed there now from the present you'd probably be wondering what the weekend had in store.

Thag was resting. The hunt had been good and his belly was full. Of course, he had no notion of what a weekend was. He needed to conserve his energy, for tomorrow he would move from hunting duties to dragging duties. A few hundred metres away, although distance for him was measured in how long it would take to get somewhere, the current dragging party was getting ready for the last big pull to get the giant stone to its position in the circle. No one remembered why the ancestors had decided on this spot, but it seemed like a good place to celebrate and worship, and when finished would be the perfect place for the big family groups and local tribes to come together.

Get-togethers were the only times when Thag felt truly at ease. He enjoyed seeing old friends and meeting new ones, especially when they brought all the exciting things that they seemed to create or find. Carefully carved antlers could be blown and made new sounds, and some of the visitors could create noises using animal hides that had them all swaying together, long into the night. The stones were arranged in what we now call a circle and were positioned so that on special nights the sunlight and moonlight would shine through them to enhance the revelry. The people always came, it was what they were supposed to do, and when it was time to go they left. That was how it had always been and probably how it always would be.

'I wonder if there's anything else we could do?' thought Thag as he idly hit a small stone against one of the large stones that was already in place. He always felt slightly empty when the dancing stopped and he dreamed of a never-ending celebration, when he could feel the specialness that the get-togethers left him with forever. The stone-on-stone sound was pleasing to him so he did it again. And then again. And then again. He just kept on doing it, hit, hit, hit, hit, hit – he was absorbed in the rhythm and it helped him think about the other sounds he enjoyed *and how they'd fit in to this pattern. When he looked up he saw that he'd been joined by several others, some tapping along, some just staring, but some were swaying. The beat seemed to have a hypnotic effect on everyone and left them all feeling energised. After a couple of hours Thag rested and the beat was picked up and carried on by others. The elders looked at Thag and his striking stick with renewed curiosity, and Thag was approached by some of the females who had never shown any interest in him before.*

This new sound had a profound effect on the tribe, with this beat becoming an important part of their culture. The kind of stones and rocks they used and the positioning of them is what made this sound so unique, and although this new 'technology' spread far and wide those in the know made the journey back to experience Thag's groove, which seemed to sound better when he tapped it out. The echo that was created enhanced the sound and the energy that seemed to emanate from the structure that we now call Stonehenge and was part of the attraction to the tribal dancers. The repetitive beat was born.

Thank you, Thag – you rock!

Over the millennia Thag was forgotten and people felt that the human desire in coming together to hear music and to dance was as natural as eating and sleeping. Instruments were made in every shape and size and from every known material, and played in a multitude of styles. At the same time dance became one of the foremost methods of social interaction and a part of courtship as well as celebration, which meant that fashion became an essential part too. Throw in changes in communication, technology and the 'rules' of society in the mid-part of the twentieth century, zap it with some electricity, 'invent' the teenager, give them very little to do and to call their own and we are nearly ready to discover what 'it' is.

HISTORY IN THE MAKING

THE (FIRST) SUMMER OF LOVE '67

All across the nation
Such a strange vibration
People in motion
There's a whole generation
With a new explanation
'San Francisco' by John Phillips of The Mamas & the Papas.
Sung by Scott McKenzie.

'If you're going to San Francisco / Be sure to wear some flowers in your hair'. Everything has to start somewhere, and the junction of Haight and Ashbury, San Francisco, was the epicentre of the Summer of Love. On 14 January 1967 artist Michael Bowen produced the first mass gathering of 'hippies' at Golden Gate Park. His Human Be-In attracted over 30,000 people and publicised the hippie look, fashions and way of life to the nation. It was at this event that LSD pioneer Timothy Leary first urged everyone to 'turn on, tune in, drop out', which was a perfect case of right phrase, right time. The music scene had been the driving force throughout '65 and '66 and the new sounds made the division between youth culture and everyone else wider. Students across the country started to drop out and headed to San Francisco with the expectation of sex, drugs and rock 'n' roll. Within a couple of months the numbers of people converging on the Haight-Ashbury district was out of control. And not in a good way. Very quickly the neighbourhood deteriorated, with vast numbers of people having nowhere to stay and nothing to eat and with the new homelessness adding to the growing drug problems and localised crime wave. Some local groups and residents tried to alleviate the suffering and formed the Council of the Summer of Love to help with housing, food, medical supplies and sanitation, and inadvertently gave the whole experience a name.

So the original Summer of Love was essentially a local welfare group with the uphill task of trying to get thousands of people who had little chance of focusing on the immediate present to focus on their future. That could have been the end of that, another footnote in humankind's long history of destroying everything they come into contact with. However, at the same time as thousands of people concentrated on growing their hair and kicking back, the political landscape quickly encompassed social, racial and sexual changes which shared media coverage with the goings-on in California. This now included festivals like Fantasy Fair and Monterey where artists like Jimi Hendrix, The Who, Janis Joplin, Jefferson Airplane and the Grateful Dead created the soundtrack to the summer. The media like catchy phrases and the Summer of Love fitted the bill. This also meant that it wasn't localised to San Francisco and encouraged 'kids' across the USA to 'tune in'. The US government had a lot on its plate in the latter half of the 60s and by the time they realised that the clean-cut youths they'd marched off to Vietnam were now long-haired free-thinking freedom seekers it was too late. With its own uniform, soundtrack and ideals, youth culture had become a force to be reckoned with and one that any politician looking for votes couldn't ignore. And not just in the States. Music was the driving force and music doesn't stop at borders.

Across the pond the UK was at the very forefront of what was going on – although what exactly was going on was anybody's guess. Little happenings popped up all over the place and the psychedelic music scene started to find places to call home like the short-lived UFO Club in Tottenham Court Road, which ran from December 1966 until October 1967. Venues across London suddenly enjoyed psychedelic lighting, a switched-on crowd and music that still stands strong today. Getting to America was something that most bands wanted to do, with the growing scene there reported across the UK's media – even in black-and-white on fuzzy-screened TVs it all looked so exciting. Events like the Technicolour Dream at Alexandra Palace, where bands like The Crazy World of Arthur Brown and Pink Floyd with their light shows entertained the eclectic crowd for fourteen hours, still seemed very British.

Everything in the UK seems to have a football influence and 1966 was the year when football changed everything after the World Cup was won. In other football-related news, at the end of 1966 a former footballer, Brian Thompson, wanted to book Geno Washington and the Ram Jam Band. The band's management didn't make it easy and in the end they convinced him to book three lesser-known bands in support. A more experienced promoter would have said no, but Thompson ended up also booking the Jimi Hendrix Experience, Cream and Pink Floyd.

Unwittingly he had booked three of the greatest bands of all time, featuring three of the greatest guitarists. Thanks, Brian. With the princely sum of £1 per ticket, the unusually named Barbeque 67 held on 29 May in Spalding, Lincolnshire, attracted 6,000 ticket-bearers and another 12,000 who turned up but didn't get in to what was the UK's first rock festival.

The Summer of Love was in full swing and by the end of it what had started as counter-culture became the mainstream cultural way of life for the majority of young people. Young now wasn't an age thing, it was a feeling – if you felt young and wanted in then you were in. Different scenes sprang up with their own music, fashion, crowd and clubs driving them in different directions. Rock, soul, jazz, blues all had their place, with everyone dancing to a different beat – but at least they were now all dancing.

The Summer of Love lasted one glorious summer and didn't have enough time to take hold firmly before it fragmented. With nothing to compare it to and without enough time to create a space for hindsight, the youth didn't have the opportunity to realise how powerful their collective voice could be. This kept the emerging music and social culture on the fringes, made it seem more subversive than it was, and with less visibility came less influence. People had quickly gone from being participants to being spectators and with the loss of momentum the scene fizzled out. The Second Summer of Love wouldn't make the same mistake.

THE BIRTH OF DANCE MUSIC ...
AS WE KNOW IT

People have always danced and we can assume that, from its inception, music played a part in this. From mating rituals and tribal dances to shamanic shufflings and victory celebrations, dance has been a part of the human experience since before the dawn of recorded time. The dance music that we're exploring here is predominantly electronic music and that means – the clue being in the name – that for this we need electricity. So fast-forward to the twentieth century.

Dancing in clubs was nothing new. The First World War had helped jazz from the USA spread to Europe, and gramophones and radio kept those feet a-tappin'. Localised bands like Sweet Emma and Her Preservation Hall Jazz Band could now be heard anywhere on 78rpm with electricity or anywhere you could crank a handle. The Jazz Age of the 1920s and 30s was all about dancing to the latest sounds from what we now know to be some of the greatest musicians ever. People danced up close to legends in the making such as Cab Calloway, Duke Ellington,

Louis Armstrong and Charlie Parker. By the 40s people were also dancing to gramophone records in clubs and some clubs became famous for having the hottest American discs before everyone else. These clubs moved away from the big-band and dinner experience towards continuous dancing, with the selector entertaining the crowd (and, at some point, steering the crowd and riding the dancefloor thus gaining the title of Disc Jockey). Sounds familiar. By the end of the Second World War, clubs were springing up based around someone playing records. In 1947, the enterprising Paul Pacine launched his Whisky à Go-Go in Paris, the forerunner of London's WAG club, with records only. The popularity, coupled with low entertainment costs, allowed him to open up several more of these places, which were known as discothèques.

The 1950s saw teenagers burst onto the scene as a whole new species that didn't seem to have existed before. Long hair, short hair, zoot suits, surfing, rock 'n' roll, reefer madness, pimples, Italian coffee, pop music that your parents didn't like – the possibilities seemed endless. As the 60s began, all over the world everything new was embraced – from the Beatles to the miniskirt, sexual liberation to scooters, Cliff Richard's (prophetic) 'Summer Holiday' to space exploration, Elvis Presley to Muhammad Ali, there was a breaking down of cultural barriers as the youth came together. Magazines, radio stations and above all television and albums brought everything that was new and exciting straight into people's homes and hearts. The youth rallied against Vietnam and were captivated by the Summer of Love and then marvelled as the 60s came to a close and a human being walked on the moon. The possibilities seemed endless. The future was most definitely theirs and it was most definitely now!

* * *

Maybe it was because of the amount of happenings and gigs that were taking place everywhere, the invisible barrier between white and black, the sheer volume of great bands or the fact that the hit parade was the focus for most artists and labels, but the underground club scene was one area that didn't fulfil its potential. That part of the counter-culture seemed to go into a slump. It was in a funk, which was both the problem and the solution. The decade following the Summer of Love saw an explosion in musical experimentation. The 70s are now associated with struttin' one's stuff to a *Saturday Night Fever* disco vibe but it was also the time when reggae, funk, real disco, early electro and punk went global and changed the cultural landscape. From the Sex Pistols and David Bowie to Parliament/ Funkadelic and James Brown's Super Heavy Funk, people were coming together and dancing. By together, I mean mostly within their style tribe. On the streets of New York DJs were putting beats, breaks, samples and records together to create what we now know of as hip hop. For the most part the scenes didn't – I should probably go further and say couldn't – mix. Despite this, things were happening and it is here that the beats that would shape dance music came together.

Like chemists in the lab, drummers were experimenting with new rhythms, designed to keep people moving. Disco was creating a euphoric dancefloor atmosphere that was moving at about 120bpm. This speed, as it turns out, is the optimum tempo for dancing to, allowing the body to react to two beats per second. We now take this for granted and subconsciously dancefloors fill and stay full at 120bpm. This is the speed of the heartbeat at exercise and induces a trancelike primeval state that dancers can sustain for hours.

Two drummers stand out for their contribution to the dancefloor. Clyde Stubblefield, the original Funky Drummer, created such a solid groove for James Brown that I'd say this was the eureka moment which was also the backbone for hip hop, rap and sampling. Clyde's long, repetitive, minimal solo, punctuated with the odd grunt from Mr Brown and backed by the band, was like Al Jolson talking at the end of the song recordings for *The Jazz Singer*. How could this have not happened sooner? It showed what was possible and the clean beat was like a blank canvas waiting for the likes of Public Enemy and NWA to get to work all over it with their spray cans. James Brown calling out for the band to 'give the drummer some' and calling his track 'The Funky Drummer' helped give Clyde the recognition he so rightly deserved. Their amazing live shows put Clyde front and centre alongside the J.B.'s, some of the funkiest guys (and gals) ever, including Fred Wesley, Maceo Parker, Bobby Byrd, Pee Wee Ellis, Vicki Anderson and Bootsy Collins.

Our second stickman was much more behind the scenes. Earl Young was the in-house drummer at Philadelphia Records. He created a revolutionary new sound which became the basis for disco and the dancefloor frenzy that would become house. He based his beat on a marching band, which he realised makes you keep the rhythm. What was revolutionary about Earl's groove was that the music was secondary and had to fit around his beat. The first track to use this Philly sound was 'The Love I Lost' by Harold Melville & the Blue Notes, which became a massive dancefloor anthem. Rather than simply releasing albums and seven-inch singles, the extended-play (EP) twelve-inch version, often with bonus tracks or different mixes on the B side, became a viable format. Clubbers and partygoers rushed to buy these extended tracks, which meant that singles could chart with minimal promotion and radio play. Suddenly music was being created directly for the dancefloor.

At the same time, there was a growth in musical experimentation using European artists like Kraftwerk as a model (pun intended). Kraftwerk will always be recognised as one of the most influential acts in dance music, whose cutting-edge use of electronic sounds and technology influenced the originators and influencers of the electronic dance music scene. Kling Klang Studio in Düsseldorf is electronic music's Graceland. Electronic music had been experimented with since the start of the twentieth century, and as confidence in what could be achieved grew, so manipulating the speed of the tapes and adding in loops made the new sounds more usable. By the 1960s bands including the Beach Boys and the Beatles were incorporating some of these techniques into their music. The Moog synthesiser was the next big step. Used by bands like Pink Floyd and Yes, the synthesiser shaped a European sound being created by the likes of Tangerine Dream, Can, Brian Eno and Kraftwerk. The German Kosmiche Musik movement (sometimes referred to as 'krautrock') often worked with a 4/4 beat that had a heavy bass drum. Pioneered by the drummer Jaki Liebezeit, it was first used on the debut album from Neu!, the band formed in 1971 by Klaus Dinger and Michael Rother after their split from Kraftwerk.

In 1972 the most important technological breakthrough happened, one that would change clubbing for ever and without which the scene could never have taken off. The Technics 1200 turntables were launched in Japan and were an instant hit. Direct-drive rather than belt-driven, and with easy-to-use (and see-in-the-dark) pitch control, they are just so good, amazingly robust and well designed, the latest versions are almost identical to the forty-year-old originals. The Technics decks gave the DJ all the control needed to mix seamlessly and to create new sounds with spin-backs and scratches. 'Ffff-Freshhhh!'

* * *

Drums, beats, turntables, technology and DJs – no matter which way you mixed these ingredients there could only be one outcome ... and the prototype of modern clubbing was it. DJs could now concentrate on painting a picture with their music and people began to expect this on a night out. The DJ on the mic introducing the next song and injecting the crowd with their own brand of humour, which showed why they hadn't gone into comedy in the first place, was on the way out. The musical craftsman was on the way in. A landmark moment in the rise of the dance music DJ was in February 1983 when Greg Wilson, a jazz-funk DJ on the Wigan Pier and Manchester scene, who later on would appear at the Haçienda and apparently taught a young Norman Cook (then called DJ Quentin) to scratch, was asked to demonstrate a two-turntable beat mix on the influential music show *The Tube*, which would be the first showcase of this new artform on British television. Under the watchful eye of presenter and Squeeze keyboard player Jools Holland, who would go on to showcase every new genre of music for the next thirty-five years (and is still going strong), Greg felt the pressure. Admittedly he was only mixing two identical records and had practised the fader up / fader down move several times, so surely here he could show that this was the future, the way forward. When asked how he did this he came back with the eloquence of a true artist, a champion of the scene and a shining light bringing clubs out of the darkness with his reply: 'You bang them in.' Progress indeed.

The high-profile clubs like Studio 54 were not really about the music. They were playgrounds for the rich and famous to show off, hedonistic but largely safe environments, the places to be seen. What we are more interested in are the places that were the scene. When social anthropologists look back at the origins of club culture they will zero in on one location. Not a club or a venue but an apartment. The New York apartment of David Mancuso, a DJ who threw invitation-only music-driven dance parties in the 70s at his place, known as The Loft. The Loft was all about music. Young clubbers like future superstar DJ David Morales would go to dance and dance and sweat and sweat. It was here that the unifying musical culture and club life of our era was born.

Not everything was glitzy and mirror-balled. There was a whole global scene of what we now call one-nighters, party nights put on in an assortment of venues and spaces bringing fashion, music and like-minded people together. Often unlicensed, these parties were organised by the partygoers themselves and meant that they could spring up with little notice and move to a new location when needed. It was all about word of mouth. Some people reading this now would not believe that everything was promoted with flyers handed out in the streets and in shops and by people hanging around looking for the next happening to go to. Even more amazingly, people actually danced and talked with not a handheld electronic device or selfie in sight.

The one-nighters became a staple of London's nightlife. A big multicultural city with a myriad of creative people looking for something to do was the perfect pop-up party location. In the late 70s, a young man from Wales, funk-loving and zoot-suited, by the name of Chris Sullivan, started throwing all-night parties. Chris was (and still is) a mover and shaker who was able to connect the dots that helped unite the 'it crowd'. He was surrounded by a bunch of people who wanted to have fun and express their individuality. Chris himself was as happy to be front and centre with his Latin-inspired band, Blue Rondo à la Turk, as he was spinning his funk selection behind an unlit makeshift DJ booth. It was Chris who would spot an opportunity to make this legit when he took over the Whisky-a-Go-Go in Wardour Street and renamed it the WAG. It doesn't seem revolutionary now, but Chris had different club nights with different promoters on different nights, which brought clubbing to life for so many and provided the regulars with a smorgasbord of musical delights. The club hosted a massive range of ground-breaking nights and was at the forefront of the early hip hop, house and acid jazz scenes; carefully curated by Chris, it ran for twenty years. The WAG was probably the first place in London's West End where you could hear dance music.

Not everyone had the luxury of four walls and a licence. Some didn't want it, preferring the added danger of the fly-by-the-seat-of-your-pants approach. This underground scene wasn't especially hidden, it was front and centre with thousands of people partying round the clock as long as they could find where that night's party was. They say that the best place to hide is in plain sight, which could be why Dirtbox was so successful. Phil Dirtbox is very tall, made taller with his signature *A Clockwork Orange* style bowler hat, worn at just the right angle. Always smiling, he didn't look like the kind of person running an unlicensed after-hours party and the venues he picked were so visible that it would take a while for the powers that be to cotton on. Like the WAG, Dirtbox's secret recipe was the music. Jay Strongman, one of London's most cutting-edge DJs, was often at the helm and the crowd, invariably made up of clubbers from venues that had just closed, were there to party. There was no intention of going home any time soon and Phil was happy to oblige.

JAY STRONGMAN: Music was really important. So from an early age I associated image with good music. I was really influenced by the whole David Bowie thing, great style and image. I became more aware then of what people were wearing. I went to all the Motown and funk clubs and I remember the importance of reinforcing style and music together. The music was so great. Definitely posers were attracted to clubs like the Mud Club and the WAG but people had gone to those clubs that still loved funk and soul, and a lot are still DJing. With any youth movement you get poseurs.

NANCY NOISE: Before I went to Ibiza I was going to RAW. It was one of the first West End clubs I really got into. I went there for quite a long period. In between the summer of '86 and '87, in London, me and my friends, we were doing RAW, Shake 'n' Fingerpop, the Family Function, Sunday at the Africa Centre. I loved Jazzie B. I was a real Rare Groover, black jacket with the orange lining, a big scarf around my head. I loved all those clubs with Norman Jay.

TERRY FARLEY: When we first started going out, the DJ was very important in the fact that he needed to have the right records and that's all he needed. He had to have all the new records as they were coming out.

As long as the DJ had the right records, the number-one thing the club needed to succeed was to have the best dancers. Every town outside of London (as well as in London) and up until kind of the south Midlands, had their own really good dancers. They were like little crews, but the real stars were this kind of band which had Tommy Mack in it. Tommy was probably the oldest one, he was about twenty-one, and none of them seemed to work. To keep the lifestyle going, they were [allegedly] selling stolen coffee. It sounds ridiculous now, but there was a coffee shortage, and they could get hold of those big tins of coffee. They were just thieves really, but all these kids would dance from Monday night to Thursday night, with Thursday's spot being upstairs at Ronnie Scott's. Sunday would be Crackers and Saturday night would probably be the night they all stayed in because back then most clubs on a Friday and Saturday, if they didn't have a colour bar would have a quota. If I turned up with my black friend, you probably would get in, but if you turned up with four black guys and a white guy, it ain't happening.

Club culture stemmed from the very British acid house scene but the big influence, the daddy of all sounds, the thing that made acid house possible, was house, and that came straight from the USA. In 1977 a venue was opened in New York by Michael Brody that would change everything. The Paradise Garage was the first club to put the DJ front and centre and focus solely on dancing. People didn't go there to look good and stand around talking, they went there to dance and that was all they went there for. It doesn't seem revolutionary now but back then it was unique and could easily have failed. When you entered and felt the power of the sound system created by the legendary Richard Long you knew that you were in for something special. At the centre of this was one of the most special DJs ever – Larry Levan. He didn't just play the records, he composed with them and took his audience on a musical journey that quickly gained him and the club cult status and a loyal following. Larry Levan was all about the music, it made no difference if you were straight or gay, Hispanic, black or white, as long as you danced. Poseurs, pullers and players were still welcome but they had to dance.

TINTIN CHAMBERS: This openness was extremely important. It's what lit the fuse, the roots of it all.

Levan was the world's first superstar DJ, although totally localised to people in the know. Larry was slightly oblivious to his growing global reputation. The club ran for ten years and during that time Larry inadvertently spread his DJ style across the world. In the last year or two of the club it attracted the new breed of up-and-coming UK club DJs.

PAUL OAKENFOLD: That was an incredible experience, really starting to understand a great DJ like Larry Levan, and how he puts his music together. I commissioned him to do his last ever record before he died.

Levan was responsible for the musical direction and cemented the club's position in New York when he brought on New York's number-one DJ, Nicky Siano, who had just been fired from Studio 54. The other DJ he brought in was a guy who loved life and oozed music so much that it dripped from the ceiling. Frankie Knuckles.

Frankie was so special. Everyone that saw and heard him felt this and his influence was instantaneous. Without Frankie, dance music might well have stayed underground in New York. But it didn't. The Paradise Garage was the go-to place for visiting musicians to check out and many took some of the spirit away with them. Tony Wilson's Haçienda, which opened in May 1982 in Manchester, came after he visited the US and people started to get into the music and the style of playing.

Other US cities had small, imitation-version club scenes springing up, but they struggled to get the energy of New York into the dancefloor. Robert Williams, a New York-based club promoter, moved to Chicago where he felt he could do something to change that. He opened a club at 206 South Jefferson Street and called it the Warehouse. He also brought over his secret weapon as the DJ with full creative control over the dancefloor: Frankie Knuckles. It was at the Warehouse where Frankie really made his mark – 'I was born and raised in NY but I grew up in Chicago.' Frankie introduced European electronica like Kraftwerk and Depeche Mode as well as his own production touches into his sets. Frankie's sound was unique and he worked the crowd hard, manipulating the levels and the lighting to supercharge the atmosphere. He was just a pure innovator who understood how to entertain the crowd. One of his well-known party tricks was called 'The Train'. He'd turn all the lights down and play a record called 'Sound of the Vanishing Era', which was made up of stereo recordings of locomotives. He'd manipulate the speakers so that the sound started at the back of the club and made its way to the front. It was as if a train was hurtling towards you. People were screaming and anyone that went to the club regularly remembers their first 'train'. But even when he was messing around it was all about the sound, the likes of which had never been experienced by most of his audience before. Suddenly it wasn't a New York thing any more and people flocked to worship at Frankie's temple. Record shops, bars, everywhere wanted you to know that they had the music you wanted and signs saying 'House Music' started appearing in shop windows. House music was the music of the Warehouse and the Warehouse was the sound of Frankie Knuckles.

Robert Williams also opened the Music Box, with a harder and louder sound, and brought DJ Ron Hardy to give it shape. These two clubs are pivotal and the music produced by the DJs and the clubbers started to appear wherever people wanted to dance, including Ibiza and the UK.

Suddenly, making your own music was a thing. Chicago became a hotbed of young producers creating tracks. They didn't even know they were producers, it was just bit of fun, but the quality of the tracks and the interest from clubbers created a whole new market within the music industry. Frankie had shown them the way and now the likes of Marshall Jefferson, Farley Jackmaster Funk, DJ Pierre and Steve 'Silk' Hurley, with vocalists like Darryl Pandy and Robert Owens and machines like the 303 and the 808, helped spread the message.

In 1982, aged eighteen, Vince Lawrence met Jesse Saunders when he was doing the lighting at a club called The Playground, which was aimed at a teen audience, and where Jesse was the DJ. They started writing music together, producing it, pressing 500 copies at a time and selling the vinyl in clubs and through record stores. After several trips back to the pressing plant, Precision Records, the owner, Larry Sherman, asked them what they were doing with so many records. When they told him they were selling them (at $4 each) he partnered up with them and Trax Records was born. To maximise profits they bought second-hand vinyl for a couple of cents, took the labels off and ground them down before melting them and recycling the vinyl for their new tracks. If you are lucky enough to have an original first pressing of Marshall Jefferson's 'Move Your Body' or Ron Hardy's 'Sensation', then chances are that deep in those grooves there are microscopic traces of thrift-store staples like Liberace and David Cassidy.

Jesse Saunders released 'On and On' in 1984, which is widely considered to be the first house record. The influence of this was enormous. Suddenly, anyone could try to be a star. You didn't need a band, you just needed a beat and a way to make the track. Artists like Marshall Jefferson quickly started releasing tracks and, with a growing club audience to test them on, hits like 'Move Your Body' rocked dancefloors everywhere. Discontinued bits of kit like the Roland TR 808 and the Roland TB 303, which hadn't been popular the first time around, could be picked up very cheaply and suddenly a bedroom was a fully functioning studio. DJ Pierre's squelchy sounding 'Acid Trax', which he created with Spanky and Herb J under their Phuture name, was about to lend its name to a new musical genre that was about to kick-start in the UK. With so much music being produced it wouldn't be long before underground Chicago became mainstream in the UK, and no one could have imagined that the UK would adopt the US sound and export it around the world as well as straight back to the States. It was a bit like the blues sound of Britain's Rolling Stones 'introducing' the blues to big audiences in the country that originally created it.

What the mainstream media, record industry and critics of

house music couldn't understand is why it worked. Theories about the hypnotic effects of the beat, the drugs, the dumbing-down of the youth and even the collapse of civilisation were discussed, and it was widely believed that this was just another fad of club culture where kids on the pull were looking for the next trendy thing. Not on your nelly. A casual observer of the club scene could see that house was not going away and, while it might evolve and develop, it was here to stay. The success of house music and then the explosion of dance culture is easy to explain and you didn't need to be a genius to do it. Just look at any dancefloor. People just like dancing to house music. Full stop.

* * *

There was one more piece of the puzzle that completed the musical tapestry needed to make it all happen. Three high-school friends in the suburb of Belleville, just outside Detroit, came together with a shared love of technology and music. These school kids were not clubbers. They loved music, loved sci-fi and were interested in how we would live in the future. Musically, their big influence was a radio show called *The Electrifying Mojo*. Mojo was/is an enigmatic legendary radio DJ who may or may not actually be Charles Johnson from Little Rock, Arkansas. Mojo played music you just didn't hear anywhere else on the radio in Detroit, including Prince and Kraftwerk.

He had a special relationship with Prince, often playing several hours of his music continuously, including entire albums and all singles plus B sides back to back. Prince, who wasn't speaking to any press, even gave Mojo a full on-air telephone interview in 1986. His show was on WGPR, a black radio station, but Mojo and his audience were colour blind and only cared about great music. If he liked it, he played it, and you could expect George Clinton and Parliament to land with their *Mothership Connection* alongside Gary Numan and the B-52's. This is where the Belleville Three were introduced to electronic music, mainly European, and they saw this as the building block for a futuristic soundscape to a bright new world. To these guys, isolated in the suburbs of Detroit, Mojo was accessible and the key to a musical freedom that they needed to be part of. As early as 1981 Mojo played 'Alleys of Your Mind' by Cybotron on Deep Space Records (created by Juan Atkins, who had been introduced to Mojo at a café after the radio show by his friend Derrick May). You couldn't get more encouragement than the man who was championing the multi-talented genius Prince around the time of 'Sexy Dancer', 'Dirty Mind' and 'Controversy' plugging your music. Especially as Mojo stuck to his guns and played what his heart knew to be right even in the face of audience and critical indifference. While Mojo was championing the *Controversy* album on air, Prince was having a hard time on the ground. The first of the three support acts for the Rolling Stones US tour, Prince, arguably the greatest live performer and dancing multi-instrumentalist ever, was forced off the stage in Los Angeles only three songs into his set when the audience pelted him and his band with garbage.

Kevin Saunderson, Juan Atkins and Derrick May – the Belleville Three – considered themselves agents for change. They experimented with production techniques and different styles which resulted in monumental tracks that still rock the dancefloor, including the very London sound of Kevin Saunderson's Inner City track 'Good Life' and the 1987 masterpiece by Juan Atkins, 'Strings of Life'. The Belleville Three's music was driven by technology and was meant to be a stepping stone to the sound of the future. It was new and didn't have a name. They called it techno for short.

House and techno were finding their place but outside of the small club scene and the few standout crossover tracks the music was struggling to take a firm hold. Leading London club DJs like Noel and Maurice Watson played the early house records at clubs like Delerium but they didn't always go down well. Even the hits struggled to reach a wide audience. Influential London club DJ Mark Moore went on to form S-Express and his 'Theme from S'Express' became a global smash. Purely driven by the club scene, it reached No. 1 in the national charts with the supposed barometer of the country's taste and champion of new music, Radio One, playing catch-up.

Mark Moore is one of the nicest guys you could ever meet, someone who is always smiling and someone who loves music with every fibre of his being. He loves how it makes him feel and how it has shaped his life. Without sounding dramatic, Mark Moore is someone who finds hope where others might see despair. Super-positive, behind the decks at some of the most happening London clubs including Philip Sallon's Mud Club and the WAG, Mark was the right person in the right place to be a very early pioneer of electronic music and early house.

MARK MOORE: We had this brilliant upbringing of pop music. Then after that I got into pop and rock, everything went wrong. My mother got quite ill and they put my brother and me in a home and I became really angry all the time. I remember I put on a record and it sent shivers down my spine, it was talking directly to me. There was this anger that I had heard and suddenly I was affected at a visceral level and I thought suddenly, 'Someone understands what I'm going through,' whereas I hadn't felt that before. Then I thought, 'Let's listen to the Sex Pistols,' so I put on 'God Save the Queen' and at the end of the record, it goes 'no future, no future, no future for you'. How I interpreted that as a fourteen-year-old was that there is no future for you unless you get up and do something about it. I saw it as a positive rather than a negative thing. And then I became a punk overnight. I got into it a bit late. Of course, punk is dying out by '78. We thought we were seeing all these bands that were still punk. The Human League were huge and unknown and underground. The Normal was an electronic record but it was still punk. I found out later that this was actually the recording name of Daniel Miller who went on to set up Mute Records. All this electronic music was making a huge impression on me, I had previously only heard soul and funk in clubs.

TERRY FARLEY: Basically I started going out properly in about '76. All the records were rare groove. I loved the records, the James Browns and the first couple of years of rare groove was great because you're hearing all this stuff you really love, and they are playing them next to hip hop. It's like the 'old school' house events now. I can tell you what they are going to play and I play on a lot of these because I have to do what I have to do, but I really do think about what I'm going to play, how can I play records that I know they know but maybe they haven't heard for a while and that they are going to love. Things like James Brown's 'The Boss', I will love these records forever, but by '87 I was thinking, 'Come on, there's got to be something more.' I was DJing with Paul Oakenfold in about '86, '87, before his holiday to Ibiza. Paul was the resident alongside Pete Tong. I was the warm-up, then Paul, then Pete. Pete was releasing *House Sound of London* then on FFFR so he would play house music. I was playing a bit of reggae, a bit of rare groove, just kind of bubbling the floor up. I used to like the house stuff but the very early house stuff that we were buying didn't sound like that. The very first one I used to play was 'Jack the Groove'. To me, this just sounded like an electro record, it was just faster but made on the same drum machines. The trigger for it all was ecstasy and that was almost like a glue that brought everything together ... I sold my reggae collection to a guy in Slough 'cos I wanted to buy loads and loads of new records. It seemed to me, 'When am I going to play these records?' I wish I still had them because now they are worth a fortune. I think that basically suddenly you could have a whole night of house music and the DJ would mix it up. If you were playing Public Enemy, James Brown and Steve 'Silk' Hurley, you would cut them, that's how it was, like an amateur hip hop DJ. So my moment came later and was when I was hearing this music played at Shoom where Danny Rampling was mixing records together. Then it made sense.

PETE HELLER: I used to go to Glastonbury quite a lot in the 80s and I remember thinking that if only the same vibe was available outside of that short three-day festival. Well, suddenly it was. Of course, the drugginess and escapism complemented things, but essentially, as with punk, there was a desire for something different and that's what was being offered.

January 1987 saw the first house No. 1 in the UK national charts with Steve 'Silk' Hurley's 'Jack Your Body', which took the clubbing community (and Steve) by surprise.

JAY STRONGMAN: We were really lucky because the crowd that Philip Sallon encouraged were really open-minded in the first place. Before the house stuff came out we could play anything from Run DMC to ABBA. We were basically playing everything. It wasn't too difficult for them to adjust to the fact that we were playing these very heavy percussion tracks. The sound engineer at Busby's used to show me how to scratch. He said that you want to kind of mix bpm that are similar. Beats per minute. A lot of disco stuff is between 115 and 125bpm and I realised you could actually mix in some of the disco stuff. I realised you could mix the disco stuff with some of the house stuff as it has got a very similar bpm. My mixing was never great but it wasn't so hard to mix because it was mainly percussion.

MARK MOORE: I've been told I'm a pioneer. I am aware of this pioneer status that people have put on me. I think it's lovely.

Dance music seemed too hit and miss and too localised a scene. Sound, venue, DJs and audience were all in place but in a very fragmented way. There was no coherent electronic music movement and while house had established a niche in the USA which it seemed quite content to stay in, the UK club scene was a whole different animal. Everyone wanted something new, something exciting, something that the diverse fashion-, style- and music-driven groups could unite under. The scene couldn't sustain lots of little cliques going off in every direction without the quality of the clubbing experience becoming too diluted. It needed something big to bring it all together. Not just the next big thing for the club faces and style icons but something for the masses, and not the few. Something that could make you dance together, with friends and strangers, and be part of a collective experience that you could own and contribute to. Ironically, it would be something very small that fuelled the dancefloor explosion, united a generation and broke the shackles holding everything and everyone back.

* * *

You must know what's coming up (wink, wink) at this point in our story. This is a social history that looks at a cultural point just as a nation of youths took a long, hard jump in unison into an unfamiliar world that sways, spins and struts – moving to an organic rhythm that built a thriving global community and brought unity to all. The full-on draft how-to-party communication map was almost in position. All that was missing to light us up and launch our dynamic mirror ball into clubland's orbit was a tiny spark, our most common marking according to any Anglo dictionary, your most important symbol in all of your writing tools and a sign that you won't find within any word in this paragraph. It's a singular monogram, a solitary mark, an initial on its own. Introducing the magic up-all-night party potion in disco biscuit form, a pill with colossal cultural kudos, an almost insignificant small round thing, known to us simply as an …

… E.

MDMA

Looking at the birth of acid house without looking at the ravers' drug of choice would be like a team photo of a cup-winning Chelsea FC team without the manager being in it – they had all the skills needed to win, scored all the goals, made all the plays and dazzled the crowd to come out on top but to make all those things happen in unison they needed their coach to provide the extra wow factor – that special something that would unite such a diverse group of people and make them move as one.

The thing about a book like this is you don't know who is going to pick it up and whether they need things spelled out, and so to avoid any confusion we'd better make something very clear. The drug that fuelled the media hysteria around acid house was not acid or even LSD or anything like that at all. The acid house recipe had elements from a diverse larder that included the 60s, Chicago, Detroit, Ibiza, soul and disco, and would no doubt have found a niche on a dancefloor or two. But like any special recipe it had its own X factor, an ingredient that would take every dancefloor by storm.

With acid house, ecstasy is that ingredient. You could call it E, Adam, X, XTC, Mitsubishis, club burgers, molly, hug drugs, mandy, Jack and Jills, doves, Bumble Bees, bumbles, disco biscuits, pills, Scooby snacks, rhubarb and custards, flying saucers, Blue Dolphins, 007s, Armanis, or any one of hundreds of variations and you could drop one, take one, do one, neck one, be on one, get on one or even get right on one (matey), but in each case you'd be referring to the same thing: MDMA.

No matter what you call it and whether you love it or hate it, are for it or against it or are indifferent to it, it was the recreational drug of choice for a generation of clubbers and has remained so for every one that followed since 1987. You are less likely to call it by its correct name, the rather catchy, grown-up 3,4-Methylenedioxymethamphetamine. Yup, you guessed it, the little round pill or dabbed white powder that fuelled the underground dancefloors was man-made in a lab by scientists, and initially by government-approved chemists in a legal, official and businesslike way as opposed to the demonised, mad, drug-fuelled back-street inventor the tabloids focused on. It could be straight out of science fiction, men in white coats working in secret, making mind-altering chemicals of no real practical use that could be used to subdue and control while making sure it doesn't fall into the wrong hands or slip into the water supply or result in a *Planet of the Apes* type scenario. That backfired just a little then.

It was all started by Anton Köllisch, who was working for German pharmaceutical company Merck when he first synthesised MDMA in 1912. Merck clearly didn't believe in winding down for the holidays and filed their patent applications on 24 December 1912. Merry Christmas, world.

Like the monogrammed hankie/sock combo and granny's hand-knitted jumper, this Christmas package would sit untouched in a drawer, gathering dust, for years. There didn't seem to be a good use for MDMA and with hyper-inflation, even more bonkers leadership than usual, a couple of red-hot world wars plus a worryingly Cold one among the many distractions affecting the German pharmaceutical industry, it was largely forgotten. Moving forward to 1970 in the USA and chemist Alexander Shulgin picks up the MDMA mantle. Shulgin had enjoyed mind-expanding mescaline-driven moments in the 1950s and was an advocate of exploring the hidden depths of the mind using recreational pharmaceutical methods. He felt that the insights he experienced could not have solely come from the drug but had to have been locked inside his mind, body and spirit. The drugs merely provided the key.

He had obtained a DEA Schedule 1 licence, so allowing him to have his own laboratory and to possess illicit drugs. He set up a chemical synthesis lab behind his house and started creating, using himself to 'test' the drugs. Worth thinking what this means – the US government are hell-bent on controlling everything and in particular making sure that nothing falls into the wrong hands be they counterculture or communist. They make it difficult for scientists to work without being heavily regulated. So far we can see how this works for them. So, what do they do? They issue a DEA Schedule 1 licence to a guy whose research is all about getting wasted and allow him to build his own lab behind his house. He then gets to 'work'. By the late 60s he's also synthesised MDMA but it hadn't excited him as much as other psychedelics. In 1970 a chemical company in California asked to see his synthesis instructions and they in turn passed them to a client in the Midwest, and by the end of that year recreational use of MDMA had been recorded in Chicago.

In 1976 Shulgin introduced MDMA to a psychologist, Leo Zeff, who tried it and then started using it as a therapy aid. If Shulgin was the inventor (or re-inventor, to give Köllisch his dues) then Zeff is patient zero. Zeff had not had the mind-altering experiences that Shulgin had had in the 60s and so felt the full potential of MDMA. You can almost visualise Leo, shirt open to the navel with his tie around his head, eyes rolling around and around while he's skanking across his living room to the sounds of Walter Murphy and the Big Apple Band with their 'Fifth of Beethoven' from the *Saturday Night Fever* soundtrack.

Zeff could see that this thing could be used to create a feeling of openness and well-being. He meant well and decided that he would share the love, and after encountering the purest of the pure MDMA he had a lot of love to share. He started to introduce it to other therapists, and not one or two close buddies but hundreds of them all across the USA. These hundreds of therapists in turn had hundreds of patients. We're now up to the thousands. It was particularly popular in couples therapy where it was often called 'Empathy'. These hundreds of patients didn't have patients of their own, but they did have mates. Hundreds and hundreds and hundreds of them. It didn't take a genius to see what would happen next – MDMA was suddenly everywhere. And these people also travelled. It was the 70s, people wanted to find themselves and suddenly MDMA was cropping up from Ibiza to India. The thing about prescription drugs is that people don't generally tell their doctors when they are passing the drugs out to friends, so despite Zeff's plan to keep this professional (and not in the 'Psssst! Need anything for the weekend?' kind of way) it quickly spread from the therapy room to the dinner party and from the dinner party to the party scene. I imagine there's a whole lot of medical data that says that, contrary to what you'd expect, people were suddenly keener to see their therapists before the weekend rather than afterwards, which is probably for the best as by the sounds of things the therapists would most likely also need to chill out a bit on Monday.

There are obvious parallels here between this story's hero, Shulgin, with ecstasy, and Timothy Leary with LSD. LSD had brought the Summer of Love to life, changing the consciousness of those who tuned in and influencing some of the greatest music of all time. *Sgt. Pepper's Lonely Hearts Club Band* would have been very different and Woodstock's genre-defining performances may never have happened. Advocates of LSD had their eureka moment and shouted about it from the rooftops (remember, kids, rooftops and LSD don't mix). High-profile figures like Leary saw that it had immense potential and could teach us about ourselves. It seemed like everyone was experimenting and that was the big problem. It became something for everyone and not everyone was ready for it. Demand needs supply and supply needs suppliers. Suddenly you didn't need to drop out to experience it, LSD was readily available on your college campus. What should have been examined in the college lab was now being 'tested' at college parties instead … with predictable outcomes. That is to say, predictable in its unpredictability. The mind is a delicate thing, and unlocking its potential is not the same experience for everyone, even for the initiated and headstrong; quality, quantity, location, circumstance, expectation, influences – there were too many variables. For many, the dream quickly became a nightmare. Some locks are not meant to be opened.

Shulgin decided to keep MDMA under wraps. He thought that

it could be studied while being consumed in a safe environment and, as it was legal in the USA, it had the potential to be developed as a regulated therapeutic treatment. Unfortunately for him, not everyone could keep it quiet. It started to appear *in* wraps rather than under them. Before long, it was being manufactured and sold across the USA, especially in Texas where it was marketed as a party drug under the catchy name of ecstasy. Bars and clubs sold it openly and X club nights were everywhere.

During this time MDMA became widely known on the US club scene as ecstasy or XTC, names designed to explain its effects and make it appealing. After ecstasy the second-choice name was makes-you-dance-all-night-like-a-loon-with-eyes-like-saucers-and-hug-everyone-while-dripping-with-sweat, but it didn't catch on. It was around, but not in the same way that cocaine and LSD were, and was only readily available in the USA. As the 80s got under way it started to appear in very limited numbers at a few localised parties in the UK, mainly in London. In 1982 Marc Almond and David Ball, the extraordinarily talented members of Soft Cell, were in New York recording an album. Marc met the aptly named Cindy Ecstasy, who introduced him to the drug. It started to be brought over more and more and, by 1984, most people out and about on the scene had heard of it.

By now the mainstream media had taken on a full-scale anti-drugs stance as recreational drugs had enveloped Western societies, destroying lives and fracturing communities. For the first time drugs were seen as a classless problem and not just something that blighted people on the wrong side of the tracks. After all, it was the people with money who drove across these tracks to buy their drugs, and as they had money but often little time they had their drugs delivered straight to them and in ever-increasing quantities. America was having a rude awakening.

Social problems like drugs, AIDS and gangs were not the storefront showcase that the planet's most powerful nation wanted to display. US President Ronald Reagan, leader of the free world, spearheaded the global 'Just Say No' campaign and in the UK, not wanting to be outdone, the cast of popular kids' TV series *Grange Hill* released their 'Just Say No' single after fictional character Zammo succumbed to heroin. The problem with reducing everything to a catchphrase is that no matter how good they are they get worn out and tired. 'Am I bovvered?', 'It's Chico Time!', 'Whatsssuuppp?', 'Is it cos I is black?', 'Schwing!', 'Just Do It', 'You're Fired!', 'How do you like them apples?' – slogans were and are everywhere. 'Just Say No' became a victim of its own short-lived success and pretty soon some clever spark had come up with the slogan 'Just Say Yes!' Hasta la vista, baby.

Looking back at the 60s and 70s, the drugs that went hand in hand with the scene are viewed in a strangely positive way, almost with affection. The scale of the drugs and the social impact they had are often neglected, as well as the fatalities. When you think about a roll call of great musicians like Hendrix, Janis Joplin, Jim Morrison, Tommy Bolin, Sid Vicious, Keith Moon, you don't focus on the drugs that killed them. It's almost as if the war on drugs started after the death of Elvis Presley and that his drug use has been hoovered away. He is still 'The King' in the USA.

* * *

MDMA was a drug and drugs were bad. MDMA was to be banned, although this was slightly delayed when academics tried to fight this by saying that its benefits to humanity would be lost. 'Seriously?' said the government, and on 1 July 1985 the US Drug Enforcement Administration imposed a ban on MDMA. Like Prohibition in the 1920s, they imagined that this ban was the end of the road, and like Prohibition they learned nothing about what banning something that people want does. Little did they know the party was just beginning.

Leigh Bowery's club, Taboo, is considered the first place in London where ecstasy became an intrinsic part of the night. This was 1985, a full two years before acid house was even conceived.

Australian born Bowery was known for his artistic excess and ecstasy added to the experience rather than heightening it. Drugs or no drugs, you'd walk into the canvas that had spewed forth from Leigh's mind and within a short time you'd be as wide-eyed and sweating as the next person, which could be anyone from Boy George to artist Lucian Freud. His events were such an assault on the senses that drugs almost didn't seem necessary, although that stopped no one. To understand the experience you have to imagine Leigh walking on stage in front of a packed club of the 'beautiful people' buzzing on ecstasy. He's wearing one of his hand-made creations that makes Lady Gaga look like a nun (of the Mother Teresa variety rather than the Benny Hill kind), collapsing to the ground and giving birth to a real live woman, who he'd secretly carried around all evening strapped under his clothes. This woman, Nicola Bateman, who would go on to be Leigh's wife for the last seven months of his life, arrives from between his legs covered in stage blood as Leigh proceeds to bite his way through the string of sausage umbilical cord. Ta-da!

But ecstasy was not confined to Taboo. The glamorous party crowd wanted to experience everything that London's nightlife had to offer. The scene was all about funk, jazz, electro pop and hip hop led by DJs like Colin Hudd, Jazzy M, Jay Strongman, Rusty Egan, Noel and Maurice Watson, Colin Faver and Mark Moore, who were starting to experiment with house music in their sets. London was a 'trendy' place and people stuck with the new sounds – after all, if everyone else liked it then maybe we should too. West End clubbers were smartly dressed, the rest less so but still, going out meant putting your best foot forward. Sound systems run by the likes of Norman and Joey Jay, Soul II Soul and Carl Cox and clubs like Crackers, the WAG and the Camden Palace were helping give platforms to a new breed of DJs like Paul Oakenfold and Trevor Fung, and promoters like Nicky Holloway were shaking up the scene with parties like Special Branch and his Doo's. The airwaves were crackling with the sounds of pirate radio and like-minded people were starting to turn into mini-tribes, following Terry Farley, Andy Weatherall and Cymone Eckel's *Boy's Own* with its own fanzine. Young record scouts like Pete Tong were scouring record shops for new artists and tunes from Detroit and Chicago were becoming easier to get hold of. Ecstasy wasn't widely in use among any of these groups, it was both hard to come by and expensive, but it meant that if and when it did come it wouldn't be an alien concept and would fit right in.

For a drug to be successful it needs two things: people wanting to take it and easy availability. Supply and demand. As 1987 dawned, demand was greater than supply. MDMA was like a secret handshake, something shared by like-minded people. It was provided rather than pushed when you could get hold of it but there were also plenty of other recreational drugs out there, mostly easily available. Drugs were always on the sideline, an accompaniment, the bread roll next to the main course, something to add a bit of naughtiness to a night out or change the direction of a night in. MDMA was just another drug, a mood-enhancing party treat for the few in the know who could not have imagined that it would become part of a global cultural phenomenon that would elevate the simple E and make it synonymous with a new way of experiencing music that would go on to conquer the world (although at the last moment, due mainly to a misinformed national press and Gary Haisman's dancefloor-uplifting crowd-rousing battle cry, what should have been XTC house became acid house).

Much has been said of the importance of ecstasy in the creation of house music. For a brief time it went hand in hand with acid house, and disco biscuits became a staple of the club and rave scene, but the quality of the music and the talent of the DJs, producers and artists created their own momentum, with the mighty E losing its importance while maintaining its influence and relevance. It's like a blazing inferno – once it takes hold and spreads, the kindling and twigs that got it going are forgotten.

Dance music is that inferno and is now BIG business. A multibillion-pound machine that has spawned global empires. It supports countless industries and is here to stay. Forever. We are its raw materials and we are also its customers. We are its champions and we are its critics. It shapes us and we shape it, helping it to evolve and grow and then to revolve. You can't capture what exactly it is and there isn't a formula you could write down to explain how it came to be. It wasn't started around a boardroom table, created by boffins in white coats, thought up by marketing gurus, discovered by business strategists or delivered by record companies. Early house – and to some extent techno – paved the way, but the music and club culture we enjoy today came straight from acid house. It wasn't introduced by movers and shakers, it didn't have big money behind it, it didn't know where it was going and it definitely didn't think that it would have any longevity. It came by accident, with no planning and no warning. It came from a lads' holiday to Ibiza.

DANNY RAMPLING'S SECOND SUMMER OF LOVE

No matter where you stand on the who, why and where of dance music there can be no argument that 1987 was *the* pivotal year. The building blocks were in place and the sounds of Chicago and Detroit were filtering, albeit slowly and gently, from the local audience into clubs all over the world and could be heard on (mainly pirate) radio stations. There was no plan to create a movement or share a moment and no strategy, which makes what happened even more amazing. It was the summer of 1987 and four young guys planned a holiday to the island of Ibiza hoping to come back with suntans and a few stories to keep them going.

Danny Rampling was one of the Four. Now a multi-award-winning legendary DJ regarded as one of the godfathers of acid house, his holiday to Ibiza sits in lists of iconic music moments alongside Queen at Live Aid, the Beatles on *The Ed Sullivan Show*, Sly Stone at Woodstock, Michael Jackson's first moonwalk at Motown 25, the Sex Pistols at Manchester Lesser Free Trade

Hall, Jimi Hendrix at Monterey Pop Festival, Nirvana on MTV Unplugged and James Brown's *Live at the Apollo*.

Danny is a softly spoken, thoughtful individual who loves music. He loves making music, playing music, discovering new music and listening to music. He's amazingly modest for someone who championed a new scene, spearheaded a musical genre, introduced an iconic logo, created his own dance, boasts the best of the best in global DJ 'royalty' as his peers and was the first winner of the No. 1 DJ in the World award from *DJ Mag*. But back then, he was just another young guy out to have fun. I asked Danny to talk me through his own Summer of Love.

DANNY RAMPLING: I'm still amazed that a bunch of lads going on a short summer holiday could come back and start something that would very quickly have such a massive impact, not only on them and their friends but on people all over the world, and that the ripples continue to spread and grow.

The Second Summer of Love is a fitting title for what was going on. We all knew about the original Summer of Love with hippies, flower power and love-ins. We'd listened to the sounds of Woodstock and marvelled at the creativity of Jimmy Hendrix, Sly Stone, Richie Havens and Joe Cocker, but they had already become a part of history – great music, great attitude, but not really relevant to us, the youth of Thatcher's Britain. We had a mish-mash of things to pick from and new places to go to. Punk, new romantics, rare groove and northern soul were some of the sounds we could hear at clubs, and occasionally at some clubs and on pirate radio a little bit of Chicago or Detroit dance music.

We were all part of several tribes. You could be a soul boy or a skinhead, a punk or a blitz kid, a casual or a West End trendy, and then you had your football team and local club scene which helped define what you did, what you listened to, where you went and what you wore. What we didn't have was a shared thing, something that could bring us all together.

The magic that we experienced at Amnesia in '87 was where it all came together. The freedom of the open-air club coupled with Alfredo's music was like stumbling across a diamond in the sand. We weren't looking for it but when we found it we couldn't put it down. By the time we came back to the UK it was all about the Balearic spirit and we needed to keep the feeling alive. To start with it was just for us and for those who had also experienced the magic. We were the Amnesiacs and like some many youth movements before us we felt that we could change the world, and like all the others we really believed it. The difference is, looking back, we really did!

This was my Summer of Love. I'd just survived a terrible car crash, which made me want to embrace all the positives that the future had to offer. I'd found my calling, realised that my goal was attainable and was having the best time of my life. I never looked back and fell in love with the world, dancing under the stars on the open-air dancefloor at Amnesia.

People always assume that it was all about house music – but it wasn't. Alfredo did play some great stuff from the USA that he'd picked up but it was his eclectic mix of anything and everything and the way he played the records that created the feeling. It was almost like he was able to create a soundtrack that was personal to you while doing the same thing for everyone on the dancefloor, be they straight, gay, white, black, old or young. That was what made it so special – we were having a shared experience with people that we couldn't have imagined connecting with. This was what the Balearic sound was all about.

Like with most underground scenes, there was a mood-enhancing element and MDMA was present at Amnesia, but not everyone was on it and they were still having the time of their lives. You didn't go to these clubs to take drugs, you went there to experience the feelings that the music and people generated and bounce off each other's energy. When I started to DJ I was overwhelmed with emotion – I was doing what I set out to do, playing music I loved to an audience who loved it – and some records would send me into an almost trancelike state. For me, music was my drug and I couldn't get enough of it!

Coming back to the UK was hard. We'd found something that we didn't want to lose and made new friends who shared the magic with us. I knew I wanted to be a DJ before we went away and now that was the path I felt I had to go down. Nobody was playing our sound and I realised that I would need to create my own environment to play my music, and I hoped that there'd be enough of an audience of Amnesiacs and those in the know to make it a success. I didn't know it then but within a few weeks I'd be the DJ at my own club, Shoom, inspired by the feeling we had at Amnesia.

Once Shoom became established we suddenly found that people were feeling what we felt – that they too were part of something special. All the Shoomers became part of a special family and the regulars formed close friendships, many of which exist to this day. Some people never missed a night. Nancy Noise, as she had now become, didn't miss a night at Amnesia across the summer of '87 and back in the UK was at Shoom every Saturday.

The word spread like wildfire as the scene started to form. By '88 the scene had grown to the point where the new music was topping the charts, fashion was led by the club scene, cultural and creative media couldn't get enough of it, the mainstream media decided that acid house was enemy number one and hundreds of thousands of people were getting involved. This is where you'd expect what the press dubbed 'a fad' to end as people invariably look for something new – but it didn't go away. It just kept on growing, quickly spawning different sounds and party crowds, all united under the house banner and then under the dance culture banner when subcultures of house music themselves morphed into new scenes. Everyone was looking for something to call their own and you could be enjoying a total different vibe at Shoom or Nicky Holloway's Trip or Paul Oakenfold's Spectrum or Mr C's Clink Street parties or even the sound system events like Jazzie B's Soul II Soul parties, yet still know you were part of a future which was inclusive and driven by the partygoers, just like you.

The Second Summer of Love would last several

summers as our vision took hold and then morphed into numerous different music genres, something for everyone, but all under the banner of dance music. The Ibiza Four, as we became known, went in different musical directions, but we remain friends and often perform together on the same line-ups, often alongside other original Shoomers including Carl Cox, Pete Heller, Terry Farley, Andrew Weatherall, Norman Jay and Nancy Noise, who shaped the Second Summer of Love and helped electronic music conquer the world. The Shoom ethos still resonates. At the time of writing this I am preparing to head over to Amsterdam where DJ Pierre and myself are playing at Shoom Amsterdam, celebrating the thirtieth anniversary of the Second Summer of Love.

This has all followed on from my special summer, when I stood mesmerised on the dancefloor at Amnesia with a bunch of friends. We wanted to take a little taste of our experience back home and share it with like-minded people – we never expected that the spirit and sound would go on to conquer the world.

IBIZA — WELCOME TO PARADISE!

Make a list of twentieth-century cultural epicentres that championed new movements in art, music, fashion, film and performance and you'd expect to have major cities like Rome, Barcelona, Venice, New York, London, Paris, Milan and Berlin represented. A bigger list would probably include the likes of Nashville, Liverpool, New Orleans, San Francisco, Los Angeles and maybe Manchester. These are places with big populations that had the infrastructure in place to support big ideas and big talent. You spend centuries bringing lots of people together under the banner of civilisation, create stability, encourage some basic freedoms, allow some of the exceptional citizens to think and do (but not too many or too much), provide lots of resources and the by-product should be a few clever people doing a few clever things. That is the way the world has always been. There is an exception to this rule. The Promised Land, the small Mediterranean island of Ibiza.

The Phoenicians established a port on the island in 654 BC

and over the next couple of thousand years it was variously invaded, captured and ruled by some of the big boys from history: the Carthaginians, the Romans, the Vandals, the Byzantines, the Moors (who brought Islam with them), Norwegian crusaders and eventually the Spanish. Lots of premiership players from the historical world stage but they didn't leave much of a mark or a lasting legacy. What they did do, however, is something that they rarely did anywhere else. They left the place unspoilt.

* * *

Ibiza is a special place. It had long been considered to have a unique energy, and from the 1950s onwards it began to attract a small number of tourists who could experience its unspoilt scenery and the old-world charm of this Balearic island. It wasn't exactly off the beaten track but it wasn't high on the list of those looking for a typical Mediterranean holiday. In 1960, all the hotels on the island combined had just 30,000 registered guests. As the 60s progressed, Ibiza attracted free spirits. Hippies gravitated to remote spots as they tried to find themselves or whatever it was they were looking for, and Ibiza had good weather, deserted beaches and beautiful sunsets. An emerging reputation for open-air parties, friendly locals and an abundance of drugs was all it took for the island to attract a new wave of visitors, many of whom would never leave. These visitors were spending money, often foreign currency, and in 1967, while the Summer of Love was in full swing in the USA, the powers that be decided to encourage tourists to come over by building an international airport. Bizarrely, the power in question was wielded by none other than Spain's fascist leader General Franco, military dictator from 1939 until 1975, who also brought the police over to try to discourage the parties and to oversee the new tourist industry. His death saw the re-establishment of the monarchy and a nation finally ready to let their hair down. So when you jet into Ibiza ready to dance, you could say that it is all thanks to a military dictator.

In fact, it is actually down to another military dictator, this time from the other side of the world, that we dance the way we do. Jorge Rafael Videla, remembered as a torturer, Nazi shelterer and murderer, seized power in Argentina in 1976. Among those who fled the country was a young journalist by the name of Alfredo Fiorito. He made his way to Ibiza, put down roots, had a family and never left.

Luckily for all of us, Alfredo decided to become a DJ. His understanding of music and the dancefloor in front of him was the benchmark that everyone would try to emulate. His influence would be heard and felt across thousands of dancefloors. It was his calling and would change the world. But not just yet. There was no bolt of lightning, no eureka moment and no instant success. In 1983 he managed to get a week's work as a DJ at Amnesia. The following year he was booked for the whole summer season but things didn't start well. Alfredo would play for up to six hours straight to a predominantly empty club. Everyone was heading up to the hottest club, Ku. To make matters worse and rub salt into the wound, Alfredo had to wait until 7am to get paid his £20 when the manager showed up. To pass the time Alfredo would keep on playing his tunes, and that's when it happened. People leaving Ku still wanting to party would pop into Amnesia. Within days he had over a thousand people dancing to his sound. Suddenly it was all change. The club would now only open at 5am and run on into the day. Amnesia was always packed and Alfredo was the star. The crowd came from all over the island. They were old and young, rich and less rich, black and white, straight and gay, and all wanted to dance in the open air in the sunshine.

ALFREDO: We didn't give a preference to any type of person.

[Alfredo played an eclectic mix of everything from electronic music and rock to Latin jazz and reggae, and everyone loved it. By 1985 Amnesia was the hottest club on the island and Alfredo was experimenting with house music and building it into his sets.]

ALFREDO: My best club experience as a DJ was in my first year at Lola's. It was a small club in the old town. I don't know what it is about Ibiza that adds the magic creative ingredient. I went to visit because I have some friends and I met painters, writers, musicians – a lot of musicians – but not DJs because there weren't many and everything you could want was around. To get involved in the island you have to get involved in the music. I've seen sunsets everywhere in the world but I think it's a whole organisation that's important to the sunset in Ibiza. Of course, there is a magic feeling from the ancient people when this was the places where the women go to procreate, the place to party from the ancient times. Since ancient times they've been doing these parties. The sunset is really nice. Then I read in the *Independent* newspaper that I was a pioneer. I was just happy to get them dancing.

NICKY HOLLOWAY: Alfredo and I always stayed friends. Alfredo is probably in the same boat as me. He's still working but we aren't earning the big dollars like the others. We are the statesmen. Alfredo probably feels more ripped off than anyone. Everyone talks about him, but we are struggling to pay bills sometimes.

DANNY RAMPLING: The way that Alfredo weaved a texture of music, mixing different genres and styles of music and making that work, that's a real skill and Alfredo really had and still has it to this day, that creative flair of crossing genres and mixing it up, and I think his South American roots … the actual rhythms of South America, I think that really comes through in his music, that Latin and techno feeling. In Amnesia he just blew us away with the way he was playing and really that was the first time I had experienced house music and techno in a club, and also it's the first time I had been to an open-air club like that so it was really special.

Alfredo had singlehandedly created a scene, but it was a local scene. The audiences were international but when they left Ibiza they left Amnesia behind. Maybe it was the impossibility of replicating the open-air experience back home or perhaps the sun-plus-music-plus-drugs-plus-Alfredo formula seemed uncopyable, but whatever the reason the experience remained unique to the dancefloor at Amnesia. Nothing came close to it and '86 was very much like '85 – packed dancefloors, happy clubbers, fantastic people. The word was spreading, with holidaymakers heading to the club to sample the delights and some clubbers coming to Ibiza for the Amnesia experience.

NICKY HOLLOWAY: Alfredo, he's a good guy. He falls out with people and is very passionate. Sometimes he loses his rag, but not with me. I think it's 'cos he didn't have the blinkers on that we had. We were hearing music we never listened to before. He was playing Rick Astley and Queen, he played lots of Kate Bush. It probably opened our ears. If we would have been in England we probably would have thought: 'Who is this wanker?' It was a little bit like that. We were black music snobs. He was playing white music. It wasn't cool for us to play white music. Later on, I still didn't play Rick Astley but did play Carly Simon, Yello and things like that. It did take the shackles off being a black music snob because that's what we were. We only listened to black music.

The early-morning start at Amnesia created a late-night culture with people dancing, listening to music, taking drugs, having fun and getting ready for Amnesia. By 1987 there was a prominent English contingent hanging out at bars like The Project. The Project was run by Ian St Paul and his cousin Trevor Fung. Trevor was already a known DJ on the island and they attracted a bunch of British clubbers who quickly bonded over a shared love of music and a shared enjoyment of ecstasy. They'd eat, sleep, laugh and cry together, and the day would build up to the moment when they would head over to Amnesia. Deep friendships were formed and, without realising it, the pioneers of the global dance music scene were starting to converge on what has to be one of the most important dancefloors of all time. Holidaymakers like Nancy Turner (soon to become DJ Nancy Noise) and City whizz kid Lisa

McKay (who'd reinvent herself as DJ Lisa Loud) were hanging out with Trevor Fung and then spending every night watching Alfredo in action. Everyone was in full holiday mode. They dressed down, forgot their differences, tried new things and made the best of everything. Of course, not everyone dressed down and it was the eclectic and flamboyant mix that attracted an international party crowd. Jon Cooper, aka Jon Pleased Wimmin, first experienced Ibiza in '87 and experienced the glamorous side of Ibiza's club life.

JON PLEASED WIMMIN: I had a good friend called Darren Courtney who was studying hairdressing at the London College of Fashion and I met him there as I was studying fashion design. We loved clubbing and dressing up and when we left in 1987 we decided to get a cheap flight somewhere and have a two-week holiday. Totally by fluke, we ended up going to Ibiza. We stayed in Ibiza Town and fell in love with the drag bars and that Euro vibe. We were already obsessed with Italo Disco and Eurobeat before we went there. The seed was really sown on that trip and a while later I was working for fashion designer Rachel Auburn, who DJed at Kinky Gerlinky. Without much coaxing we got another friend, Peter Jordan, on board and started going out as a trio and causing mayhem. It seemed natural that we just ended up on stage, doing all manner of stupid stuff. I think our youthful exuberance and bare-faced cheek was infectious and people just wanted us at their parties ... we were real party-starters at that time. It all worked well as I made the outfits, Darren did the hair and Peter was excellent at make-up.

Some of the London soul-boy crowd had gone out for 'fun in the sun'. Even open-minded future Shoomers like Terry Farley were much more likely to come back with a cuddly sombrero-wearing donkey and sunburn than return somersaulting through the airport having seen the light.

> **TERRY FARLEY:** I first went to Ibiza in 1982, I was going out in London on a Friday night and I was dressing in La Rocka from Johnson's, in that kind of rock 'n' roll style, but I never had good hair, I had the really shit hair that I still have. We went in '82 because someone had told us it was really good. We stayed in San Antonio. We went out in San Antonio dressed in our La Rocka clothes, ripped jeans. They sell for a lot of money now. We heard that there was a club called Ku and that it was pretty good. None of us had money. San Antonio is not what it is now, it was still quite quaint and there were some little open-air bars playing the kind of music we liked, which was soul and funk, and there was a coach that took you to Ku at 10pm and brought you back at two in the morning. We talked about going and talked to someone who said that there was a reason it leaves at 2am when the club doesn't shut 'til seven or eight. It brings you back because they want to get all the English people out before all the cool people turn up at 3am. So we were like, 'Fuck that, we aren't being mugged off.'

Ibiza was great, the sunsets were beautiful, Café del Mar was special, Ian St Paul was a visionary, Trevor Fung had an enviable record box of the finest tunes, and at the end of the day they made their way to the dancefloor where Alfredo held court. They were the Amnesiacs, disciples of a sound that was more than music and a feeling that was more than chemically induced. It was very much an Ibizan thing – something to enjoy there and then. In fact, Trevor and his mate, Paul Oakenfold, had tried to launch an Ibiza-influenced club night, Fun City, in London in '85 but it hadn't worked out. Trevor had met Paul on a coach trip and the DJ (Trevor) immediately hit it off with the aspiring chef (Paul). Paul confided in Trevor that he wanted to try to break into the music business and it was Trevor who gave Oakenfold his first DJ gig at Rumours, a wine bar in Covent Garden. London and the wider world weren't ready for something so radical. It seemed that the Ibiza sound would stay where it was. For now.

NANCY NOISE: I'd already been there in 1984 on holiday twice. Once with family and once with friends. That was the first time I'd ever been abroad on my own. Then we decided to go for the summer in '86. There were four of us. I arrived in San Antonio in the May, we were there just hanging out and rented our flat for like four months. Back in London I was already working in music and we were enjoying it, but the clubs were kind of – it was a bit like people dancing around handbags, Star Club was very much like that. We were having fun, but I ended up at Café del Mar one day early in the summer and I met one of Trevor Fung's brothers, I think it was Rudy, he knew a lot of the workers I knew. They were all slightly older than us. They said, 'We are all going out on Thursday and everyone has to wear black.' Bar crawl, club crawl, out all night together. I went back and told my friends. We all got ready and met them, went round bars and clubs in San Antonio and then ended up going to Amnesia, which was out of town. We walked in there and it was quite late in the night and it was changing from day to dusk. I thought, 'Hang on, this is really good,' there was no roof, loads of flamboyant dressers and people, different characters, so I enjoyed the rest of the night. It blew me away. I remember thinking, 'I'm gonna come back again.' There were little tickets that said 'Amnesia' and they got you in free if you went in by a certain time. I went as many nights as I could. I'd get there really early and there would be about four people in there. I couldn't afford a drink – drinks were obviously really expensive and I was out there for the whole summer, I wasn't into buying lots of drinks – but yeah, I'd be in there all night to watch the night grow. At the time I wasn't thinking that but when I look back I think that's what I wanted to experience. We spent the whole summer there so I totally got into the music.

1987 was an exciting year musically, with landmark moments like the Beastie Boys telling us that '(You Gotta) Fight For Your Right (To Party!)', Prince releasing 'Sign o' the Times', Terence Trent D'Arby being (prematurely) touted about as if he was the Second Coming, and MARRS encouraging us to 'Pump Up the Volume'. Even a normal bloke in a raincoat like Rick Astley could storm the charts with a bit of production behind him. Anything seemed possible and whether you were experimenting, sampling or collaborating it looked as simple as just getting yourself in the right place at the right time.

The most extraordinary example of this was when the cheeky upstart with the rather grand name of Ben Volpeliere-Pierrot and his band, Curiosity Killed the Cat, managed to blag their way in to meet legendary pop artist Andy Warhol at a rare UK appearance and convince him to direct the video for their single 'Misfit'. The band ended up joining the many hangers-on in the company of Andy and his friends at his Factory in New York, with the Cat in the Hat hanging out with Drella (Andy's nickname to his inner circle which was a mash-up of Dracula and Cinderella). Warhol was handing them cash to go out and play and, in the end, for all his creative flair, he tried and failed to copy an old Bob Dylan theme in the video. The track bombed but the publicity gave them a second chance at their fifteen minutes of fame and luckily, for them at least, 'Down to Earth' was a hit. Back in the UK, record scout Pete Tong was hearing early house tracks in London's record shops and a new breed of young record company employees were hearing DJ sets at the trendy clubs that included music by artists they'd never heard of playing a sound they'd never experienced.

On the club scene a few clubbers had discovered MDMA but it was still something that was almost unheard of and didn't have the effect on them that it would have the following year.

> **NANCY NOISE:** We had a funny one the year before it all kicked off. We already had some ecstasy, in powder form, and had taken it before the club started. We were on the way to a Philip Sallon night. Early days, this was before Future, before Spectrum, before anything. There was a little crew of us, ten of us all going crazy, when we caught sight of this boy, dancing like us and

wearing a baggy jumper. He winked at us. He was the same as us! So there were a few floating about. We found out in the end that he was a friend of someone from Ibiza.

Oakenfold had also made it into the music industry. He had a column, under the name Wotupski, in *Blues & Soul* magazine and had a job in music promotions trying to get club DJs to play hip hop records. It was a start and one that kept him in the UK over the summer of '87, but he still managed to book a two-week holiday to Ibiza to meet up with Ian and Trevor so that he could celebrate his birthday with friends.

Earlier that summer Trevor Fung and Ian St Paul opened a small bar in San Antonio called The Project. The bar became a focal point for the British contingent in Ibiza, listening to Trevor's DJ sets while enjoying the laid-back freedom of Ibiza's nightlife scene, which was totally different from the UK's see-and-be-seen (or is that scene) trendy West End clubs and a million miles away from the suburban discotheques.

TREVOR FUNG: I let the music speak for itself.

ALFREDO: Trevor was doing his job in San Antonio, he was like a pioneer of the new sound.

TREVOR FUNG: It's been a really amazing journey. I've always loved music. I was looking for a change. In the early 80s I used to play a lot of soul and funk. I first got a job working in Ibiza in '82. Back in the UK I was picking up all the Trax Records coming out of Chicago from Jazzy M who had a shop in Croydon.

NANCY NOISE: I didn't know Trevor that well. I met his brothers and in 1987 I hung out loads with Ian St Paul. Trevor, Paul and Ian are really good friends, they all grew up together – there was a whole crew of them. But in Ibiza, Trevor and Ian had a bar called The Project and lots of people used to go down there before we went to Amnesia. I was with Ian a lot more than I was with Trevor. He was the reason Ian and Paul went out there. I don't know how long Trevor had been out there. I think he'd been DJing. I wasn't a DJ, I was a music lover. I think Trevor invited them out there. He gets a lot of props for that.

Oakenfold had been to Ibiza before. It had been an eye-opener. Paul had been working for a small label called Rush Release who had signed Divine, who was to perform at Ku Club over the summer. 'Send the new guy,' they must have giggled as Paul arrived to meet the 22-stone, semi-clad transvestite who rode onstage on a baby elephant. All in a day's work. He'd experienced the specialness of the place and enjoyed observing the goings-on, and there was no reason that this trip would be any different. He'd have a supercharged cosmic break, go to some clubs, party with the lads, drink some booze, laze in the sun, get a tan, spend all his money and then head back to the grind of London life.

PAUL OAKENFOLD: There is something about the island that has a great spirit and energy. I'm sure it's got a lot to do with the hippies. They were going there. It's an international playground. When I first went there it was a lot of like-minded people going there, dancing in the open air, under the stars, you're on holiday so it just captures all those moments where you feel good.

As it was his birthday, he and some of his friends decided to book a villa. They'd only be four of them flying out in the end as some people couldn't make it, like good friend Carl Cox, who couldn't afford the ticket. Paul was joined by Johnny Walker, who worked club promotions for Phonogram, established club promoter and DJ Nicky Holloway, and Danny Rampling, who was playing soul on pirate radio station Kiss while learning the club promotion ropes from Nicky. Danny had survived a major car crash in the States, was doing odd jobs and looking for a path of his own, preferably as a DJ, when Nicky invited him to join them.

> **DANNY RAMPLING:** I learned the ropes with Nicky and I was already visualising my own career before, but unwittingly that was my vision, to become like Nicky and have my own crowd and for people to enjoy the music and loving what you do. Everyone that aspires to be a DJ dreams of having an audience.

A bunch of lads, much like the countless others before and since, jumping on a plane to head out for fun in the sun. But these were not any old group of lads and this would turn out not to be a typical holiday.

When the Beatles landed in the USA and came out to the screaming fans, this had been cleverly orchestrated by the record company and the media to ensure that the planned 'British Invasion' seemed like a reality, with the next day's headlines already written and the Fab Four looking surprisingly stylish and refreshed, if not a little bemused, after a long transatlantic flight. Ringo, Paul, George and John, already global superstars, went to an America that was ready and waiting for them. Two decades later, Paul, Danny, Nicky and Johnny, pretty much unknown outside of a tiny group of London clubbers, went to Ibiza to have a bit of a laugh. There was no record company plan, no strategy, no screaming hordes, no police cordon, no limo, no nothing. What they couldn't know, as the plane landed on the island, was that the very moment of touchdown was the ground zero of acid house and that they would become immortalised as the Ibiza Four.

THE IBIZA FOUR

akenfold, Rampling, Holloway and Walker. Four names that have gone down in electronic music history following a holiday that has gone down in dance music folklore.

What can possibly have happened, over the course of what was supposed to be a normal holiday, that would change these guys so much they felt compelled to try to introduce the experience to everyone they met when they got back home?

The first thing the Four noticed was that their friends had changed. A lot. They were more relaxed, more open-minded and in a sense seemed freer. The sun was shining and the people were euphoric. Everyone was living for the night and recovering in the daytime and they were taking a new drug called ecstasy. They were happy, chatty and more sure of themselves. Drinks in the clubs were expensive but everyone seemed to be having a great time without much alcohol.

NANCY NOISE: Amnesia was like five quid for a bottle of water. There was an area there with all these tables and chairs and groups like Italian film stars. When I went back to England, I bought a lot of the records that I loved from '86. I'd saved all winter. Amnesia starts in June and the crowd had got a bit bigger because more people had heard about it and there was a few more people in the crew. Then Paul, Danny and Jonny and Nick came on holiday and I already knew Nicky so I hung out with them too.

Trevor Fung was showing them the sights and after a couple of club stops at Nightlife and the Star Club they headed over to Amnesia. They weren't big on drugs but it all seemed so harmless and they would all keep an eye out for each other. And the pills were legal, weren't they? Oakenfold and Rampling were the first to swallow an E. Holloway, who was strongly anti-drugs, saw that they seemed happy so he threw caution to the wind and tried one. Johnny Walker was even more cautious and waited, but when he saw his friends hugging each other with big smiles across their faces he took one too. Lift off!

To the four of them Amnesia was pure magic. The crowd was diverse and international. Transvestites mixed with European club kids, London soul boys with models and movie stars, international jet-set playboys with buffalo girls. Straight, gay, black, white, rich, poor, all coming together as Alfredo shaped the mood under the stars. Everyone was smiling, laughing, dancing and rejoicing. Alfredo's music was eclectic, with everything from Prince and the Woodentops to house music and Latin percussion lifting the mood – records you'd never imagine hearing in a club, like 'Josephine' by Chris Rea, suddenly became incredibly important. Things that you'd normally think were very important became unimportant. Throw some pure MDMA into the mix and let the alchemy begin.

So here they were. On the magical Mediterranean island of Ibiza, experiencing their first E, and a really good E at that, at Amnesia, on a dancefloor powered by Alfredo, dancing in the open air under the stars, in a club full of beautiful, like-minded people, surrounded by friends. And that was it. Something changed in all of them that night and they would never be the same again.

The next day they were at the villa, listening to one of Alfredo's mixtapes and discussing what had happened the night before. They had shared something that was almost inexplicable; in their former lives the four of them were quite different and so each one had a slightly different take on what had transpired. Using the phrase 'former lives' after one night in a club may seem strange but their lives had changed for ever. They climbed into the pool, holding hands, and listened to 'Moments in Love' by Art of Noise. During the course of their conversations they jokingly spoke about ecstasy bringing world peace and then more seriously about how they needed to bring the club experience back to London and how they could do it. It would be no mean feat, transporting an all-inclusive, open-air, all-night party experience to the London club scene with its strict licensing laws, tough door policies, terrible weather, cliques and rigid musical styles. Danny Rampling was perhaps the most affected. A lightbulb exploded over his head as he listened to U2's 'I Still Haven't Found What I'm Looking For' and realised that he had found what he'd been searching for.

As the holiday continued they got more and more into Alfredo's music, took more Es and met more people having the same experience they were. Oakenfold had become friendly with Trevor's friends and had Nancy go over to Alfredo repeatedly to ask what the various records were that he knew he'd need back in London. The stand-out tune of that summer was the Amnesia anthem, 'Jibaro' by Elkin & Nelson, an extended, exotic Latin-jazz-funk workout that would soon be a call to arms across London's underground club scene. It starts with an acapella that has a unique mesmerising magic to it and a promise of a great tune to follow. Throw in the open air, Alfredo's string-pulling, the international crowd of hedonistic partygoers, the holiday spirit and the 'how many tickets for the party do you want?' from the medical bag of Dr Ugs and you had no choice but to dance.

NANCY NOISE: It's all a bit of a blur and I did take loads and I was out every single night. First year was loads of LSD and second year, '86, ecstasy started coming in at the end of the summer ... They did play the same records every night. Me and Alfredo only met in 1987 because in 1986 I never met him, I was just there all the time. I used to just wander over to the DJ booth and have a little peek and look at some of the sleeves and look at the records because I wanted to buy them back home. But in 1987 when I went there, I danced in the same spot by this speaker. Quite early in the summer, one night I was dancing away and looked round and Alfredo was in front of me dancing and he was like, 'Who are you? You're here every night.' And I said, 'I'm Nancy.' After that I would go up and say hello and he gave me a few mixtapes which I had in my apartment – that was our first proper meeting.

Alfredo was the ringmaster at a circus of pleasure that held his audience spellbound. Without knowing it, his expert ear and eclectic taste had created a new genre of music, the Balearic sound that is easily recognisable but hard to describe. The closest would be a lifestyle-based rhythmic compilation that is half music, half concept and half feeling!

PAUL OAKENFOLD: Alfredo is a great DJ who has a wonderful way of telling a story through music. He really pulled you in, he is a truly great DJ.

ALFREDO: The feeling is a feeling. I mean, like bringing together the people in a situation where they feel like they are together. I went to many places I never thought I would go. I used to say, 'Mama, don't do this to me because I'm going to go to China,' and I went to China, to Japan, I have friends from Japan, from all over the place. All that I knew was because of music. Nancy Noise, without her the Ibiza Four wouldn't have happened. She was not afraid to come to the DJ booth or shy like the other boys. Danny wasn't a DJ and Paul was somebody in the industry. Nancy came to me for records, she was my friend. In terms of feelings she was very important. She was the connection between me and the English people like Trevor Fung who used to come to the club.

DANNY RAMPLING: Balearic is about openness and a sound that evokes that feeling and that spirit. If you really listen to music, it's about the way that music travels in Ibiza; without wanting to sound esoteric or hippyish, there is something about the energy in Ibiza that also transforms the sound. You can hear a record played in Ibiza and elsewhere in a European city and that record can sound very different. It's about the feeling and the spirit on the island.

The regulars had become known as the Amnesiacs and they became as much a part of the club as the music, encouraging Alfredo to keep the pressure on the dancefloor and to push himself to new heights. They were so loyal that Nancy didn't go to Oakenfold's birthday party at the villa as she felt she couldn't miss a night at Amnesia. Nancy Noise is still very much an Amnesiac to this day (and with her big smile and passion for music, one of the nicest DJs you could ever meet).

> **NANCY NOISE:** It was funny because I was in there every single night basically. The first night they arrived I bumped into Nicky. And he says, 'What you doing here?' and I was like, 'What do you mean, what are you doing here? I've been here since May.' It was August. I knew Nicky because he used to do the Royal Oak in London Bridge and that's where I'm from. I used to go see Nicky play. So he knew me from when I was really young, like at school. Then I met Paul and Johnny and Danny and I really clicked with Paul. I was having lots of fun with him but at that point me and the others weren't really clicking – we weren't really having lots of conversations. I got invited to a villa party for Paul's birthday but because I was such a die-hard Amnesia fan I said I might not make it. 'Don't worry,' he said, 'we will come on after.' And they did.

The Four spent most of the holiday going backwards and forwards between Amnesia and Café del Mar. Ian and Trevor closed down The Project, and the Brits, who by now were becoming a very close-knit group, all embraced this new freedom wholeheartedly. They met other similar-minded kids from all over – Manchester, Stoke, Germany, Spain – all united in the special feeling that the summer of '87 in Ibiza was generating.

MIKE & CLAIRE MANUMISSION: Ibiza was a little-known island in the Mediterranean when we first arrived. Tolerant of whoever was 'invading'. Back then it was international Bohemians. It was untouched in many parts, beautiful and affordable. The gay scene was vibrant.

DANNY RAMPLING: In my eyes, the Ibizan sunset is the same as anywhere else. It's your moment alone with friends to take a moment to reflect on the day and the anticipation and excitement of night-time beginning.

NICKY HOLLOWAY: We felt like we belonged to something, I suppose. It's like how 60s rockers all know each other and are still hanging out together. Facebook has been good for that in a way because there are lots who wouldn't be in touch had it not been for Facebook. There was a big gap. If you were doing a party, you had to go out every night to bump into people. Then Facebook made all these people come out of the woodwork, 'cos you don't necessarily wanna talk when you're out but it's still nice to keep in touch.

Then it was time to go home. Going back to reality is always a sobering moment, when the summer sun fades and the grey skies take over. But this was no ordinary holiday and the reality that the Four were going back to was inside them – their new reality was the dancefloor at Amnesia, the freedom to dance and to be open-minded to what you danced to and who you danced with. To them the party was only just beginning, not just for them but for all of us. For you.

BACK DOWN WITH A BUMP

So here we go ...

The Ibiza Four return triumphant to the UK where they are met by representatives of Her Majesty's Government and whisked straight to Buckingham Palace to be knighted for services to mind expansion and social freedom. The establishment decides that having happy citizens is the only way forward and our heroes embrace each other before taking the helm of their new superclub as the entire population, no, the entire world, rejoices.

'Paul, wake up, wake up, mate, we've landed.' The plane bumped to the end of the runway. Bleary-eyed, the lads step off the plane to the familiar icy blast and greyish sky. They join the seemingly motionless solitary customs queue as two other officers sit joking with each other behind a small sign saying, 'This Position Closed. Please Use Next Door Window' with a hand-drawn arrow pointing to the left. The next-door window has the same sign but with the arrow pointing to the right. Time for the post-holiday blues to set in, to forget about the fun and for the amnesia to kick in. 'Did someone say Amnesia? Wait, I rememb...' Someone in the queue breaks wind – it's an 8 out of 10, silent but deadly. Danny looks at Paul, who shakes his head. A couple in front misinterpret this. Nicky doesn't help by pointing at Paul. The couple look at them in disgust and start tutting while looking back accusingly. Secretly, the husband wonders why they had taken the blame for something he had done. Welcome home!

OK. So there was no big welcome, no fanfare, but more worryingly there was no Amnesia. But Danny, Johnny, Paul and Nicky were so affected by what they had experienced that they single-mindedly set about spreading the message in their own way.

GRAEME PARK: They helped popularise the whole movement that we now know and love.

CYMON ECKEL: They brought the openness, warmth and incredibly diverse playlist back from Amnesia – remember, house wasn't really played then.

They were united by a common goal but although they were together on this mission they went about it in different ways. Johnny and Nicky had work to go straight back to – after all, this was meant to be a little summer holiday. Johnny was due back at the record company and Nicky's club nights needed him at the helm. He was quickly back in the swing.

Paul opened up The Project club as an 'after hours' thing, kicking off when the club officially finished at 2am and running until 6am for the Ibiza crew and their new movement. Carl Cox provided the sound system and, not having been with Paul in Ibiza, he was seeing the Balearic style for the first time. Carl wasn't fazed, he was used to a mix of styles from his time as a mobile DJ at weddings. Carl could see people dancing and having a good time and that was good enough for him.

TREVOR FUNG: Me and Paul are really good friends. We started Fun House and The Project in Streatham – our warm-up was Carl Cox! What I liked about Paul was that he was a bit like me, we always wanted to drive new music. Where we're different is that he's more overground and I'm more underground but that's the only difference. I'm proud of his achievements, and of Carl's. Loving the trade and loving what you do, that's where it can get you.

CARL COX: Basically, I used to hire turntables for my system set-up. I never had the turntables, just the sound system. Paul said he'd hire me for the sound system and pay me for the turntables. He'd buy them and I'd pay them off from the money he was paying me. At that time they were so expensive. I think they were like £1,500 apiece. My car only cost ninety quid!

Paul also invited some of his mates along from football, fellow supporters of his beloved Chelsea. Terry Farley came down with Andy Weatherall, Cymon Eckel and Steven Mayes. The lads had started a fanzine in 1986, *Boy's Own*, which was a mix of music, clubland, football and fashion written in a humorous style. *Boy's Own* started to document this new Balearic style and without knowing it created a way for non-clubbers to get an understanding of what was going on. *Boy's Own* was the only tangible thing in the whole scene that the record companies could access. It became known as 'the village newspaper of acid house', the showcase for the various elements that made the street scene tick and a real indicator that there was no one thing or person that was the catalyst for change.

PETE HELLER: I think it was a combination of things. Definitely a response to the general moodiness in a lot of London clubland at that time – a reaction against the overall level of over-seriousness and poseur side of things. The Ibiza vibe was all about tolerance, anything goes, no one gives a shit, be whoever you want, which may have been there in the gay scene but was most definitely missing from the rest of clubland. And of course there was a hippie aspect – peace and love was a terribly seductive idea, coming at the end of the 80s which was quite a violent period in society. A lot of confrontation politically: Thatcher transforming Britain into something quite ugly, football hooliganism etc. It did feel like the bad people were winning, so yeah, the new vibe was definitely a fuck off to all of that.

TREVOR FUNG: The UK was going through a cultural change at the time so it was the right time. My friends used to go to football, they were mainly Chelsea supporters, used to a bit of a fight, the next thing I'm seeing them in clubs cuddling and kissing Arsenal supporters. It was the right time for change – it was perfect timing.

CARL COX: When the idea of this movement happened

it did start off at The Project club. Nowhere else was playing this music. Paul was there obviously, Johnny Walker, Nicky, Danny, everyone else around the music had transformed. The Project Club used to be all about rare groove and hip hop every Friday night. But Paul had the idea of throwing everyone out after two o'clock, onto the streets, and letting in only the people who understood the music that Paul had experienced in Ibiza. They booked Alfredo to come play from Amnesia in Ibiza. He travelled two hours to be there from the land of the sun and he played with his shirt open! He came in with this aura about him, he knew that these people who had booked him had been to his club in Ibiza, danced outside in the stars, enjoying his music, enjoying this moment, and bringing that whole vibe to south London at that time was unheard of. Basically, everything was transformed: lights, strobes, the music was lively, fresh, it makes you feel like you're at the top of the world and we're at the cusp of all of it. What I was experiencing was right in front of my eyes, it was happening right now and I loved it.

Things were going well and by the sixth week Paul felt confident enough to fly the maestro, Alfredo, over. This was to be the defining moment that would fast-track the new sound and way of doing things. It was also probably the first (and possibly last) time that Paul willingly stepped back to play second fiddle. Paul invited everyone and the expectation was high. Of course, Alfredo didn't disappoint. He rocked up, he rocked the dancefloor, making new converts as he played, he lifted the crowd higher and higher ... until the police raided the place and shut it down. Someone had parked blocking the local supermarket's goods entrance and with the early-morning deliveries piling up they called the police. Alfredo had to stop mid-set. Game over! Turns out Paul had convinced the manager to open up for this after-hours 'private party' outside of the venue's licensing hours, so there was nothing that could be done. And that was the end of that.

There weren't many places for the Amnesiacs to go to and experience the uplifting sounds they craved. Nicky was incorporating a Balearic feel to his out-of-town nights. He already had a solid organisation in place and so it made sense that he would have the platform to experiment and see if this could work.

NICKY HOLLOWAY: I was already doing this. We did a sort of thing down in Chessington, a little club down there, once a month on a Tuesday. People that had been to Ibiza that summer were getting what we were doing but the ones that hadn't done it didn't get it at all. It was kind of divided. But in the end, everyone got on board. Even before the acid house thing started out. If you'd been to Amnesia you got what we were doing but most people hadn't. I sort of dropped the soul thing because I wanted to do the other thing.

Thursday night at Heaven was the place to be for Maurice and Noel Watson's Delirium. They'd come from the warehouse scene and honed their skills as DJs at some of the most successful underground parties that had happened to date. The night wasn't particularly busy but the music was great and their style of playing suited the Ibiza crowd. The Watson brothers couldn't have known what was around the corner and didn't understand the comradeship between the Amnesiacs. With dwindling numbers, they pulled the plug just as the scene was about to take off, which ironically would have given them the appreciative audience they needed.

DANNY RAMPLING: The Thursday when Delirium closed was actually the best night. I didn't really fully appreciate what was going on. It was the foremost stage of the scene. Delirium had a great set-up and for some reason they decided to close Delirium just as the scene was ready to explode. We used to go there on the Thursday night at Heaven. All that crowd, the Ibiza crowd, the Amnesia crowd, went to Delirium as well. The music was great, played by the Watson brothers. It was just a little too early. I think the best night was the last one, but we didn't know it was going to be the last one. If I remember, there was only about three hundred people in Heaven. It wasn't super-busy, but the energy created on the dancefloor, it was all of us collectively, really enjoying the music that was being played and the excitement of the scene that was just coming together in its formative stage.

MARK MOORE: The different scenes were in the same room but it was still very separate. The soul scene boys, which was very straight, came back from Ibiza. It was very heterosexual, they weren't really frequenting the clubs we were going to. Our thing was much more stemming from the first clubs I ever went to: Billy's, then to the Blitz and to Philip Sallon's clubs. He used to do a wild night in Piccadilly called Planets, so we came from that kind of thing. Then obviously the WAG club and Heaven's gay nights. It was a very gay scene, very fashiony, not mainstream, but up-and-coming designers like John Galliano. Taboo was great, so we came from a very dressed-up, post-punk kind of scene that was very different from theirs; our people weren't coming back from Ibiza like that.

TERRY FARLEY: I was a black music enthusiast. I very flippantly remarked I was 'a gay black New Yorker trapped in the body of a white gasfitter from Slough', which people seemed to like at the time. I was always a black music fan from very young. I grew up on Latimer Road. Little kids where I grew up were black boys, one of my best mates when I moved to Slough was a black guy. I felt quite drawn to black culture, black music culture. I'm not sure whether it was the times, rebelling; my dad went nuts when I played reggae, which made it more exciting. I felt that I was living a double life. The kind of working-class culture I'd grown up in at school ... kids in school would know the leaders of all the London ends [football terraces]. People would know these people's names, they were stars in their local areas. These people were legends, I'm not saying it's right but that's how it was. We grew up with a culture of going to football with your mates and knowing who the leaders were. There was slang, dress, fashion around it, the slang that only went with that culture. I'd have to go home after football to change to go clubbing.

The returning Ibiza crew were starting to make themselves seen and heard. Ibiza had changed them all and this was apparent to people who knew them from before.

> **TERRY FARLEY:** The year before acid house, they [the record companies] had me driving round buying records, which is how I met Johnny Walker. Steve Mayes from *Boy's Own* would have to drive from London to Manchester, stopping off along the way, and we would buy stuff. Bananarama was our group! We would stay there and drive back. Johnny was a really straight bloke. We were getting a bit pissed or something and Johnny was really straight. Acid house comes in and suddenly he was joining in … Danny [Rampling] was standing behind whoever was DJing and Johnny was in the bass of the speaker curled up in a foetal position. He was the definition of a lovely bloke.

Converting the youth of a nation to something new would always be an uphill struggle. If there's one demographic of people who don't like being told what to do it would have to be the group who had spent most of their lives in schools being told exactly what to do. How the incoming Balearic ideal and the influential hedonistic party crowd would merge couldn't be straightforward. Could it? Perhaps a series of near-cataclysmic events were needed. It was time for some *force majeure*.

* * *

Late 1987 was an exceptionally miserable time by any standards. Firstly, Rick Astley's 'Never Gonna Give You Up' was No. 1 for five consecutive weeks and you couldn't seem to go anywhere without hearing it.

GRAEME PARK: People like what they like.

Then, on 15 October TV weatherman Michael Fish told the country to ignore rumours of an impending hurricane. Fish was clearly no relation to Nostradamus and obviously hadn't paid any attention to his briefing notes, misreading 'Run! Hide! It's going to be the mother of all storms!' for 'A good night to leave your washing out on the line and enjoy a nice, chilled glass of rosé in the garden.' A few hours later that night a major storm smashed into the South of England with such ferocity that seventeen people were killed, tearing down buildings, flipping cars, and leaving trees that had stood for hundreds of years lying on the ground, destroyed among the carnage that a few hours earlier was the picturesque English countryside. By the end of the weekend people had managed to get their aerials back onto what was left of their roofs just in time to hear about the arrival of what we now refer to as Black Monday, when the British stock market crashed and the 80s boom was officially over. More tea, vicar?

The future looked bleak. It said so in the newspapers, so it must have been true. Was the glass half full or half empty? Hard to tell as it was lying on the ground, smashed to smithereens. Thank you, Michael Fish! People needed something to look forward to. People were looking for something new, something life-changing. Just what Danny Rampling had been thinking a few months earlier as he boarded his flight to Ibiza.

NICKY HOLLOWAY: Danny wasn't a DJ then. He was just my mate. He always wanted to DJ but I didn't really know that at the time. He came back and started up [Shoom] at the fitness centre. Paul was doing Heaven and I got the Saturday nights at the Astoria.

IRVINE WELSH: People were bored of the Thatcherite right-to-buy, home-and-garden, individualistic culture and wanted to connect with each other and have fun. The history of Britain has been about the ruling classes being pompous, boring, controlling cunts and the masses mostly conforming but occasionally saying, 'Fuck you, we're having it.' This was one of those moments.

In November, Danny Rampling and his soon-to-be wife Jenni opened Klub Sch-oom at a fitness centre in Southwark in south London. Off the beaten track, the sound system was provided by Carl Cox, who also opened with a DJ set to be followed by Danny Rampling. The flyer proudly announced that you needed to 'present this invite plus 4 spondoolix' and that 'the plastic [would be] – hard, fast and unexpected'. No DJs were named on the flyer but the plea was 'let the music take you to the top'. Heavily influenced by his heroes Frankie Knuckles and Alfredo, Danny's ability to read the crowd and take them on a musical journey was unparalleled at that time. It wasn't something you could learn, Danny was his own target audience and played what he felt worked; and if it worked for him it worked for the crowd. The crowd had been expertly curated by Jenni, who ruled the door with a rod of iron. It felt like a members' club, which is what it was technically supposed to be to get around licensing, and the hand-drawn membership cards and flyers added to the intimacy. Klub Sch-oom became Sch-oom which became Shoom, and the regulars became known as the Shoomers.

Two weeks later Oakenfold and Ian St Paul opened Future in the back room of Heaven, Richard Branson's mega-club situated in Charing Cross in the centre of London. Future was 'members' only but not like any other central London members' club. Ian and Paul made sure that anyone coming knew why they were there – emblazoned on the card was the order of business: 'The Original and Only Balearic Club – Dance You Fuckers!'

> **TREVOR FUNG:** Ian St Paul is a fantastic guy with a great vision. He's always ten steps further ahead than everybody else. He's got a kind spirit, loves to party and loves to travel. He's a visionary and a very nice guy to boot. When it came to the clubs he always wanted to do something very different. Like going to Heaven, a gay club, and making it a mixed night was unheard of in the UK. But it was happening in Ibiza all the time. The best clubs there were the gay clubs.

They came, they saw, they heard and they danced. Then they wanted more. Paul quickly became an in-demand DJ on the scene.

> **NICK HALKES:** Considering it was a pre-internet era, word of mouth spread fast. After each significant club night there must have been many conversations where person A said to person B, 'Man, you gotta check this thing out,' or words to that effect, and so the scene grew.

MR C: People have been dancing to tribal rhythms as a part of human evolution for fifty thousand years and it's not about to stop any time soon. Disco music had already done the hard work and in the late 70s and early 80s disco started to become way more electronic with Italo disco and of course the American stuff too, which of course was a precursor to the scene we know and love. With house and techno being a natural evolution of that with new technology coming through, it could only keep progressing.

FATBOY SLIM: It was very much a word-of-mouth thing for ages, which kept it underground long enough to really develop and mature before the lowest common denominator explosion driven by the tabloids.

PAUL OAKENFOLD: It's difficult to pinpoint one special time at Future, there was a lot of moments with friends, moments where I started to become a popular DJ, moments where I was getting asked to remix bands and producing music for other people. The first thing I did was a Happy Mondays remix called 'Wrote for Luck', the Future remix. That was pretty special.

'Wrote for Luck' won the Best Dance record at the 1989 NME Awards and *Pills 'n' Thrills and Bellyaches*, produced by Oakenfold, won best album the following year. Looking back, you could say this album was the peak of the whole baggy clothing Madchester thing, and the album still sounds good today. The fashion fared less well. A young entrepreneur, Shami Ahmed, had originally seen a gap in the market and created a whole range of loose-fitting T-shirts and baggy jeans for the rave market, which he marketed under his Joe Bloggs brand. Shami's big moment, in terms of sales and marketing, was during the Stone Roses concert on Spike Island where he sold boxes and boxes of T-shirts. The Joe Bloggs brand was very specifically tied to the rave scene, with little thought of where the brand could go. While brands like Gio-Goi and Chevignon were able to ride the acid house rollercoaster and emerge at the other end, Shami fared less well. When rave died, Joe Bloggs died. Gone, but not forgotten.

* * *

Joining Paul behind the decks was Nancy Noise, who the previous summer in Ibiza, as Nancy Turner, had been part of the Amnesia experience. With all the DJs in London to choose from, Paul selected someone who had never DJed before but who loved music and brought the Balearic energy to the room that Paul needed.

> **NANCY NOISE:** I think because I was crazy about music, about the club, I knew all the crowd so when we get back to England I was always on the phone, 'Who's coming out?' and ringing round. I moved back home but then I got a flat quite quickly in Clapham and I remember being on the telephone or downstairs on the call box phoning everyone saying, 'Who's up for it?' I used to do my own flyers if it was someone's birthday; it would be part of the Future night but I'd do an extra one that I'd give out to people.

The official flyer introduced 'New DJ's Terry Farley [and] Nancy Noice'. So Nancy had gone from Turner to Noise to Noice and in the time it takes to say, 'Sorry, mate, I don't do requests,' she'd gone back to being Nancy Noise.

PAUL OAKENFOLD: Nancy was very important because Nancy was instrumental in bringing the community together. She is musically talented and that's why she became more than the girl that's dancing on the dancefloor, she became the fellow DJ that played alongside me at the Future club. Lisa Loud was also important, credit where credit is due, we went on to open a club called Loud Noise for Lisa and Nancy. She wasn't a DJ. We turned her into a DJ. Me and Ian St Paul opened the night in the West End, opened it for them. It was Tuesday night, we had Future on Thursday, Spectrum on Monday, and Tuesdays was Loud Noise where they would play. Nancy is more alternative, more Balearic. Balearic is inspired by what we heard in Ibiza, not necessarily what I'd heard from Alfredo 'cos you'd hear rock, pop, reggae, house music, all under this umbrella of Balearic. I would go to this bar to hear Pink Floyd and Bryan Ferry and then you'd go to the club and hear Alfredo playing house music. To us at this time the future (and Future) was Balearic.

NANCY NOISE: When it is happening you don't really think that you're someone special. I've had people say that to me but when it's going on it's just what you're doing. I never used to think, 'I'm this, I'm that.' I never used to take notice. I would just be with my mates.

Nancy Turner had gone to Ibiza for a holiday and fallen in love with the place. She wasn't a DJ and hadn't thought she ever would be, so for her the musical revelation was as genuine as it could be – she just loved dancing to the Balearic sound and that was really all there was to it. Renamed as Nancy Noise by Paul Oakenfold when he first convinced her to DJ, she went along with it because she didn't need to think about it too much, after all this surely wouldn't amount to much. Future, Spectrum, Stella McCartney's birthday party ... all a bit of a dream. It wouldn't be long before bootleg tapes of Nancy's mixes were being sold in Camden market, she formed her DJing partnership with Lisa Loud and would be on a world tour co-headlining with Graeme Park and bringing her sound to locations as diverse as the former Yugoslavia and South America. Not bad for a non-DJ!

The first mention of Balearic in the press came, naturally, in the *Boy's Own* fanzine, with an anonymous article, actually written by Paul Oakenfold, proudly declaring (and misspelling) 'Bermondsey Goes Baleric' – so not off to a good start.

TERRY FARLEY: Paul wrote an article for *Boy's Own* about Ibiza. He wouldn't let me put his name on it because it was about drugs. My writing skills are legendarily poor on grammar and spelling. I spelled the headline of 'Bermondsey Goes Balearic' wrong. Everyone laughed at us. Anyway, Paul wrote it about Ibiza. He gave me some pictures of him and Nancy Noise. We printed it and it was the first ever story or article in print about acid house. It took *i-D* two issues before they did their first one.

Spelling aside, *Boy's Own* was brilliant. It mixed a deep understanding of the club scene with insights into fashion, football and anything else that took their fancy, all told with a certain working-class meets *Monty Python* meets mad-for-it style. It was also a good place to find out about parties and a good way for promoters to tap into the growing *Boy's Own* following. Nicky Holloway used the fanzine to promote his ongoing Special Branch 'Doo's'. He pulled together a stellar line-up of clubland royalty for his 28 December All Day Doo at Le Palais Hammersmith. He name-checked each club, which brought him into the widest circle of the trendy London club crowd possible. From Special Branch he had himself and Pete Tong, Gilles Peterson and Derek B from the WAG, Norman Jay from Shake 'n' Fingerpop, Dave Dorrell from RAW, Ben and Andy from The Boilerhouse and Jay Strongman from The Mud Club, and billed it as 'London's Most Successful DJ's Together Under One Roof'. Things may have been getting a bit Balearic but it wasn't all or nothing. The scene had already grown big enough to accommodate everyone.

GRAEME PARK: Paul has always been very focused. He has an idea and he does it.

NANCY NOISE: At the beginning, the basis for Future was the tunes which myself and Paul played. They were the things we loved, stuff that we had heard in Ibiza mixed in with stuff we loved as well. Mine would be a mixture of warehouse-y style mixed with the stuff from Amnesia, mixed in with stuff from Glory's – there was another club in Ibiza called Glory's with a DJ called Nelo that I used to go to. With Future, anything went, really. The crowd originally was the Ibiza crew because the first week we did it was like a private party, really. Everyone paid £5. Then there was a one-week gap and Future started and I was asked to play by Paul. I always remember finishing. There was loads of whistling. High-energy atmosphere, lots of people. I used to go down there with pockets full of badges, I remember giving out flowers one week. That's the drugs thing, where the hippie Summer of Love thing comes from because it was that sort of sharing thing. I got Youth down to the club. I introduced all those people to Paul. I had stayed in touch with Youth. I rang him up and said I'd become a DJ at this club, he came down and actually met Chloe in there, they ended up being together and he married her, and they wrote 'Sunshine on a Lonely Day'. I brought them down to Future and he said, 'OMG, Nancy, this is amazing.' They brought Alex Paterson down, I introduced Alex to Paul and Ian and he said he wanted to DJ. This is how the Orb thing came about. He did his first thing in Spectrum with the oil lamps and the visuals.

GRAEME PARK: One night at The Garage in Nottingham there was this bloke and he just hovered around the DJ box. He didn't know anyone, he wasn't talking to anyone and he kept looking up at me. 'Who is this weird bloke?' At the end of the night I grabbed him ... 'Alright, mate, my name's Paul, Paul Oakenfold.' He was sending me records. 'The reason I'm here is because I looked at your chart return and I can't believe that someone is playing these records

… but this is an amazing night.' Straight away he got me really annoyed with this London-centric view and very quickly turned it around by saying we should do something together. We started arranging coach trips to his night in Streatham at Ziggy's – he said, 'Bring a coach to Streatham and you can do a bit of a DJ set and we'll bring coaches up here.' That was my first encounter with Paul.

Suddenly it was all going on. The club scene in London didn't know what had hit them as free-spirited, dressed-down ravers started popping up at the trendiest clubs. When people first thought they'd discovered rare groove, they hadn't. It had 'always' been there and they'd just discovered the DJs like Norman Jay who had been playing funk, soul and hard-to-find grooves at their own parties. With acid house it was different. People were discovering it at the point in time that it was being created.

TINTIN CHAMBERS: At the time acid house broke in London, there was an incredibly vibrant club scene, where young and old people involved were, I would say, pretty forward-thinking in terms of cultural reference and fashion. Clubs like Delerium and Enter the Dragon were playing early Chicago house alongside rare groove, whilst the dancefloor provided a melting-pot cross-section of urban culture. But it was Shoom and Spectrum ultimately that provided the pure, unfiltered acid house experience that the scene could coalesce around.

Not everyone in the rare groove scene would jump into the house pool. There was a big place for some of the cornerstones of clubland, particularly the music-driven side. Gilles Peterson had the record collection that you'd do anything to see, let alone listen to. Jazz, funk, fusion, Latin and blue note – he was the man. From his legendary 'Wired' parties at Dingwall's in Camden to his Monday night at the WAG – Gilles could get anyone dancing. Rumour has it that he was DJing with another jazz funk DJ, Chris Bangs, at one of Nicky Holloway's parties on the same bill and in the same room as Pete Tong and Paul Oakenfold. Behind the decks there's a screen with clubby visuals. Gilles starts to play a fast Latin track (possibly by Sabu Martinez) and as he does so the word 'Acid' starts flashing within the visuals, ready for Oakey and Tong to deliver the goods. Chris Bangs grabbed the microphone and shouts, 'Fuck acid house – this is acid jazz!' They spent the rest of the night playing to a chorus of 'acid jazz' and a new label and genre was born. Other labels were quick to sign artists up as the club scene began to run nicely alongside the acid house movement. Very much a London thing at first with acts like The Brand New Heavies, Us3, Young Disciples, Galliano, Jamiroquai, JTQ, and Incognito, it quickly spread with crossover artists like United Future Organization from Japan and MC Solaar from France before arriving in the USA and influencing a more hip hop orientated version that included artists like A Tribe Called Quest, Digable Planets and Guru.

NICKY HOLLOWAY: Loads of my friends would go to their thing as well. They were kind of like friendly rivals because there was a crossover. This is what I was saying about how other scenes emerged from it like the whole acid jazz thing. That started when Chris Bangs started playing this thing ... maybe 'Iron Leg'? [by Mickey and the Soul Generation.] They started a label called Acid Jazz. It was a way of keeping it moving forward.

By the start of 1988 Hedonism were starting to hold their illegal warehouse parties and the acid house scene took off in Manchester with the Haçienda's Hot and Nude nights. At the same time, in London the RIP parties were started in Clink Street by Paul Stone and Lu Vukovic, which had a harder sound than Shoom and Future with the music mixed and selected by the likes of Evil Eddie Richards, Kid Batchelor and Mr C. Pretty soon they were also holding parties on the Sunday so you could party through the whole weekend. But if you wanted to experience the true essence of acid house in the most magical way there was only one place to try to get into: Shoom.

DANNY RAMPLING: Clink Street was much darker than Shoom. It was a darker, after-hours vibe. Shoom was a lot lighter music alongside the house stuff, you know, we had punk to indie, all kinds of music. Clink Street was just very deep, moody house.

Saturday night at Clink Street was called RIP and within three weeks it was packed to the rafters. They opened up the Fridays too under the A-Transmission banner, which was supposed to be more techno and acid than Saturday's house and garage, but the music could go either way on either night. It was all down to the DJs. By August of '88 every Sunday was called Zoo as they figured that anyone who partied all weekend long had to be an 'animal' – 'A great philosopher once wrote ... naughty, naughty, very naughty!'

MR C: After kicking off in April of 1988, the party was packed by the third week. By June we'd started A-Transmission on Friday nights and by July we were doing Zoo on Sunday nights. The crowd was like nowhere else. People of all colours and backgrounds came to let loose and as the music was New York house and garage, Chicago house and acid, Detroit house and techno and also old school electro, the crowd was a lot blacker than most other parties, which added a real urban feel. Many other parties were a lot whiter than RIP and felt in some ways less inclusive. There were many parties spinning up but most of those exploited the more obvious and mainstream side of house and techno music, so they just [weren't] quite the same until we got into the early 90s. That same musical open-mindedness and progressive attitude could then be found at Release, which I did with Nathan Coles and then later at Heart & Soul, Wiggle and Vapourspace before The End opened in December 1995.

Mr C (who was also on MC duties), Kid Batchelor, Eddie Richards and Colin Faver played a more underground sound than Shoom, reminiscent of the underground Detroit and Chicago scene, and didn't include the pop side much, almost looking down on the selection and seeing their sets as more serious. Little could they realise that within a few years the mainstream pop charts all over the world would be dominated by dance music tracks. Even Mr C went on to have a No. 1 hit with The Shamen and one of the most controversial hits ever, 'Ebeneezer Goode'. In the song he either says, 'Eezer Goode ... He's sublime, he makes you feel fine', or 'Es are good ...

E's sublime, E makes you feel fine'. When they appeared on *Top of the Pops* Mr C was asked to tone down the last line, 'Got any salmon?' which is rhyming slang for snout ('salmon and trout'), which in turn is a slang phrase for tobacco. For reasons best known to him he came out with 'Has anyone got any underlay?' He was asked if this too was a drug reference with 'underlay' linked to speed via cartoon character Speedy Gonzales, and replied in all innocence that it was not, it was 'a rug reference'. Like at Clink Street, Mr C knew how to push those boundaries with his club, The End, and continues to do so to this day with his acid house inspired global Superfreq parties.

> **NICK HALKES:** I was already deeply into dance music when acid house emerged so it didn't provide an entry point to a new world for me but rather an exhilarating new chapter of a book I was already in love with.

> **MR C:** What was achieved at RIP was nothing short of ground-breaking. Paul RIP did an amazing job. Of course I helped to promote as any proper resident DJ should, and I truly believe that RIP was the foundation for all good cutting-edge house and techno parties to follow.

To document the scene's shenanigans first-hand or, as they called it, 'acid house scrapes and capers' and immortalise the players, especially the supporting cast, fell neatly at the feet of dance music's very own diarists, the *Boy's Own* bunch. The *Boy's Own* fanzines, which ran from 1986 until 1992, are nothing short of a work of modern art. There was a lot of input from writers, designers, photographers, promoters, DJs, blaggers and assorted waifs and strays who helped maintain the strictly 'no trendies' policy and reinforced their position as 'The only fanzine that gets right on one, matey!' There was a big team behind it, involved in creating, printing, distributing, writing and designing the thing, but part of the charm was that they didn't directly put their names to it and treated the whole thing as a family-run collective. They checked any ego they had at the door. As far as we can work out the key players were Rob Leggatt, Phil Thornton, Terry Farley, Steve Hall, Steve Mayes, Adam Porter, Andrew Weatherall and Cymon Eckel.

At this point there were only three publications that catered for the nightclub crowd: *The Face*, *i-D* and *Time Out*. The first two were elegantly put together but always a couple of months behind the times and the latter was little more than a listing mag with little space available for 'Clubs' although Dave Swindells, the nightlife editor, would cram as much relevant info in as he could. The *Boy's Own* fanzine sacrificed style for substance and packed each page with the info that they wanted to share with their readers. But don't get me wrong, style was still a big part of the fanzine. OK, so it wasn't glossy, but they used the paperiest paper, le finest glue sticks, the feltiest pens and the clickety-clacketyest typewriters (for anyone under thirty-five, a typewriter is a cross between a computer keyboard without a screen and a printing press). Terry had come up with the *Boy's Own* name and Dave Little did the illustrations. Anyone on the scene could give some input and Gary Haisman had a few ideas of his own to add to Little's *Boy's Own* logo as he art-directed an addition by saying, 'I wanna young geezer at the top O with the baker boy cap on, and a little Staffie [Staffordshire Bull Terrier] in the other O.' The baker boy cap was an 'essential' part of the uniform in the rare groove scene and some nights would look like an audition to find the next Bisto Kid.

Two of the *Boy's Own* team, Farley and Weatherall, were DJs and both played at Shoom. Andrew Weatherall has always kept a low profile but behind the decks he comes to life. His deep knowledge of music shines through as he explores the known musical world and beyond in his (often epic) sets. At the Tribal Gathering at Luton Hoo in May 1997 Andrew and his Two Lone Swordsmen sound system played for eight hours straight before Kraftwerk came on for a two-hour performance, the first live performance anywhere in the world in almost a decade by the original masters of machine music, cited as a primary influence by almost every producer of contemporary electronic dance music. For most DJs this would have been a high-pressure set, made more so by the fact that the Detroit DJs including Richie Hawtin, Jeff Mills, John Acquaviva, Kelli Hand, DJ T-1000 and Kevin Saunderson were hovering near the booth to catch their heroes live. There was no other artist allowed on before Kraftwerk, they only wanted Andrew, and they could have had anyone they chose. Weatherall delivered, and then some, and I think no one else on the scene could have made this work the way he did. The recent compendium of the fanzines, that is already changing hands for silly money on eBay, describes him as follows: '... Wevvers ... an enigma ... a breeze that cools you on a summer's day ... a whisper in your ear that is barely audible ... to be honest we asked him what he was up to but he couldn't be arsed to tell us ... That's Andrew – a techno freedom fighter from the Windsor hood.'

But for acid house to exist and to spread it needed more than a fanzine, more than music (and more than the odd cheeky chap scaring the establishment). The fanzine was a good messenger but even the best messenger needs a message to deliver. It needed the kind of atmosphere that had changed something in the Ibiza Four, and it needed to be cloned and passed through to an entire clubbing generation quickly.

> **FATBOY SLIM:** I think like all great musical revolutions (rock 'n' roll, punk etc.) there was a moment when the social, economic and cultural climate demands something new to shake out the cobwebs and reinvent how people dance, dress, socialise, make and consume music. You need disaffected youth that demands better than what it has been fed.

This is what the Balearic vibe at Shoom provided. Colin Faver played at Clink Street and at Shoom and could see the influence that Shoom was having outside of the club world by the types of people trying (and in most cases failing) to get in. Already, the dancefloors of Future, Shoom and RIP were starting to move to different beats.

> **TERRY FARLEY:** Shoom and Future – the difference between them – 50 per cent were the same people but Future was more indie, they played the more rock records that Alfredo was playing, whereas Danny was playing the soulful end.

> **GRAEME PARK:** I would argue that it wasn't those two nights that created that spirit, it was already going on all round the country. In different pockets. Paul Oakenfold was coming up to the Garage in Nottingham, either late '86 or early '87, he used to work for Rush Release and

If the Second Summer of Love were a picture, this would be it – the legendary Gary Haisman at Shoom, wearing Boy's Own and a Smiley while shouting 'Acieedd!'

© Dave Swindells

Above: 'Can You Feel It?' Danny Rampling at Shoom with Anton Le Pirate dancing in the background.

© Dave Swindells

Below left: Four to the floor! Johnny Walker relaxing in a speaker.

© Dave Swindells

Below right: The look that would become known as 'acid ted' making its debut at Shoom.

© Dave Swindells

Above: The adventure begins … throwing shapes on the dancefloor at The Future. Note the brave chap wearing a thick jumper on one of the hottest dancefloors in the nation.

Below left: Paul Oakenfold in the cramped DJ booth at The Future in 1988. Usually set up in a dark corner, within a year every new club had the DJ front and centre.

Below right: 'This is really happening!' A young Terry Farley at Spectrum cross branding with Shoom T Shirt and Boy's Own bag.

Above: Above: The secret's out! The party spills over into the street outside Nicky Holloway's Trip in 1988.

Below: Dancing under the stars at Amnesia.

Above: Strength in numbers. Suddenly, ravers were seen as free-thinking consumers and voters. Using flyers and word of mouth to spread the word, the 'Freedom to Party' rally in Trafalgar Square united a new generation and terrified an old one.

© Dave Swindells

Below: Before anyone knew what 'Fake News' was, you could sit on the beach in Ibiza and have a chuckle at the latest tabloid exaggeration.

© Dave Swindells

Left: The Pleased Wimmin at Kinky Gerlinky in 1991, the most fabulous mixed club night that has ever existed.

© Dave Swindells

Below: Anything is possible. Davina McCall behind the decks at Hollywood Babylon in 1993, blissfully unaware that she was soon to become one of the biggest stars on British television and a household name.

© Dave Swindells

Inset: The original Spectrum flyer, designed by Dave Little, introducing Paul Oakenfold and Ian St Paul's Theatre of Madness to the world.

Above left: Greetings from Goldie at Metalheadz.

© Dave Swindells

Above right: A rare look at the 'glamorous' world of pirate radio with DJ Stacey and DJ Foxy on Fantasy FM. Note the state-of-the-art mobile phone.

© Dave Swindells

Below: 'Mr Good Times'. Norman Jay on the radio at the Southport Soul Weekender in 1989.

© Dave Swindells

Right: Basking in 'Danny Rampling's aura' at Shoom at the YMCA in '88. © Dave Swindells

Left: Having followed the Yellow Brick Road to Heaven clubbers were prepared to be amazed in the Land of Oz. © Dave Swindells

Right: Graeme Park in the Hacienda's state of the art DJ booth. © Dave Swindells

send records for DJs to promo. I was aware who he was and he certainly was aware who I was. In those days you had to fill in your reaction report and send it back in the mail … and 'please don't forget to include your weekly chart'.

SHOOM

DANNY RAMPLING: The club was called Shoom after the rush of excitement on the dancefloor at Amnesia.

Shoom had it all. An underground party vibe in a seemingly random venue with an incredible soundscape painted by some of the finest DJs ever assembled. Inside was sorted. Outside was a whole other ball game. Jenni Rampling was running the most difficult door in clubbing history since New York's Studio 54 and she ran it well. Jenni had to push, pull, please – but mostly push – hundreds of people who were either in or out or should have been in but weren't, and of course the club faces who expected to walk through the door. Pop stars like Bananarama and Paul Rutherford mixed with serious dancers like Tommy 'Mad' Mack, club faces like Gary Haisman and Anton Le Pirate, returning Amnesiacs, original Shoomers like Big Ade and a totally up-for-it party crowd. Jenni didn't just 'do' the door, she curated the door. She had the right mix of people in the club because she cared about the club. Here, the movers and groovers on the dancefloor were the stars.

DAVE SWINDELLS: Shoom was different to every other club because it broke the mould. It changed the way clubs worked. When I first went down there I'd already heard about it. People had told me how special it was but it's all very well hearing acid house music for the first time or Balearic beats – you've got to go down to experience it.

DANNY RAMPLING: Sade came a couple of times, Kevin Rowland from Dexy's Midnight Runners, Boy George, ABC and Jeremy Healy. Jeremy told me the other day that the first time he came down there the bouncers wouldn't let him in. That's what I'm told. They probably came down late and were told the club was full and they couldn't come in. But they came back later and were let in. [Boy] George loved it. The word was out there, wasn't it. In arts and fashionable circles and with designers like Patrick Cox. He helped put the word out there that something cool was happening outside of Soho.

TERRY FARLEY: Gary Haisman was the one that got me to go to Shoom. I'd never met anyone like him. Gary would just scream. Gary used to shout 'Acieed!' and you'd go to places and you'd hear waves and waves of people shouting 'Acieed!' He was also a good dancer. He'd go on to run the Raid club. Raid was suburban meets the West End with rare groove meeting house.

It was almost like everyone who went to *Boy's Own* in '88 came together at Raid. We already had that crowd ready to go.

Heavily influenced by the music he was hearing and the club culture he loved, Gary put on a series of events called the Raid as warehouse parties as well as at West End clubs including the 100 Club, Limelight and the WAG. Gary had hand-drawn flyers created by Dave Little, who would go on to leave his mark on the *Boy's Own* fanzines and at clubs like Clockwork Orange. Dave's flyer for Oakenfold's Spectrum at Heaven is stored for permanent record of national cultural interest at the Victoria and Albert Museum. It was one of the first nights to get fully behind house music and boasted DJs including Pete Tong, Paul Oakenfold, Terry Farley and Andy Weatherall. Sadly, Gary 'Acieed' Haisman passed away in November 2018 as he was preparing to join his friends Danny Rampling and Terry Farley for Shoom's New Year's Eve in Amsterdam.

DANNY RAMPLING: Shoom wasn't illegal. They had a licence. Unbeknown to us, the council, because it was a fitness centre gym, had granted it an events licence. So they could stay open 'til 5am – five was the cut-off. Shoom wasn't illegal but it felt like it was. It wasn't in the trendy area of London, the Soho area, it wasn't a nightlife hub at the time.

Pete Heller was the warm-up DJ and would play the guitar over the tunes. Having worked at Our Price he'd 'accumulated' a healthy record collection and had been influenced by Jay Strongman, who'd signed Chuck Brown & the Soul Searchers to Flame Records. Pete had embraced the club scene, getting to know the movers and shakers while making a name for himself, and even getting his hair cut at the must-go-to place, Vision in Kensington Market, where Paul Daley (who would go on to form Leftfield) worked. Pete Heller meeting Terry Farley would result in one of the most important production pairings in house music and lead to the iconic Junior Boy's Own record label that spawned acts like the Chemical Brothers (formerly the Dust Brothers), Underworld and Fire Island.

CARL COX: It was important to have someone with his [Danny's] vision. Obviously, he took his career path in the way he went and I took my career path in the way I went but we were trying to fight the same cause. When you've got someone mixing records, to mix them now, it takes years. Danny was always a great programmer, at that time it was infectious, I really loved to see how he rose above where DJing was supposed to stop. It was his own creation, he made a sound for himself, knowing that it was something that he owned and no one else.

DANNY RAMPLING: The first night was with a rare groove DJ and we were going to go into it as a partnership but it didn't work and there was only about fifty to a hundred people there. He played his records and I played house. Carl [Cox] and others were there too. I was nervous as hell. Shoom wasn't formed into the Shoom that it became. There were two events. The first one wasn't as promoted – that was the rare groove one, and the next one the plan was really to move forward and focus on house and Balearic. The first one in December/ November with the Shoom spelled Sch-oom – that was the true first one and that's the one Carl Cox played on.

MARK MOORE: The first time I went, it was just full of dry ice, you couldn't see two feet in front of you, couldn't see what people were wearing or who was there. There would be a moment when suddenly the dry ice would clear and you could see and look around and suddenly you'd realise that everyone was on E. I was like, 'This is really cool,' because the music was great, fantastic, with the flashing strobe lights and the dry ice, it was like a sensory deprivation tank. It made complete sense, it's almost like they had taken what they did with disco, the flashing lights, to heighten the experience and they had done it in such a way that it was almost like a psychedelic trip.

DAVE SWINDELLS: As a photographer it was hard to take pictures in there because it was so bloody hot. You had to wait about half an hour for the camera to warm up to the temperature of the room, otherwise all you got was steam.

DANNY RAMPLING: The name was changed in December or January and then it became Shoom. I'm sure Carl played on two of these. I was very nervous but I did enjoy myself because I was there partying. I had borrowed some money because I wasn't out there working on the circuit, so I made a bit of money and that went straight into the club night. It didn't work on the first one but it didn't lose money and the second one it broke even and the third one in the New Year, '88, was the turning point, when it really, really took off, I think that was January. The word was out. We were out promoting it at art colleges and places where we'd find interesting people. It was always different, but every Saturday was one of the greatest Saturdays of my life. It's hard to define it, but every week the energy was amazing. I'd had to practise to become a professional DJ. Creating this club, that really broke down so many barriers and that came from my own zest for life, seizing the day. *Carpe diem.* That's where a lot of that came from, my own energy and approach to life and that is reflected from behind the decks and that's what people loved – a DJ standing there and playing records. There was something much greater than that – the energy that was transferred around the room.

MARK MOORE: It set the blueprint for the future. The way people club now and the way people clubbed from then onwards. You know what's funny, when acid house happened, the Second Summer of Love, people thought clubbing didn't exist before that time, they thought clubbing started in 1988. That's why people called it ground zero, because in a way people did not know all this stuff was going on before.

DAVE SWINDELLS: The real thing that made it different was the love in the room – you knew it was basically ecstasy that was breaking down barriers and letting people experience clubs like they'd never experienced them before. The other thing was that they had such an amazing approach – Danny and Jenni – getting the regulars to respond to what they were experiencing. That was really different, they really encouraged people to turn a club into a lifestyle. This was something really different and I remember Danny telling me about Fraser Clark coming down, he was editor of the *Encyclopaedia Psychadelica*, and how he responded and instantly saw that this was the new-age moment he'd been waiting for since the 60s.

DANNY RAMPLING: I had seen Carl Cox play at Project in Streatham and Carl was the opening support DJ. I was blown away by it. I didn't really know him at the time, but I was like, 'Who's this guy?' and I introduced myself to him and I just thought he's technically brilliant. In that period, the mid-80s, mixing as it's done today was not as commonplace. Carl gave me a few tips, particularly about bpm. Back then we only had turntables and that was it – so yeah, Carl gave me some good advice.

Once they'd moved the gym equipment to the side of the fitness centre (oh, the glamorous life!), the smoke-filled room was captained by Danny Rampling and steered by the crowd, but to get in you had to go through Jenni. From all the hype, you may have expected that getting past the gatekeeper and going through the gateways of Shoom was to enter into Nirvana. A bit like the thousands of late-nineteenth-century immigrants arriving in the United States of America expecting to find the streets paved with gold, or the music press believing that the follow-up album to the 1992 Stereo MC's *Connected* would be delivered before the end of that decade. People really do hear what they want to hear and see what they want to see. The reality at Shoom was very different.

CARL COX: It was just a box room like a gym and all the walls were covered in glass. I remember them putting all the banners up. There wasn't much more production in there, there was a smoke machine and some colour, it transformed the room. We put the decks up and away we went.

RUSTY EGAN: A sweaty room, no air conditioning. Of course, I enjoyed it. I knew them all because they had come to my club. I was the generation before.

CARL COX: There was a toilet, there was a bar – end of story.

But strangely enough, you *were* entering a sort of Nirvana. It was definitely Danny Rampling's 'land of dreams' and it was his single-minded belief in himself and in the goodness that the crowd would bring that made Shoom the sort of place that promoters with lavish venues and huge production budgets would try to copy. If truth be told, they rarely came close.

DANNY RAMPLING: What I did was transport the feeling and the experience of Ibiza back into the basement and created Shoom, and Shoom was very colourful and attracted a diverse, wild mix of people. From art students to street kids to fashionistas to creatives to 80s pop stars and young clubbers. It was all about the mix of people in the club, that's what made it very special, and our host at the time. Myself downstairs, playing music and talking to everyone who came into the club, and my wife at the time, Jenni, on the door upstairs, selecting people to come in. Actually, Future and Spectrum also had elements of Ibiza as well. It was a free state.

MARK MOORE: My nights at Shoom were all amazing experiences. You'd just go there and see these great new people, hear these great new tunes, it was always fantastic. There is no best experience. Every night was the best.

DANNY RAMPLING: I used to open my set with Barry White's 'Ecstasy', with the lyric 'It's ecstasy when you lay down next to me'. That would be the call to get to the dancefloor.

CARL COX: My best time at Shoom was when I was first there. I treated it as the party I knew Danny wanted to set up. It was like I was being hired for my sound system. Danny did approach me when I was playing in Kingston for the music I was playing at the time, which was early house, early acid house and garage music. I really concentrated on finding as much music as possible at that time. I wanted to play for a crowd that was moving things forward musically. With Danny he was thinking, 'OK, I have Coxy and I want his sound system.' I can't remember how much he paid me but it was more that I felt honoured he asked me to do that for him. I remember going outside and half of these people, all dressed in funky clothes, wearing big platform shoes, and thinking, 'You guys have no idea what you are in for 'cos one thing's for sure, there is no rare groove tonight.' But I think Danny wanted to have some support from me, he knew I could play and that I had the sounds. Half the people there in their funky shoes just sort of stood there and went 'Ugh?' – it was amazing what went on, people just had a really good time. We knew that there was something good going on at that time. It was rare groove OUT and house music and Balearic beat IN.

DANNY RAMPLING: With Carl Cox it's all about his skill, it's his energy, he's like a Roman warrior, he's like a gladiator behind the turntables. He has relentless energy and a really big massive sound, and his mixing is ferocious, the energy within the mix is amazing. Everyone has their own unique style. Back then when I saw him in that club in Streatham I knew immediately this guy is really, really talented. Even that young.

NANCY NOISE: Shoom was mad, Shoom was brilliant. It was like a complete sweatbox, full of smoke, strobes, mirrors where you used to get really confused, was it a wall, was it a mirror? Then there was the bar. In the bar there was like a pool table. We had a corner called speaker's corner where we used to talk. I was there every week. It was great. They had Fingers Inc and Bam Bam doing PAs and you never knew they were on. There were a few times I was dancing and then suddenly I came face to face with the guys from Fingers Inc and I didn't even know they were there. Then one week, Bam Bam did a PA on the table. I actually found five pounds on the floor and he said, 'You keep that, darling.'

TERRY FARLEY: Within two minutes you knew every person at that club. That wall completely went down with Shoom ... I knew straight away that this was completely different to anything else and this was going to blow up massively. A lot of Shoomers were saying, 'Don't tell your friends. This is our thing. Keep it to yourself.' And the first thing we did, of course, was tell everyone we knew.

CYMON ECKEL: I grew up, I realised that pretty much anything you want to do, is down to you, it is your door to open.

MARK MOORE: I felt like I was somewhere where they were going to get exactly what I was playing. It didn't feel like you were performing or on show, it felt like you were part of a family, a group of people. Many a time, whoever would be on the decks, was completely off their head, and would slide down on the floor unable to put on the next record and that was all perfectly fine, you didn't have to be perfect. You didn't have to be a pro, you were playing for family. If you fancied passing out during the middle of your set, that was fine.

TERRY FARLEY: Shoom was definitely more spiritual than the other clubs that came along later. Some of those early Shoomers were like disciples of Danny's. I remember one girl telling me she could see his aura while he was DJing and, do you know, to a certain extent maybe you could.

Danny was unknowingly building a solid movement with disciples, a message and a place to worship. Danny and Jenni stopped using Carl Cox for the sound, having brought Joey Jay in with his sound system. Joey's younger brother Norman, that's Norman Jay to you and me, was often helping to set up and can be seen, Zelig-like, in early Shoom photos standing behind Danny while he was DJing. The sound system would go on to be the backbone of Norman and Joey's 'Good Times' sound system, which became one of the key features of the Notting Hill Carnival. Most movements need a logo, an identifying symbol that lets people know you're part of it all. So of course Danny managed, by chance, to 'discover' an iconic one that is still as relevant today as it was then. In January 1988 Danny introduced us to the smiley. A yellow circle with two dots for eyes and a wide curving smile.

> **DANNY RAMPLING:** It was the adopted symbol of Shoom. Wherever you are, something will just stand out. Smiley had been forgotten about – it was very special to most kids in the 70s – a lovely, happy symbol, that's what it was about. Happy, happy, happy, it was the happiest that I've ever felt in my life, in fact. But the smiley influence came from seeing my mate Barnsley wearing a waistcoat covered in smiley badges and I thought, 'That looks cool,' and then it brought back the stickers as a kid and I thought that was the perfect symbol for this. Barnsley is a well-known stylist in London and in Japan. I saw that symbol and I thought: 'That's it! That's the symbol for Shoom!' and thereafter, it became the symbol for the whole movement. And it represented the whole

movement. The emojis of now must be the direct descendant of our smiley.

Smiley T-shirts appeared everywhere and very quickly. Seen as a bit of fun, you could pick up a 'Where's the Acid House Party?' shirt on a Sunday afternoon at Camden Market and wear it without people knowing what it referred to. Even the tabloid press started to cash in, with the *Sun* newspaper bringing out their own version (although not long afterwards, when they turned on the scene, they turned their smiley upside down and you could then just as easily pick up your 'Frowny' T-shirt). Everything seemed to the masses and the media to be deliberate, but most things from the night at Amnesia to the smiley logo just happened by chance. The ravers' drink of choice was Lucozade and a common misconception was that this was chosen for the energy it gave you.

Of course, the last thing these clubbers needed was more energy. The Lucozade thing came about because that was what was available at the fitness centre by day and so that was what there was by night too. Had it all happened today it would be all flavoured waters and your five-a-day. Suddenly everything felt new: what you wore, what you listened to, where you listened to it, who you listened to it with, what you drank, what you took – even what you thought. DJs were mixing long sets, using the mic less, building a crowd who were hearing less and less music they recognised but were there for the experience and discovery. The DJ wasn't twenty feet above you, he was among you with the booth at ground level. Danny at Shoom was something to behold and he would often be seen with his hands in the air, sometimes waving a record around or sometimes reaching for something visible only to him, floating within the music itself. The 'Danny Dance' became part of the spectacle and was the forerunner for the big fish / little fish / wrap it up rave move. Soon the Shoomers were copying Danny and then it popped up in clubs all over the UK and beyond.

DANNY RAMPLING: Well, if it did, I just didn't notice! In Shoom, I was just immersed in the music, I remember being very animated behind the DJ booth. It was so dark down there. It's what I'd call a trance dance, the music would evoke a trance-like state.

TERRY FARLEY: Danny had a dance. The whole acid house dance is an Ibiza dance. All these kids from south London estates went to Ibiza and stayed there all summer. They are copying the Eurotrash, the rich people and the hippies waving at the open-air sun. Danny had a dance (I was quite into my dancing, but my dancing days had kind of gone) and everyone got on to this dance and I was like, 'What the fuck?' Nicky Holloway could see that Danny had caught the wave now and he could see that he was never gonna make any money from it. Danny was the first person to dance like that. I'm not saying he didn't get it from someone in Ibiza, who knows, but that dance was done at Shoom, people probably started looking at the DJ and thinking, 'What the fuck is Danny doing?' I think Nicky could never have done Shoom. Shoom had to be done by someone that no one knew because it was so fucking new. People needed to love or hate Jenni and she needed to be on the door. You had to want to get in.

NICKY HOLLOWAY: Anton Le Pirate was a great acid house dancer. He used to look great with all his dreadlocks. Also, Nino, the old guy in Ibiza. Everyone knew about him, he would wear dungarees, dancing like a madman, at about seventy years old, he looked like Father Christmas. You looked at him and thought, 'That's what I want to be like at his age!'

NANCY NOISE: I'd seen Danny in Amnesia and I saw how into it he was so it wasn't really a surprise for me. I didn't know him. I just knew Nicky. For me it was like we were all just so passionate and we fell in love with the sound, so I probably wasn't really looking at him too much thinking anything because I was just enjoying what was going on, we were all in it together.

Danny concentrated on perfecting his style and in one of those 'I can't believe it even though it really happened' moments from dance music folklore, Carl Cox would give him bpm mixing lessons before Shoom opened its doors.

CARL COX: Me and Danny got on really well. He was a part of the funk mafia, Nicky Holloway's thing. Paul Oakenfold was different. Paul used to come off the back end of their style of music and rip up the rulebook, but at the time Nicky Holloway was one of the best promoters in music for funk and soul. Hip hop was rife. As soon as it went from 98bpm TO 120/122, you were either in it or out of it. So, all the people were out of it to begin with. At the end of the day it's out with the old and in with the new. Any venue you did you normally got kicked out at 2am. Any venue where you could stay meant you were on a proper night out until you came out at eight in the morning – the music took you through.

By March they'd outgrown the venue so moved to the YMCA on Tottenham Court Road. This made it easier to get to but you still had to get past Jenni, who by now was married to Danny, and there were often more people dancing outside the club than in. Another move was urgently needed and Shoom found its way to Busby's, where it became a showcase for the new music and, being more accessible, became more of a destination for other DJs and in particular for visitors from overseas.

TERRY FARLEY: My favourite night at Shoom, I reckon, has to be when Tony Humphries first played, which was at Busby's. I was playing upstairs with Andy Weatherall. We would play 'E records', Danny had dropped the Balearic thing and was playing a lot of New Jersey, New York spiritual house music, and we were upstairs playing slower stuff. I was playing some reggae, like Dennis Brown's 'Love Has Found Its Way'. Everything that I could connect vocally, musically, to that ecstasy experience, it was really good fun. You could find northern soul records or reggae and the crowd connected. You didn't need to take ecstasy to have a good time in a club because that wave of energy is infectious, but Tony was playing downstairs. He was a revelation, he blew my mind to hear him. He was playing a really wide spectrum, he played Talking Heads' 'Once in a Lifetime' and mixed it really well, much better than anyone else, London DJs, northerners, it was very special.

JAY STRONGMAN: Yeah, I went to it. I can't really remember, it's such a blur because I was out almost every night. Everyone was in those days. Once you knew the bouncers and the DJs, it wasn't hard to get in. It seemed like a logical progression, because there is only so far you can go. It had been so fashion conscious from '81 to '86, there was bound to be a natural thing because these crowds, the English and the British, took the best of the new music and acid house and adding to it the drugs, the energy, that European beach look, created something completely new. I went to Greece for the first time and some guy said to me, 'You English are always ahead of everyone.'

Shoom was at the forefront of the scene, with Danny bringing in DJs including Colin Faver, Carl Cox, Andy Weatherall, Terry Farley and Pete Heller. Clubs and nightlife had been all about the music. Sure, some DJs had the best records, but people came to listen. Suddenly, people were worshipping the DJ more than the records and were coming to see Danny in action.

DANNY RAMPLING: I think there was a strong element of that because I'd go out of my way to find music. I was the first to go to Italy and buy Italian productions and bring them back, cover them up and they became hits. I spent a lot of time and money covering up the labels. Therefore, in some circles, it was rather pretentious and arrogant on my behalf. So it kept the music elusive and exclusive for a while because there was a mystery as to what it was, and then on those tracks, people were asking, 'What were they?' There was no Shazam or the internet then. Eventually I would uncover them.

MARK MOORE: Danny Rampling was very important to the underground scene. Like I say, Danny and Jenni set the blueprint for how clubbing became. The thing about it there was that whole kind of loved-up, spiritual, unity side of things, being one family. All that carried on for quite a few years. There was a consciousness that people were trying to bring in. We'd have conversations in the club like, 'How are we going to save the ozone layer?' It was very conscious. I think later on we kind of lost that.

Those in the know were able to get hold of MDMA but it was still an 'exclusive' drug used sparingly by the inner circle. These early house clubbers had this additional shared secret which bonded them together and helped break down barriers, both musical and cultural.

DANNY RAMPLING: There's no denying it, it was part of it. It was part of it. Like psychedelics were part of the 70s and amphetamines were part of the 60s, that was part of the 80s. I think everything collided and came at the right time. The whole stage was set. I did believe that if that wasn't part of the development of the scene, music still would have created the scene with or without it. The tabloid newspapers scandalised one of the most popular and empowering British youth cultural movements that possibly we have ever seen. The tabloid newspapers attempted to smear the scene; well, they grew the scene, large and wide.

The increase in publicity started to attract people from different scenes to experience this phenomenal club that turned football hooligans, street kids, celebrities, middle-aged hippies and city slickers into dancefloor buddies. It was a spectacle and the showmanship and audience reaction was something that hadn't been seen in clubs before, so it was inevitable that many of those leaving Shoom would go on to try to replicate the feeling that they had experienced.

DAVID GUETTA (IN *FORBES* MAGAZINE): I discovered house music in the first wave, way back in '88 ... I went to London and saw a DJ, Danny Rampling, at a club called Shoom, which and whom were leading this counter-culture acid house revolution in the UK. He was centre stage with a crowd going wild like I'd never seen before. I was transfixed; it was my epiphany moment.

PETE HELLER: Well, obviously it's had a fairly huge impact. It inspired me to believe I could make a living out of being creative. I was lucky in that I was in the right place at the right time. But in terms of the music itself, the idea of being able to make something like that wasn't so far-fetched, you just needed the right equipment, which was reasonably affordable. You certainly didn't need to be particularly musically proficient. You just needed to be able to capture the spirit of the dancefloor. And I think, certainly on the dubbier side of the sort of music we were making, that spirit was what we were trying to achieve.

DANNY RAMPLING: I never did recreational drugs at Shoom. Music is what lifted me up in that room. Also, as a DJ you can't play on that. I didn't drink really. I'd go out on Thursday night – that would be my night of recreation. Then Friday I'd be on the radio and then Saturday Shoom. We had a responsibility to everyone that came through that door. We looked after people. Anyone who was overcome by heat … Well, the heat in Shoom in the summer is intense. Contrary to public opinion, because of my energy behind the DJ booth, it was only joy and happiness and love, there was enough of that going on in the room for me to reciprocate. I was absorbing the crowd's energy and giving it back to the crowd, by the way I danced and played and kept the energy levels high.

Acid house even had its own uniform: oversize T-shirts, loose clothing, dungarees and, of course, smiley. A pair of Kickers on your feet and clothing labels like Big Jesus Trashcan and Sign of the Times were part of a whole baggy look that came out of the hot summer clubs in Ibiza. Long before Joe Bloggs kitted out the Madchester scene the look was created by the Amnesiacs just bumming their way around Europe. This was at odds with the underground scene that existed where the 'cool' crowds tended to go. In London, the epicentre of acid house, promoters like Philip Sallon and his Mud Club and Rusty Egan, whose motto had been 'It's better to be looked over than overlooked', suddenly saw a shift, both musically and aesthetically. Philip knew how to fuse music and fashion to great effect. On his opening night in 1983 he had Malcolm McLaren doing a live performance of 'Buffalo Gals' and a couple of weeks later Afrika Bambaataa did a one-hour set. Philip had always allowed his DJs like Jay Strongman and Mark Moore total musical freedom and they had experimented with house, but he wasn't prepared for the changes that the Second Summer of Love would bring. No one could have predicted the rise and rise of dance music and the emergence of a whole new clubbing generation. Suddenly, there was a division between the scene that was used to being trendsetters and these new partygoers who were 'on trend' but oblivious to it.

JAY STRONGMAN: I guess there was a rift. I remember Philip [Sallon] having a difficult time because no one was dressing up because all the kids looked the exact same in a way, in baggy trousers and T-shirts. I think he had a good seven years before he closed [Bagley's]. He actually did it 'cos he loved dressing up, making an effort. It wasn't so much about the money, he's the king of kitsch. He really put a lot into these nights, would spend a fortune decorating the place, making sure everyone really made an effort.

RUSTY EGAN: I was dressed stylishly, I still looked like me. Mark Powell suits, I smoked Dunhill in cigarette cases and then there [were] girls sucking lollipops wearing the smiley T-shirt on the dancefloor and I've got my hands in the air and I'm loving the music and they are like, 'What are you doing here? You don't fit in here,' and I didn't say anything, just gave them a look like 'stupid question'.

NANCY NOISE: It was all about the baggy stuff. We all used to wear long jumpers and people would stand out to you if you liked their jumper or their top. You'd be thinking, 'Oh wow, they've got something on that's really cool.' I had this black cut-sleeved tank top and it had black and white squares and I remember loving wearing it with black trousers and a black hat on – sorted, comfortable. Jumpers were important.

TERRY FARLEY: I was going to football before I went clubbing. So kind of '85/'86, casual had changed from kind of tennis gear like Fila and Ellesse into European casual clothes which was stuff like Chevignon, Best Company, Chipie, etc, and so I went to football dressed like that. Almost a year later when acid house kicked in you'd go to Shoom and see people in clothes that I was wearing to football. So I was more than happy, actually. I got my wish, I didn't have to go home and change. I literally stopped going to football when acid house kicked in. By then my buzz was so opposed from shouting at a man playing football and other supporters that I just didn't go. It was very easy for me to feed into that fashion. Yes, it was baggy jeans, dungarees but they were Lee dungarees. There were rules. By the time the thing went nationwide, the rules were out the window – the kids were wearing any old dungarees and baggy T-shirts. Shoom, Spectrum, the Future were still for fashion connoisseurs but the rules had changed. All the girls at Shoom wore cool stuff like Vivienne Westwood Care Bear T-shirts. There was a great label called Big Jesus Trashcan. All kind of distressed, with paintings on, it was like, 'Wow, look at this.' So the rules had changed but you still had to wear the right stuff. Of course, by the time this meets the M25, it's a look now. But very early on it had to be the right T-shirt. I like rules. I think they are important in club culture. They keep people on their toes, people have to make a bit of an effort.

Rules were important to some degree. Vivienne Westwood's designers and assistants were likely to be found at Shoom, as were the teams from other leading designers, so translating what they saw into what they would wear themselves was a logical step. The clothes shops were also the places to pick up the latest flyers, so a mini collaborative industry, feeding off each other, began to take shape. One of the most important shops was Sign of the Times, which had been started by Shoomer Fiona Cartledge in Camden Market before moving to Kensington Market and then on to Covent Garden. Fiona designed the iconic jackets with religious iconography for Big Jesus Trashcan's shop in Kensington Market, and these ended up being worn by the likes of Danny Rampling, Bob Geldof and S-Express. Sign of the Times was born out of Shoom and was a great example of the 'anything is possible' attitude that the new scene created. Alongside displaying flyers they started selling mixtapes from DJs, tickets for raves and fanzines. Before long they were throwing their own first-class parties under the Sign of the Times name.

With so much going on it is easy to forget that Shoom was

relatively small. You had to actually get in to experience it and Danny wasn't a gun for hire – to hear and see him you needed to get over to Shoom. The London club scene was in full swing and dance music was starting to be more present at mainstream clubs. While this sounds like a good thing, the UK electronic scene didn't have the solid foundations that had been laid in Chicago and Detroit, and there was a real danger that the music would be too diluted to make the impact it would need if it was going to spawn a whole new genre and mindset.

DANNY RAMPLING: There was a lot of spiritual energy going on in Shoom, and quite a bit of tripping going on as well, but that's a side. I was really vocal, I was the spokesperson for the right things and the positive things about the scene and life and the whole message behind Shoom, which was about positivity, hope, fun and opportunity. That had an effect on people because I'd be relaying positive statements, I engaged with people, that's what it was about. I was engaging with people on the floor, people could get really up close.

PETE HELLER: I think it was huge. The other element, in addition to the attitude shift, was the futuristic sounds coming out of the electronic dance scenes in New York and Chicago. This was mainly due to the availability of affordable electronic instruments, which up to that point had been restricted to the more experimental or *avant-garde* scenes or mainstream pop. To be in a club and hear an almost completely new sound, with the energy behind it, was to experience something extraordinarily different. In combination with the drugs it gave that feeling of abandoning yourself to the groove, and knowing that you were safe because everyone was tuned into the same frequency enhanced that. So it wasn't just about coming to dance and losing your inhibitions – it was abandoning everything to be *part* of the dance, being connected to something bigger. It was quite pagan in that sense. And the music, being so new and so different and hypnotic, provided that by stripping away all your reference points. It was massively liberating.

JAY STRONGMAN: It was kind of gradual. You noticed more and more people dressing down, that whole Euro look. Mark Moore and myself were really early on playing house music, it kind of fitted in with our disco stuff, there was only a bunch of DJs doing it. I think they were calling it garage before the name house became more apparent. Mark would continue that. More and more people were saying, 'Let's play the house stuff all night' – I noticed that. I definitely thought this was the new wave, I was aware enough of youth culture to think, 'Oh, how quickly do things change.'

With this new sound the established club figures and the ultra-trendies suddenly started to seem like cultural dinosaurs, teetering on the edge of a precipice and looking up unblinking as a massive meteorite headed straight towards them. To be fair, it wasn't always possible to embrace the change. Many of the movers and shakers were so established that to change was to admit that they were wrong. This was most apparent in the music industry. Some of the younger guys like Pete Tong were able to use their youth and knowledge to make things happen, but in most cases electronic music was not something that major labels took seriously.

> **RUSTY EGAN:** Now here it was coming from everywhere. The record industry didn't consider a DJ to be an artist. 'Who's the singer?' they'd say. I actually made a record at Island Records, a cover version. It must have been 1989 or something. So that's the point, I was embracing this music. I got Richie Rich to remix an extended version of Led Zeppelin's 'A Whole Lot of Love' and I put acid house graphics on it and I wrote, 'Every generation is a musical revolution. Rave on 1990.' Guess what happens. The record company said, 'Forget it.'

Rusty Egan is a clubland legend. A pioneer of several music scenes, he used his skills as a drummer and his love of electronic music to try to get the industry to embrace house. Rusty has a good track record, giving bands like Depeche Mode their big break and being an early influential club DJ at places like Blitz and Billy's, but the industry couldn't seem to get to grips with sampling and the ownership that went with it. They saw DJs as people playing other people's music rather than creators and remixers of a new sound.

> **RUSTY EGAN:** In the late 70s, a drummer played and then the guitar player played and then perhaps a synthesiser. Basically, they recorded them all separately. Then we made 'Fade to Grey', which was a ground-

breaking record at 104bpm. We made records with drum machines but still recorded things separately. Now we're in recording studios which cost a fortune, in a pre-production suite which costs a fortune, while suddenly you could make a record with a little drum machine, get it pressed and stick copies out. There wasn't a proper sampled tune until I made a record which became 'Wildstyle' by Time Zone which I made in Germany when I went to sign Yello in 1983. I then sampled bands like Kraftwerk, Chic and Blancmange. I did the whole thing. That was possibly the first one of these. At that time out came a record called 'Rockit' by Herbie Hancock, and then on the B side there was a mash-up between 'Rockit' and 'Time Zone'. I got robbed of that whole record.

MARK MOORE: I'd have to say Rusty Egan was the DJ that influenced me the most. Blitz was one of the first clubs I'd been to, Blitz and the Hell. After the opening night at Hell it wasn't very busy and it was almost like Rusty Egan was just DJing for me and the fact that he mixed it up, he'd put on electronic records and then he'd put on Bowie, he was so eclectic. I loved the way he mixed it up. Another DJ that's influential was John Peel, he was a radio DJ rather than a club DJ but his eclecticism was amazing. Then Tasty Tim got me started as a DJ. He would play in places like Cha Cha. I also learned a lot from Jay Strongman at the Mud Club, who was very influential, very sweet, very helpful.

PAUL OAKENFOLD: Future never got the respect it deserved. It wasn't trendy like Shoom so no trendies were interested in it. Shoom was a Saturday-night club for trendies. We were running Spectrum on Mondays and Future on Thursdays. You had to be committed to come to those nights. Future was the workers' club. One Saturday, Ian St Paul organised a coach trip to Gravesend that would go to Shoom on the way back, and when we got to Shoom Jenni wouldn't let us in. That was it – we stopped going after that.

JAY STRONGMAN: In hindsight it's more obvious but at the time it didn't seem so obvious. I'd say Mark Moore was the first Balearic DJ, he was playing this eclectic style from '84/'85. I guess in '84 when it was all hip hop and funk and this came out '88, there was a lot of new crowd that I guess would have been a soul boy crowd, the soul mafia crowd, who seemed to go straight into house stuff, they almost bypassed the whole hip hop stuff. There was a lot of football-supporter guys. That became obvious, they would start chanting 'ECSTASY, ECSTASY'. Obviously, DJs love when the crowd is chanting but [Terry] Farley said to me, 'It's like being in a football crowd.' It worried me a little bit.

TERRY FARLEY: You all need a springboard, don't you. I always thank Paul [Oakenfold] for giving me the residency at Future. At Spectrum I was probably getting about £25 a week and you know records cost a lot of money, around £6. Basically, I was covering the records.

About six months later, Paul would close Future and wanted to relaunch it. He said, 'I want you and Nancy [Noise] and I'll give you around £100 a week each. I was earning that working five days a week. People are sometimes negative about Paul and Danny. I think a lot of it stems from the first two years. Spectrum, and Future were so important, so incredible, that when Paul moved into playing trance they felt it was too different … and of course the tough door policy at Shoom [was another factor]. The final night at Shoom was in The Park in Kensington, and Boy George sang kind of acapella, he sang 'After the Love Has Gone' and Jenni got up on the bar to give a tirade to people who had slagged them off and accused them of having sold out. I like Jenni. What they created originally was this really intense bond, almost like, 'This is your family now.' The club at Shoom is a kind of cult. People would ask to come to Shoom and we would be like, 'No'. It was almost like this was your new family. Looking back, there was a slight cult about it [he smiles]. These were really your best friends. I have best friends today that I met there. I speak to people who talk about *Boy's Own* in the same way, we had to know them and I wasn't aware of that as you don't think about it because you're in it. But Shoom, I was in it to win it and I do think that what they created then was so intense that it's really hard to recreate that. Without those two I wouldn't be, you wouldn't be talking to me now. I don't know what I would be doing.

SPECTRUM

Up until this point things were done on the fly. Quick decisions about venue, line-up and artwork could only get you so far. It needed a bigger stage and it needed a foot in the door of the mainstream club world. Paul Oakenfold went a step further and nearly a step too far. He didn't just put a foot in the door, he kicked it in and stomped on the pieces. That door could never be closed again.

On 11 April 1988 Oakenfold and his friends opened Spectrum.

* * *

On the surface, Spectrum should never have worked. It was held at a predominantly gay club, near to Trafalgar Square and Parliament. It was owned by Virgin's Richard Branson, who couldn't afford to let anything interfere with his public and political image. And it was massive, holding over a thousand people. They were given the *Titanic* of clubland, Monday night, and were pointed in the direction of the iceberg. Happy sailing, mateys!

Oakey and Ian St Paul had a vision and the determination and belief to see it come to reality. Holding the Spectrum flyer, designed by Dave Little, you knew you were in for a treat. The multicolour front had a large all-seeing eye announcing Spectrum, Heaven on Earth, and inviting you to their 'Theatre of Madness'. The back was more traditional in that it was in black-and-white. Nothing else was, as in big letters it asked you to get 'On One' every Monday and asked, 'Can you pass the acid test – Aciiieeed!' with DJs P. Oakenfold and J. Walker.

MARK MOORE: The thing about Spectrum was I remember Paul telling me, come down, I'm at this new night on Monday at Heaven. I remember laughing, thinking, 'Monday at Heaven? It's huge. How is he going to fill that out?' and we went for opening night and there was, what, 200 people there, and it's a huge place and all the haters were like, 'Yeah, we knew it was going to flop,' and the 200 people inside had the best time ever, I had the best time. Everyone told someone else about it and within weeks there [were] queues. On a Monday night!

DAVE SWINDELLS: In hindsight the thing that made it different was that it was obvious that this was going to be the club that was going to inspire change. All these club promoters were there, they were partying there, one or two of them already running clubs but the real thing, seeing all the people who had already made a name for themselves partying and you could see straight away that this is going to be the start of something huge.

Heaven was the perfect venue for them – it has the best sound system in the UK and the kind of lights and lasers you'd find in the big New York gay clubs. On the first night every clubber (between 100 and 200 of them) was given a free E. Original partners like Gary Haisman pulled out, but Ian St Paul kept his nerve and concentrated on making it work while Paul concentrated on the music. Things started slowly but the word spread like wildfire. Within three weeks there were 1,200 people inside the club with nearly as many outside trying to get in. Pretty soon they were at a capacity of 2,500, with everyone dancing in the streets when the club closed at 3.30am. London had never seen anything like it. Monday night, the quietest night in clubland, was working in their favour.

TERRY FARLEY: Up until acid house you wouldn't have found anyone in a club over thirty. Things were just building up. Then Ibiza happened and it was an explosion, like a chemistry set. House music on its own wasn't enough. Ecstasy on its own wasn't enough. People had been putting on illegal parties, they were already there. It was a chemistry set, the critical mass hits and the wave of people start going mad. The first week I got a residence at Spectrum, there were 120 people there, all for free. It was probably my favourite night ever. And literally six weeks later thousands were outside.

NANCY NOISE: I think when Shoom was on, Shoom was kind of lots of the Ibiza lot; when Future was on, I wondered how did people hear about it. The first week was just friends and stuff. I remember there was this group from Waltham Abbey and I remember thinking, 'How did they hear about this?' It was like someone in Ibiza who heard. Future was on a Thursday. Then they started Spectrum and the first few weeks was really quiet, obviously it's a really big club as well. In Spectrum, I remember arriving one night – I used to play upstairs in the Star bar. I used to do upstairs with Tony Wilson, which was a more Balearic sound, and you arrived and there was this massive queue going all the way down and around the block. The word had spread and then Spectrum was so busy. They started doing the all-dayers and then not long after that, it was kind of the beginnings of the raves. I know there was all this stuff going on in east London and there was a warehouse scene. Then I realised this was big.

Musically, it was a Balearic mix of anything goes. On one famous occasion Paul plunged the club into total darkness and played Tchaikovsky's *1812 Overture*. At Shoom, Danny and the DJs were right in the midst of the action. At Spectrum, Paul was in a DJ booth high above the packed dancefloor, playing whatever he felt like. This was the real start of the headline DJ and all that went with it, and Paul was ready for it. The boy who'd sat next to Trevor Fung on a coach trip talking about getting into DJing was a couple of years away from being on tour with U2 as their support act and becoming the world's first global superstar DJ.

MARK MOORE: Spectrum was incredible. It was kind of like Shoom but more theatrical in a way. You'd have things like a giant E would come down all lit up and sparkly, the letter E. You'd be like, 'Did that actually happen or was I tripping?' Then you'd be like, 'No, that actually happened.' It was on such a bigger scale at Heaven, it was like a Fellini film. You'd have these big musclemen on the podium, dancing and posing.

GRAEME PARK: At Heaven, Paul had this crazy idea to get myself, Mike Pickering, Johnny Walker and him on at the same time so we all had two decks each and they built four DJ booths, all in different parts of the club. Paul's mad idea was that we all DJed at the same time. Like so many nights back then, you ended up getting a bit off of it so I can't remember if it worked or not.

TERRY FARLEY: The opening night was special. I was given a residency. I was given VIP in the very top floor of Heaven where there was a glass window looking down on the dancefloor. I was playing with Alex Patterson from New York. He was playing chill-out music, I was playing reggae and it got to the point where it was only the main and the VIP open. It was empty. One week I was looking down and instead of there being a hundred people there were five hundred. I could see what was going on. I would get to a point where I had some King Tubby albums. I was putting music on, leaving it, running down for five minutes and then running back 'cos the record would run out, and it got to the point where I said to Paul, 'I've got to be able to play other music,' and he said, 'We are going to open a middle floor,' and we played an alternative to what Paul was playing. It was me and a guy called

Roger Beard, aka Roger the Hippie. He was a strange man, he had a wife called Maggie and they had several kids and they would turn up at Shoom events with their kind of trailer, and all the young girls would end up in the trailer with Maggie and the kids, cuddling the kids, and Roger would be playing these old 60s records. And me and him used to play on the middle floor. Stuff like Yello's 'The Race'. I started playing Sister Sledge, 'Thinking of You', which was an overplayed record. I played it at '86 at a rare groove thing, and it would be cool. Play it in '88, and it would be an explosion, it sounded like a completely different record. So, I think my favourite night was when they let me play on the middle floor. My sister was seven years younger than me and she was really into Madness and she had loads of their records. I went through them and she had 'It Must Be Love', which I played near the end of the night and it was like really magical. When the piano played the place went mad. The place was alive. Straight away it was this wave of positivity.

Spectrum was the place to be. Not just to show off, but to experience what was going on, whatever the hell it was. The Pet Shop Boys famously brought Liza Minelli so she could see what was going on. The balcony was shut off for her and you can only imagine that after a bottle of champagne she may have felt she was back at Studio 54. This is where U2 first clapped eyes on Paul Oakenfold, who also played host to the likes of Prince, David Bowie and Bros. More importantly, Spectrum was the place that the US DJs would visit when they were over. Normally booked somewhere for a Saturday night, Monday would see them checking out Spectrum. Kevin Saunderson was able to witness first-hand the reaction to Inner City's 'Big Fun' as the crowd lost their minds to his tune. There had been nothing like it before. People would walk in as one person and become a totally different person by the end of the night. And once you'd 'seen the light' you couldn't go back.

> **RUSTY EGAN:** Paul Oakenfold's night was Monday night at Heaven. Of course I enjoyed it, I was in the booth with him, asking him, 'What is that tune?' There was one with some bells. Basically it sounded to me like a loop and it was the same thing over and over. And there was no vocal. It was very minimal. I loved it. To be honest, I am a musician. I was only a DJ because the generation of DJs before me only played soul, funk and American imports and they didn't play what I wanted to hear. Now, there were DJs playing what I wanted to hear and I became more of a promoter. I wanted to book these DJs, promote these events.

This was the club that propelled acid house to a national audience. Unfortunately, not always in a positive way, and with such a high-profile owner in Branson the inevitable happened. On 17 August, with the '88 Ibiza season in full swing, the *Sun* newspaper, who had a few months earlier been selling their smiley T-shirts, published an investigation into Heaven. They went as far as to ridicule their own concept by saying that 'Junkies flaunt their craving by wearing T-shirts sold at the club bearing messages like "Can you feel it?" and "Drop acid not bombs".' Suddenly, the country was talking about acid and LSD, completely missing what acid house was all about. Most clubs would have kicked you out, shut you down, locked the doors and thrown away the key. But not Branson. He told Paul that it needed to 'look' closed but that he could continue. Spectrum was put on hold in London, with Monday nights reopening under the new name, 'Land of Oz'.

> **PAUL OAKENFOLD:** The reason we called it that was because the *Sun* newspaper got into Spectrum and we had called it 'heaven on earth' and they renamed it 'hell on earth'. Richard Branson said they were going to shut the club for a couple of weeks and then reopen it under another name, so we called it the Yellow Brick Road. We painted the pavement from Charing Cross train station to the club like the yellow-brick road from *The Wizard of Oz*.

Land of Oz was important. Paul brought in more DJs, like Colin Hudd who already had clubland followings at places like Flicks and Crackers and who would go on to introduce this new way of relaxing and truly enjoying a dancefloor to an ever-growing army of dance music devotees. It cemented acid house as a *bona fide* scene that wasn't going to go away. It was an important melting pot where musicians, DJs, designers and the whole spectrum (couldn't resist!) of creative types and club kids came together. Amazingly, despite the obvious market for new music and the massive publicity (all publicity is good publicity, right?) and the fact that the man behind Virgin owned the most high-profile club, the music industry were slow to get on the party bus. You had this huge, mainstream entertainment industry employing thousands of people trying to find, market and sell the next big thing, oblivious to the fact that they were a stone's throw away from a bunch of kids who were producing, plugging and marketing the next big thing – and they were largely doing it for free. Mark Moore played and partied with the acid house crowd but also fitted in with the trendy influencer hangouts and filtered some of the great dancefloor tracks back to an audience of movers and shakers who grooved to his beat.

TERRY FARLEY: It's a bit weird. I didn't know Mark Moore before acid house, I wasn't important enough to be in the DJ booth. Once Shoom happened, I never played the great pop records as they didn't connect with the underground or how we saw ourselves. The first record that people from the *Boy's Own* scene were behind was when Andrew Weatherall did the 'Loaded' remix for Primal Scream and that got played. He played an acetate of that and I remember thinking it was so amazing, so timeless. I still see it today in adverts on TV, on the radio.

RUSTY EGAN: I have been laughed at for backing punks, gays, gender-benders, synthesisers, I have been laughed at every single step of the way. Monday night at Heaven had a couple of thousand ravers loving new music. Now I recognised it. I was jumping up and down trying to get the record companies to come and see it, but they were more interested in going to see the football.

PAUL OAKENFOLD: We had this moment where there was a band called KLF who had a No. 1 pop record and they did their only ever live club show at Land of Oz.

So here we are again. The youth are trying to create something for themselves. It's based around going out with your mates, having a good time, listening to great music, dancing and meeting people. The establishment say, 'Naughty children! Don't do this, and in fact don't do anything instead. Don't have a good time and please wipe that massive grin off your face.' They do this by writing about it in the national press and include pictures of lovely people having a lovely time. For some reason, and in a tried and tested manner, this didn't stop anyone from doing anything and the kids thought, 'Hmmmm, this looks interesting. I'll check it out – and tell ALL my friends.'

PAUL OAKENFOLD: Spectrum was the true birth of acid house in Britain. We created a whole movement that turned club culture into youth culture, because the raves came the year after.

Within a month there were also Spectrum parties in Manchester at Legends, with the Haçienda's Mike Pickering joining Paul behind the decks and the nights being promoted with the same 'Theatre of Madness' flyers. Inadvertently, and without any game plan, places that wouldn't have dared play house were suddenly packed with a totally 'mad for it' crowd who wanted to be 'largin' it', just like everyone else was. It didn't matter who you were or where you were from, this was a club that was open to everyone who wanted in.

IRVINE WELSH: My early books, in particular, were conscious attempts to capture the beats and effects of house music, the dynamism and excitement. I didn't write in phonetic Scots to make some point about cultural hegemony and linguistic imperialism – I did it simply because it's an oral, performed language and used to convey emotion and experience rather than instruction and therefore has beats. It's not a Celtic thing – Chaucer was the same. The FX were my typographical experiments. No way would I have become a writer without being immersed in acid house.

THE TRIP

All of the Ibiza Four were DJs but Nicky Holloway was
also a well-established promoter. Nicky had a loyal
following who went to his Special Branch parties and because
he was so involved in an ongoing scene it took longer for him
to make his Amnesia experience an integral part of his events.
After all, it's not always wise to change a good thing.

> **DANNY RAMPLING:** From Nicky I learned how to
> read the audience and the timing of playing certain
> tracks, setting up club decors, direct promotion and
> marketing, people skills … and his cheekiness – I
> learned that as well.

Since the holiday to Ibiza the previous summer Nicky had
bided his time and had been slightly knocked for six when his
good friend and sometime apprentice Danny Rampling opened
Shoom. Nicky found out about the night at the last minute,

apparently after picking up a Shoom flyer that was lying on his own dancefloor. He came down to the opening of Shoom and must have been the only person there who didn't enjoy it.

DANNY RAMPLING: I was really upset, I was pissed off. I thought, you know, I've worked with you for a long while and I was very supportive. He didn't like it. I told him I was going to do Shoom but I don't think Nicky thought I had the capacity to do it, but I did and I went off and did it. I modelled what Nicky had taught me. That's the whole art of being in a system as an apprentice. So, I went off and did my own thing and put a lot of energy into the artwork, the design. I felt a bit wound up at the fact that I was unappreciated. I'd worked with him for four years and I helped him and he helped me, it was a two-way street. Really, he should have been proud and said, 'Your time is now,' and it was his time too! He created something bigger and commercial. He took the money. [With Shoom] I did not take the money. He may have wanted to take the route that I took.

NICKY HOLLOWAY: I found out about Shoom when Danny handed out flyers at my club. He got my security, my sound, my printers, my artwork. So we kind of fell out. He didn't tell me until I saw the flyer. I felt a bit pissed off. But I didn't take him seriously as a DJ at first. I was a little aggrieved, I felt like I was being ripped off. It was all the people I had introduced him to. I felt a bit like he had done it behind my back. I went to Shoom. I've talked to Danny about it. It's like someone who works for you going off and doing what you're doing, which goes on all the time. I didn't enjoy myself, not really, when I went. I only went a couple of times. All my friends were going. I was pissed off, 'cos he started out just before I did [The Trip] and all the people in there were people I knew. But we made up fairly soon after. I felt like I was the last one to know. The art bloke was my bloke, security, sound system, all the things that I used, connections he had made through me, but I was sort of forgotten. We are better friends now than ever. I love Danny to pieces.

On 4 June 1988 Nicky Holloway opened The Trip and, while it didn't last long and was not as influential in the long term as Spectrum, Future, Land of Oz or Shoom, it gave the nation something new. Pictures of thousands of people out in the streets dancing after the club night finished. Not because they were invited to, not because they were encouraged to, but because they wanted to. These street parties were largely trouble-free, at least from the clubbers' point of view, and fuelled the illicitness of the party scene which was just about to enter into a summer of raves that would become known as the Second Summer Of Love. The Trip was held at the Astoria, in the heart of the West End, and was the kind of venue that was 'on the tourist map'.

NICKY HOLLOWAY: When it started I'd already done a couple of parties there, but they were more of a one-off. I kind of wasn't sure if I was gonna be able to fill it up. We decided we wouldn't open up the balcony unless it was busy downstairs. Salt-N-Pepa, the rap band, were on before. We had half an hour before half past ten to put up all the decorations and we turned it around and then from the first night it was rammed. I remember standing up there thinking, 'It's not gonna get much better than this.' Sometimes I did the whole night on my own [as the DJ] and I was also taking the door money – you know, it was the first legal Saturday-night rave. When people would see them all dancing in the streets, it was special. The funny thing is, it was very organic, there wasn't a marketing plan, no one sat there and dreamt this up, just all the parts fell together at the right time. The week we opened, *i-D* magazine and *The Face* did front-cover stories about us and they were the only two style magazines out there. So it just fell that the last weekend of May, when we started, June's issue comes out the week before and the timing was perfect. It meant all these people felt they were trying it out for the first time.

TIME OUT: The spontaneous street parties have been continuing wherever three or more acid house fans get together, especially after club one-nighters. They've partied 'til 5am in Trafalgar Square, 8am in a London Bridge car park, and blocked Tottenham Court Road for the fourth week in succession after the final night of The Trip club … hundreds of happy acid fans swaying, yelling, 'Street Party! Street Party!' in unison. The police were less than amused but stayed cool under pressure, but the traffic-jammed car drivers were totally mystified. [10 August 1988]

There was a general feeling of togetherness, and being a part of the acid house scene was a badge of honour. The Trip was an instant hit, and it took everyone by surprise. There was no couple of nights to get going – Trip just took off and was seen as the most successful acid house night, even though it was over in the blink of an (all-seeing) eye.

NICKY HOLLOWAY: Probably because it was a lot of people's first experience with that sort of thing. I've got a video where we're all doing this silly dancing, but it wasn't silly at the time. Maybe 'cos Shoom was smaller. But the other thing was, Paul's was a Monday. I think it was the first Saturday legal one there was. Shoom wasn't really legal. We had a proper licensed bar. But Shoom used to stay open until 6am and nowhere else had a later licence, but you could never drink after 3.30am anyway.

MARK MOORE: I really enjoyed it. It was kind of like Nicky took it out of the underground. Before that it was Paul Oakenfold's Future, Danny and Jenni Rampling's Shoom, Spectrum. They were all underground. Suddenly, Trip was Saturday night and it was a different crowd as well. Some from the other clubs but it was more of a West End crowd, people doing their first E, experimenting, like, 'What's this all about?' Lots of the hip hop kids went as well, who said, 'I hate this music,' and then they took an E and were like, 'I love this.' To me it was looked down upon by the Aciderati, as I call them, but it was really exciting to see these kids who were kind of acid virgins having their minds changed.

DANNY RAMPLING: They were part of something that was greater than themselves and the whole spirit of it. We all were. Not they. We were. That was infectious to everybody.

DAVE SWINDELLS: We needed to document and let people know what was happening. We needed to shout about it.

RUSTY EGAN: The weekend parties were underground but if you went to clubs on a Monday to Thursday, the same promoters took the nights. Clubs were over the moon because thousands of people showed up on a Monday night and didn't drink much alcohol but paid to get in. The clubs were happy. They 'did' and they 'didn't' know people were on drugs. Without going into great detail, the raves which started out on the weekends created an audience of people who also wanted it on a Monday. It was already happening on the weekend. They wanted it Monday, Tuesday, Wednesday, Thursday, so really these people were people that came from the suburbs, whereas the West End was more people dressed up to go up West. If you just went out clubbing in jeans and trainers you wouldn't get into clubs in the West End but you would at the raves. So rave culture came into the West End and the West End had to say 'let them all in' and they were happy to let them in on Monday, Tuesday, Wednesday, Thursday, but not Friday and Saturday. Prime clubbing real estate reserved for 'grown-ups' and serious spenders. Also, the DJs playing at these raves were just starting so some of them were brought in to play for us, like Judge Jules who I got into Wall Street, a club in Mayfair. I loved him.

Being a high-profile promoter with a prime Saturday night in the heart of the West End, a night with a very lucrative door take, created problems for Nicky. Clubbing today is very different. Everything is regulated, from the bar and the opening hours to the door staff. You can buy tickets online, get there by cab with an app or public transport by tapping a card, and pay for everything (legal) by card. Your income goes into a computerised till, government taxes are accounted for and the wages come with payslips. Back then it was all about cash. Cash on the door, cash over the bar, cash for everything and everyone. If you think how many club nights there were and how many clubs there were to hold them in and all those clubs had DJs, doormen, flyers, bars, and all of those things were paid in cash, and then you imagine the cash that went into the warehouse and rave scene and you can see why the powers that be were suddenly going to come down hard. But before it could get to that stage Nicky had issues closer to home to deal with. Now remember, Nicky was a seasoned promoter, so if he says it was bad enough to stop a good thing dead in its tracks then it must have been terrible.

NICKY HOLLOWAY: In the end it started getting … In those days there wasn't CCTV, alarms on doors. In those days it was a Rottweiler and a couple of doormen. You'd be trying your best not to let certain people in but they'd be paying at the back door and get in. It got a bit heavy in the end, too many people offering you things. We lost control of our own door in the end. It got too much, the pressure of it all. The Trip went for nine weeks. Then the venue had a play booked in which stiffed, didn't do well, so they called me straight back in. Before the break we were always told we could go back, but that's when all the newspapers started doing all these acid house stories, so we thought we'd better not call it The Trip 'cos of the drug connotations so that's when we called it Sin. There was a lot of pressure on me, driving to the gig every Saturday, you had butterflies, nerves. The worst was people were paying the doormen and there was two companies of doormen. You didn't want all black or all white doormen, so we had to mix it up and they were all blaming each other. That night my car got scratched up, my new BMW got keyed.

Almost as quickly as it had started, The Trip was over ...

NICKY HOLLOWAY: It's funny, 'cos I know I have the credibility and the sort of pedigree of it that I just didn't get the money for. I feel proud. That's how I felt. But one thing I didn't do, which I didn't fucking think about, was keeping that door money. I got hit with a massive tax bill and it all came crashing down ...but it took like a year.

... but it left its mark. It gave the established, and dare I say complacent, trendy clubs and their crowd of influencers a shock. Suddenly, they were playing catch-up and had to decide whether to stay on their path or to jump into and if possible ahead of this whole new world that might end up only being a short-lived fad. Many of them had sampled the delights of Ibiza, New York, Chicago and possibly Detroit, so the culture vultures probably had a good inkling that this was a wave they wanted to ride. Some of the key movers and shakers like Jay Strongman, Mark Moore, Chris Sullivan at the WAG, Phil Dirtbox and Rusty Egan were music-led so were familiar with house. And it wasn't just a London thing. Across the UK there were early experiments in house music that were springing up in clubs throughout '86 and '87, but these club nights lacked the all-encompassing lifestyle that was the lifeforce of the Second Summer of Love.

CARL LOBEN: It's important to stress that it wasn't just Oakey's Spectrum and Danny Rampling's Shoom that kicked off the UK's acid house revolution. House music permeated the London gay scene in the mid-80s via DJs like Mark Moore, and Manchester got house well before the end of '87 via DJs like Mike Pickering and Graeme Park. Many other areas of the UK – Glasgow, Nottingham and so on – didn't just wait until London was kicking off, they spontaneously got their own thing going. However, what the fabled Ibiza Four kick-started after their holiday was more to do with the culture. It was inclusive, it was fresh, it allowed football hooligans to dance next to stockbrokers. The fact that quite a few other London music people had also been to Ibiza — and so immediately 'got it' — undeniably helped. And the Ibiza devotees had photographers around and writers for the style press, and so got the lion's share of the credit. But it was a bottom-up revolution, rather than top-down.

Some of the key London hangouts like Wall Street were all about attracting a high-fashion, jet-set, trendy international crowd, so they stayed as they were and carried on hosting superstars like Prince. However, even Wall Street caught the bug when the owner, Gerard, was introduced to a new DJ, Judge Jules, by his good friend Rusty Egan. It was promoters like Philip Sallon, creator of the incredible Mud Club, and Leigh Bowery of Taboo fame who initially struggled. For them, image was an important part of the show. The kind of people who spend the best part of a day getting ready to go out, and then head out for a night out with light bulbs on their heads or wearing togas alongside capes made of newspapers and shaving foam (and that's when they're going for a quiet one) were at odds with a crowd whose idea of dressing up was a pair of dungarees, a baggy T-shirt, an oversized dummy in their mouth and nicely topped off with an all-over dripping suit of sweat.

MARK MOORE: They didn't know what hit them because the West End was a certain way, it came from the New Romantics, it was all about dressing up and looking smart. Suddenly this new scene was about dressing to sweat, not about wearing expensive suits. It was almost like overnight they became dinosaurs. I remember it took a while for them to adapt. I remember them telling me off for playing house music at the WAG club, which I still did anyway, and I remember saying then, 'A few years ago you told me off about hip hop and then everyone loved it lots.' So Philip [Sallon], he's good at what he does, and within that year the Mud Club was even more happening. Philip benefitted because he had the biggest club ever, the Mud Club, and was doing raves. He didn't miss the boat, he knew he had to change with the times.

RUSTY EGAN: Just because music changed doesn't mean they had nowhere to go. They had the WAG club for years and the Café de Paris. What happened was another generation arrived. I tried to talk to Cymon Eckel and I went to *Boy's Own* parties at the Middlesex and Herts Country Club, I went to Paul Oakenfold's underground raves, to warehouses, I went to Sunrise, everywhere, but what did they need Rusty Egan for? They had their own thing going on. So then I went to the record companies and I was laughed out by everyone and couldn't get one person to go with me to a rave. They'll go to football though. I'd say, 'Call me at midnight, I'll meet you,' and they said, 'Fuck off, I'm going to football.' I said they have to come see this, they said 'no'.

GERARD: 'I was too busy running my club [Wall Street] to go to Shoom or Spectrum but kept hearing about this new energy being played by Paul Oakenfold and Danny Rampling. Ibiza was always a special place for me and I could see that finally London was ready to open its heart. We were already playing some US house but the new London sound needed home-grown talent with an ear to the ground to make it work. Rusty Egan always had the edge when it came to spotting DJs with the skills to lift the dancefloor to the next level. He introduced me to Judge Jules, who was also throwing parties with Norman Jay, whose selection of music I was really into. Jules was exciting to watch and the queues to get in just grew and grew each week. I could see that the DJs were becoming more important than the clubs. It was then that I knew house music was here to stay and the West End clubs could never stay the same.

NICKY HOLLOWAY: I remember standing in the club at its peak and thinking, 'It is never going to get better than this.' And it never did really, not for me.

INSIDE & OUT

FROM WAREHOUSE
TO RAVE

In the future, when historians need to put an exact chrono-logical stamp on the Second Summer of Love they will mark it down as 1988. It was a busy summer. Shoom, Spectrum (soon to be Land of Oz) and The Trip were moving to their beat and growing the scene. Chicago, Detroit and Italy were producing great records to fuel the dancefloors and a whole new wave of up-for-it British clubbers joined the holidaymakers in Ibiza. A new wave of producers were emerging, particularly in the USA and especially in New York. The hottest producer to emerge in '88 didn't come from the New York club scene. It was a kid from Brooklyn. His name was Todd Terry – he shot to prominence with 'Bango' and his skills went global with the biggest club record of the year, Royal House's 'Can You Party!'

New music was important and experiencing it under the stars in Ibiza was cool, but holidays are short-lived and people wanted more than just listening to the music. They wanted to listen to it together. Clubs were great, but warehouses and fields seemed better, more edgy, more 'now'. Before it became a 'dirty' word, you could rave indoors, outdoors, in towns and in the countryside. Being a raver didn't mean that you'd 'dropped out' (the whole crusty raver thing came in when the media put the New Age traveller thing in the same pot), it just meant you liked to rave, to dance with people, to be part of something. To have fun.

Up until this point, licensed venues controlled the moment when the lights came back up and the fun was effectively switched off. All over the world there was an unofficial chill-out scene which basically involved a 'back to mine' approach to hanging out and winding down at the end of the night. Invariably, some of these after-hours get-togethers were a little bit more lively, and lively was good. Maybe a few more friends could join us, and he's brought a couple of mates with him, and he's got some booze/birds/smoke. Before you knew it there was a scene – something that was to have a massive impact on nightlife and club culture. Something that would lead straight to the Second Summer of Love.

We need to look at the warehouse parties and the raves to understand this, and to keep the story fluid we need to do a bit of time-travelling. Not much, just backwards and forward from about '82 to '89 so that we can look at these two distinct but similar phenomena and then, having seen what they were all about, splash back down to earth so that we can take a peek at the actual summer of '88. Fasten your seat belts and prepare for blast-off!

WAREHOUSE PARTIES

Although illegal/unlicensed, the warehouse parties were relatively self-contained. It was all about the music and dancing, and the organisers made sure they had great sound systems in place and gave the party's appealing names like Hedonism. Going to these events was as important as going to Spectrum or Shoom, nobody wanted to miss out. A bit like Nancy Noise missing Paul Oakenfold's birthday party as she couldn't miss a night at Amnesia, nothing would stop a true acid house devotee from attending. As the promoters prepared to unlock the gates, the people prepared to unlock their minds. Danny Rampling and Jenni came to the first Hedonism warehouse party straight from their wedding.

DANNY RAMPLING: We got married in the morning in the Wandsworth registry office, just us and a couple of friends as witnesses, and then we went to lunch at a restaurant, and then we went to Hedonism for our honeymoon! We wanted to go to Mexico but we went to Hedonism instead. That particular night, February 1988, that was one of the first kind of raves actually. Hedonism had so many people there. Looking back, there was Norman Jay on the dancefloor, not DJing, I believe, just coming along to experience it, and here was Jazzy B and Soul II Soul. Justin Berkmann, who I met for the first time that night, had a number plate 'JUST B 4'. There was a guy playing real New York house and garage, it felt great. It all came out that night. That night was different from Shoom. Mark Moore was there and he had been to Shoom. Mark was a mixture of all the scenes alongside individuals like Norman with the rare groove thing. Reflecting back to Hedonism that night, it was a turning point. Because it was the formation of the rave scene.

TINTIN CHAMBERS: I myself was just a seventeen-year-old boy when I first walked into a warehouse in Alperton (Hedonism, February 2018). I had been a club kid in London over the previous couple of years, and was very much into electro and the early house records I had been hearing, but nothing prepared me for what I experienced in the tiny warehouse. Being met by a wall of sound, smoke and strobes, and so immersed in this that the music took on its own life. Powerful, carnal even. I really won't forget that ever in my life and in reality it changed me and the direction of my life since. This experience, I am sure, was very different to the one had by others at Shoom. Altogether a more social and harmonic experience, versus that rather insular but consuming one I had at Hedonism.

The warehouse scene was dictated by the sound systems and the availability of a friendly or easy to get into property. Lots of risk and the potential for reward, but as the scene grew and the authorities became more vigilant it became more difficult to keep the parties secret.

DAVE SWINDELLS: You'd go out, like to Soho, knowing you'd be given some flyers and who knows where you'd end up. You'd either end up at a warehouse party in some dive with one toilet for a thousand people or in the middle of the countryside.

The warehouse scene had started in the mid-80s in a relatively low-key way, organised by people with a shared love of music and eager to carry on celebrating life, mainly after hours. Many people claim that they created the warehouse scene, a sort of 80s throwback to the speakeasies of the Jazz Age, but there's a big difference between throwing a party and the ingenuity and nerves of steel needed to create a warehouse shindig. An early party was the night before the wedding of Prince Charles and Lady Diana in July 1981 when Chris Sullivan's Blue Rondo à la Turk played live in a squat and Hector Heathcote was the DJ, but it was really just a party, a bloody great one with Chris Sullivan's enviable coolness all over it, but still a party. The warehouse organisers used any means at their disposal to secure the best venues. Westworld, Bazooka Joe's, Mutoid Waste Company, Soul II Soul, Trevor Nelson's 'Madhatters', Zoom – they were all on the lookout for places and spaces. Car parks, building sites and derelict railway arches had never been more interesting. Areas that would soon be on the up-and-up like Shoreditch, Hoxton and Old Street were not up yet, and where there would soon be a local nightlife community there was currently darkness. There were lots of friendly estate agents with big bunches of keys waiting nervously (as well as hung over, exhausted, mullered and mashed-up) to get them back first thing on a Monday morning and hoping that there were no early-morning viewings at the property. The old 'change of use' thing was popular. Act like you were organising a film shoot, which would explain the lights, security and generators, and then switch at the last minute to an unstoppable party once the hundreds of 'extras' had turned up. Then there was the highly effective but less creative approach, the bolt cutters.

Claimants aside, the first proper warehouse party, the start of the scene, the place where we can start a conversation by saying 'In the beginning …' was Dirtbox, held not in a warehouse but above an old chemist's shop in Earl's Court. Rob Milton and Jay Strongman were the DJs and the crowd loved it. Jay Strongman was really the first superstar DJ and being the dance and club reviewer for the fashion bible *The Face* meant that his name was known around the world as someone at the forefront of the British club sound and scene. Looking like a rock 'n' roll star with his legendary blond quiff, Jay played everything from go-go and rap to funk and rockabilly. Jay was a draw and savvy promoters and club owners knew the value of having his name on a flyer. People wanted to hear these hard to come by funk tracks and these rare records or rare grooves quickly developed a huge following. Rare groove was what it was all about and a massive soul scene exploded across the UK.

The Watson brothers, Maurice and Noel, started holding

parties in a disused school in King's Cross. At that time the area was run-down, known for alcoholics and prostitutes, and a place where the police had better things to do (like driving away fast) than checking on a bunch of revellers. The brothers were DJs and were joined by a host of local talent as well as artists including Malcolm McLaren and Nellee Hooper. They even had Neneh Cherry doing the bar for them. The Watsons were far more experimental musically than most DJs. The venue was always packed so they could try out records to gauge the reaction of the crowd. This approach would stay with them when they eventually opened up Delirium, which was an early house club, almost before house was house, and which attracted the likes of Danny Rampling and Johnny Walker. Along with the warehouse parties, this early house music, largely created by unknown artists playing in unknown clubs in the USA, was bringing more and more different types of people together.

> **MARK MOORE:** I think it did change attitudes, it changed attitudes in Britain, hand in hand with dance music. Suddenly people who never mixed with gay people were now dancing with gay people. Slowly that changed in England. People suddenly became more multiracial, whereas in the West End it was quite a white scene. I can't stand a club that's only gay.

Some people made throwing a warehouse party into an art form. Norman Jay's Shake 'n' Fingerpop was the place to hear great music, expertly played and on a great sound system. Norman and his brother Joey had their own system so they could focus on the venue and the music. Norman had encyclopedic knowledge of rare groove, funk and soul, and an ability, when you thought that he had exhausted his gems, to pull out a glorious seven-inch record that would make even the most knowledgeable collector groan with envy. Norman's music and the party atmosphere he curated gave him the edge on most promoters in that he had a large, and growing, following. At a time when there was an unofficial but apparent colour bar in the West End stopping black promoters, particularly on the weekends, from hosting their own parties, Norman was able to sidestep that by cultivating a racially diverse crowd who all came for his music (and some just to see which hat he'd be wearing that day – my personal favourites are the bamboo pith helmet and what I call Squashed Canadian Mountie). His Good Times sound system had a bigger name but mainly as a reggae sound system and his regular crowd would have been confused by the direction that these parties needed to go in, resulting in Shake 'n' Fingerpop creating its own following.

Norman's parties brought people together, ironically they were the real 'good times'. On New Year's Eve 1985 he took over a carpet warehouse in Acton and over a thousand people turned up. His big one, called Amityville, was in an empty school in Hampstead. Set over three floors, the other floors had Derek B ('the bad young brother') and Manasseh, which consisted of three white public-school boys playing dub reggae. Soul boys and northwest London kids danced with Sloane Rangers and Hooray Henrys. The diverse crowd meant that, more than any party before it, the word of mouth spread like wildfire. This party indirectly changed the scene and brought it to the nation's attention, although the *Sunday Times* claimed it was an 'all-night sex and drugs party' – which is about as good an advertising slogan as the scene could have hoped for.

Norman partnered up with a law student, Jules O'Riordan,

who he'd met through a mate of his called Femi. Femi was at LSE with Jules and would go on to be one of the Young Disciples. Jules was a DJ with a good crowd and Norman realised that they should put on parties and DJ together. The black parties always seemed to get busted, so Norman trained Jules up so he could front the show to make it more 'acceptable' to the police. At the time it was an unusual pairing as Jules was white. Today that statement looks ridiculous, but it wasn't long ago when things like 'Stop and Search' meant that young black kids on a night out were often harassed, humiliated and turned away for no reason other than the colour of their skin. Jules and Norman were a great team, allowing the duo to promote successfully whilst Jules, now known as Judge Jules, with his legal knowledge and educated manner, deal with the police. Jules became as sought after as Norman and was at the forefront of the UK house movement, being voted Best DJ in the World by *DJ Mag* in 1995.

Jazzy B and his Soul II Soul parties were among the best, but attracted a lot of the wrong kind of attention from the authorities. Jazzy's distinctive look and the Funky Dred artwork paved the way for Soul II Soul to be held at the Africa Centre in the middle of London. Although not a warehouse party, this licensed weekly gathering was like a breath of fresh air to the club scene and would create the climate that would put funksters like The Brand New Heavies, Galliano and the Young Disciples on record company radars, and propel Soul II Soul's *Club Classics Volume One* to international chart success. The jazz and funk based grooves would have enough power to fuel an acid jazz scene and create a global superstar of Jay Kay (another cat in a hat) and Jamiroquai – complete with dance remixes – but this was really just a blip. Dance music was to be the dominant music and even the appearance of a whole new radio-friendly hip hop thing headed by Dr Dre's super-smash 'Chronic' and his two major discoveries, Snoop Doggy Dogg and Eminem (as well as major players including Tupac, Biggie and Jay Z), would still leave dance music as the clear winner.

Nicky Holloway was a DJ and promoter known for pulling out all the stops with his parties. A couple of years before the fateful night at Amnesia he pushed the envelope in what could be achieved with his 'Doo at the Zoo', a party inside London Zoo. Other 'Doo's' at the Natural History Museum and Lord's Cricket Ground made Nicky a star and his approach and vision was to influence the rave scene in '88.

> **TERRY FARLEY:** The whole thing was a reaction against the West End clubs and the strict licence laws. People wanted to get away from the restrictions of the clubs and, remember, for the majority of people it was very hard to get into clubs.

> **JAY STRONGMAN:** Dirtbox was different, like getting back to basics with the décor, the music and the clothes.

The last night of Dirtbox in Earl's Court was the sort of night that should have been filmed in black-and-white, slightly speeded up, with a honky-tonk piano and the other placard on the screen saying things like 'Crikey!' and 'Oops!' Sade was singing live that night with her band, who were still called Pride, and Jay Strongman was in the DJ booth contending with a fire extinguisher that someone had let off in there. By 4am the police had come to close it down. They were running up the three flights of stairs above the chemist shop to the West

Indian drinking club that hosted Dirtbox, while half the club were running against them in the opposite direction. Someone had turned on a fire hose, which soaked everyone.

JAY STRONGMAN: I think that was the hottest club night I'd ever witnessed.

In the days before social media and mobile phones there were three ways to promote a party. Fly posters, flyers and word of mouth. Flyers were good but ended up all over the pavements and were easily picked up by the powers that be, who then knew the who and when and possibly even where. Fly posters had the same problem, as well as having to deal with the turf wars that meant that each wall had someone who controlled what could go up and how much it cost to do this. Having your posters covered over or getting a 'visit' was an added risk. Word of mouth was by far the best way. It wasn't just a case of you telling someone and them telling someone else, it was someone who'd probably been to a previous event vouching that the party would be great, the DJs would show up, the crowd would be buzzing and that it would be money well spent.

Word of mouth had another string to its bow – pirate radio. Since the days of Radio Luxembourg, the government boffins at Radio HQ, which was probably the BBC, had actively tried to stop pirate radio stations as soon as they sprang up. They were mostly harmless and were shut down for the sake of it – the BBC are very good at keeping up appearances. The warehouse and underground club movements made localised stars of the DJs, and pirate radio was a great platform for them to share their music and give coded messages as to where the next party would be held. Standing head and shoulders over these stations was Kiss. Kiss had been launched in south London in 1985 by Gordon Mac and had shows from influential club DJs including Norman Jay, Coldcut, Paul 'Trouble' Anderson, Judge Jules and Jay Strongman. Kiss quickly became the voice of London's youth and, as well as introducing new music, it was the most direct way to reach an audience and invite them to party. It was also one of the first places people heard house. Danny Rampling, himself a Kiss DJ before his fateful trip to Ibiza, was exposed to these new sounds, played by DJs he respected and wanted to learn from. Having this radio platform gave Danny the legitimacy he needed within the scene and helped when he began to establish himself and Shoom.

NICKY HOLLOWAY: When Kiss was a pirate I used to be asked to do interviews, but I couldn't be arsed. So, I got Danny to do it. When Kiss got legal, he got a new show on Kiss. Then Radio One nicked him off Kiss. They were getting all the people from Kiss, five or six people went to Radio One from Kiss.

Kiss would go on to become Kiss FM, with a legal broadcast licence, and would be one of the most vibrant champions of all forms of street, club and underground music. It was ahead of its time and ahead of the competition. The BBC had tried hard to block it at every turn, but Gordon Mac just kept on his straightforward path of delivering great music in great shows and eventually they had to give in. Ironically, down the road, Rampling himself would be poached by BBC Radio One.

DANNY RAMPLING: Pirate radio was very instrumental in the development and marketing the scene as a whole, the only output for music on pirate radio at that time. Pirate radio was the sound of real London, that's what it was with Kiss and other stations at that time. Pirate radio was a platform.

TERRY FARLEY: On Saturdays we would walk up and down the King's Road and every shop had Kiss on. You were hearing the same DJs who were playing at the warehouse parties.

You would see the 'Legalise Kiss' stickers everywhere and once legalised the roster became a shopping list for the big stations to pick and choose from. Radio One, who had secured Pete Tong early on, brought over Danny Rampling, Dave Pearce, Lisa l'Anson, Trevor Nelson and Judge Jules. Lisa would go on to show the BBC her party credentials when she was sacked having missed her 'live from Ibiza' radio show after the infamous 'Lost Weekend' at the Manumission Motel.

The UK warehouse scene was different to the US underground scene. The UK was more inclusive and the nature of the crowd, particularly in London and Manchester, meant that the fashion press spoke highly of it, mostly because the journalists writing the articles by day were 'havin' it' at the parties by night. They helped the vibe cross borders and go international. Jay Strongman ended up being flown to Moscow and being the first British DJ to play a set at a warehouse party in Russia.

JAY STRONGMAN: It was either in '87 or '88. I was DJing in Hamburg and Berlin at a string of clubs.I was in a club in Berlin and these two guys came up to me who said they were managers of a band and wanted to book me and knew the British club scene was the best. They said it would be New York, Paris, Moscow, Berlin. The first gig we did was Moscow, with someone in the German embassy. They got this amazing disused theatre. I flew out there and played records. It was an amazing night. They got all the press to come down saying 'first DJ'. It was communist Russia, they were looking at all my records inside out. One Russian guard was obsessed with Kool and the Gang. The KGB turned up at some point in the night to shut it down but they bribed these guys with bottles of vodka and food and let us carry on. The music that went down worse was the house stuff. All they knew was the Beatles and Aerosmith and had no idea about rap or house.

Obviously, most warehouse parties weren't actually in warehouses, but the connotation of youths getting together to do who knows what in derelict buildings created a whole scene people just wanted to have fun with and be part of. Unfortunately, it painted a very different picture in the minds of the authorities. The warehouse party's success proved to be its undoing and the police were all over it. Unbeknown to them, this was just the appetiser. The rare groove scene had sound systems, promoters, DJs and followers but was a small enough scene that the powers that be could control it to some degree. But then the music changed and the parties changed and as the parties changed the numbers grew … and grew and grew. A four-letter word emerged that would make every police officer furious and would send fear through the heart of middle England. The word was 'rave'.

RAVE

Thatcher had encouraged a 'loadsamoney' attitude, so it wasn't surprising that this would spill over across the country. The kids weren't greedy; they had been told that they should aspire to be entrepreneurs and they just wanted a share. Throwing a party was an easy way to make a bit of money. Throwing a good party, on the other hand, is a skill and an art form that very few managed to pull off. A bit like your 'penny for the guy' kid and your paper round lad. Both want to make a bit of dough but one will work harder and need a whole host of skills to do this job well. The other is little more than a seasonal beggar.

The warehouse parties were not just people coming together in any old manner. There was a structure and a hierarchy from the organisers and the DJs down to the party people. They were organised by crews who were known to many of the crowd and they were contained enough so that the events more often than not went ahead as planned.

GRAEME PARK: It was harmless – there was a certain naivety about it as well. 'Can you come and DJ for me after you finish at the Haçienda and I'll hopefully have some money for you?' Before serious promoters got involved in it. The police didn't really know what to do and they couldn't really do anything anyway – if there's an illegal rave on a hill on the Pennines overlooking the M62, how do you stop people getting there? There isn't one road that goes there. They'd make their presence known but let it go on as there was nothing they could do. It was only when it became a big money thing they had to get involved.

The rise in dance music throughout '88 and the expansion of the warehouse scene meant that small parties quickly became oversubscribed to the point where the events began to be dangerous. One needs to remember that many of the promoters were in their mid-twenties with little experience in dealing with situations that could arise from the punters on one side, the police on the other and the venue owner potentially in the middle.

MR C: All of the huge rave orbital promoters frequented the Clink and in the late 80s Clink Street was on the tongues of every proper partygoer.

The key was always to find a venue, ideally with or close to a power source, that would be off the metaphorical police radar but also not somewhere that 'ruffians' could steam into. *Boy's Own* had become known for throwing great parties and with Terry Farley and Andrew Weatherall as part of the crew the music was excellent. Their parties grew, helped by their fanzine, but also they were everywhere. There was always a *Boy's Own* presence at all the key places including Shoom, Spectrum and Future, either behind the decks or on the dancefloor.

TERRY FARLEY: A girl who was coming to our parties, her dad had showrooms in Lambeth North, arches with outdoor courtyards where he'd keep these classic cars all under covers, and basically from her we were able to do a party in there. Now we had no licence, nothing, the police turned up about 8pm, came in and saw all the booze. They said, 'What's going on?' and I just said, 'We are having a party.' 'Basically, you can't sell any of this beer,' they said. So we decided we would give the beer away and charge £25 to get in instead of £15. We had people climbing over walls to get in who couldn't get in. It was a mad, rowdy affair and we got away with it and then the police turned up again as people were leaving.

Investing in an urban rave was becoming too risky. The unlicensed aspect coupled with the nationwide awareness of the acid house scene had signalled the end of the warehouse scene and the illegal rave would have to move out of the towns.

TERRY FARLEY: It was a good party but it was stressful. People were coming over the wall, and there were free drinks so people were only drinking half a can and leaving it. We had a big gang of football hooligans, West Ham and Arsenal, who we hadn't sold tickets to on purpose but they turned up and got in through our door men. It was a very stressful night. This was at the height of *Boy's Own* mania. We did flyers, we called the party 'Eggs, Bacon, Bubble with Two Slices' and that's all we had on it. Having a *Boy's Own* party in London was too mad. We thought we'd get under people's radar but we never did. We sailed too close to the wind.

For some, sailing close to the wind was not enough, they had to go through it. In August 1988, one of rave's most visible promoters, Tony Colston-Hayter, decided that he needed to be part of the scene. His main goal was making money and he could see that there was a lucrative business for him. He'd seen the queues at Shoom, and had been in and seen the euphoria of the crowd. He kept trying to get involved with Danny but they had nothing in common – Danny loved music and Tony loved money. On top of that, Colston-Hayter and his friends were fed up with Jenni's strict door policy, which often saw them excluded. He wasn't from the club scene and wasn't from the warehouse scene so decided to throw a mish-mash of the two, a big-club style warehouse party at Wembley Studios, the first solely-for-profit rave. Had he been clever and tried to understand the scene he'd have picked a name for his party that reflected the optimism and mind-expanding beauty of the scene – Shoom, Future, Spectrum, The Trip were all filled with positive energy. Colston-Hayter settled on the name 'Apocalypse Now'.

DANNY RAMPLING: He [Colston-Hayter] came down to the fitness centre and I was introduced to him through one of the Shoomers. And he said to me, 'I'll buy everyone a drink here,' and I said, 'They don't drink. They are just drinking Lucozade.' He said, 'I don't care, I'll buy everyone one of those.' He struck me as one of those characters that are on the edge and up to no good. At the time, he was working the casino. He was making huge amounts of money, winning money on the casino tables, an 80s loadsamoney character in a public-school, educated way. But he had charisma and a certain charm about him that was cheeky and you warmed to it. He was a very charming, non-pretentious character. A public-school artful dodger. He wanted to be part of this scene. Once when we left a private members' club on the King's Road he said, 'Come and be my partner in Sunrise.'

Fortunately, Danny said no. 'Apocalypse Now' is not a good choice of words if you're trying to sail under the radar. A good word to describe his next move is 'stupid'. For whatever reason, Colston-Hayter decided to let a national television news channel film the event and interview the DJs. Jenni Rampling was outside telling the Shoomers not to go in, while some diehards waved placards and protested to the incoming ravers. Having a TV crew filming with no editorial control and giving them full access to thousands of E'd up Acid Teds, conveniently bedecked in their smiley clobber, could only end up with one result. This wasn't even a stitch-up. The camera crew, who were tasked with filming something interesting, were given free rein with a loaded camera in a room where thousands of sweat-drenched kids looking like an 80s version of Mr Tumbles were lolloping around, arms flailing, and doing what looked like a new form of the old English pastime of gurning. It was as if Tony had decided to show his interior-design skills by picking up the media shotgun, loading both barrels and showing us that this was the sensible way to paint a wall, and then expecting to be able to do it all over again.

Of course, the editors dropped the interviews and focused on 'spaced-out' ravers, lawlessness and drugs: 'Would you want your son or daughter there? Would you hire your venue to these people? Look out for kids wearing smiley T-shirts.' Tony only had himself to blame, you can't lead a horse to water and then force him not to drink! The tabloid press were all over it and every regional journalist was on the lookout for convoys of cars. Apparently, some of them were on first-name terms with the guys running the petrol stations who could tip them off when a bunch of rave-mobiles pulled into the forecourt. It was all about to go 'Mental! Mental! Radio Rentals!' Colston-Hayter couldn't shake off the negative publicity. He renamed his organisation 'Sunrise' and, having seen the example of Danny and Jenni's Shoom membership cards, exploited a loophole in the law that said it was legal to throw a private party if the guests were members. The problem with loopholes is that they are easy to close down, and with all his various plans and schemes he ended up being his own worst enemy. It takes a lot of stupid to be that clever. His small team including his sister, Charlie, started mailing out cards like there was no tomorrow. He held his first event in October 1988 but this was stopped by the police. Tony started throwing events in quick succession. It was almost as if he could see that the writing was on the wall, which it was, for him at least.

MARK MOORE: That's when it changed and all the shock tabloid headlines came out. It was a wonderful, beautiful period before that, but it was inevitable: there was no way we were going to be able to keep a lid on this thing.

NICKY HOLLOWAY: Basically he [Colston-Hayter] was really good with technology, he was the first one to come up with the phone-line thing where you don't know where you're going until the last minute. He's always been a bit of a rebel. If he put as much effort into things that were legal as much as he did with things illegal he'd have stayed out of prison. He's just naughty, but he's very clever.

Tony was giving out the final details of the rave location through a pre-recorded phone-line system that had been put in place by British Telecom. The British Telecom Voice Bank gave you ten lines instead of one. He hired seven of them so they could handle seventy callers at any one time. This meant that he didn't have to put the venue or even the location on the flyers. Phoning in and getting a clue to the next location was all part of the fun. Tony being Tony, he'd also realised that BT shared the proceeds of the calls, so you suddenly found that the message would often require calling back at a certain time to get the next message. Eventually he'd move on to the premium numbers that could handle a hundred calls at the same time and had such a monopoly on them that other promoters ended up having to hire them from him. By August 1989 Sunrise had 30,000 members. Finding out about a rave would involve flyers, phone lines, pirate radio stations, following convoys, even handwritten and photocopied notes. An example of a note reads:

Freedom Fighters Present A
Free Rave
Today from 10pm — 10am
Meet at the South MIMMS service

station, junction 23 of
M25 (where A1(M) crosses)
convoys leave at 9pm.
adress [sic] will be released at 11pm
on all good pirate radio stations

Suddenly there were lots of ways to communicate a shared interest with a bunch of strangers. The police were getting increasingly frustrated. A bunch of kids using payphones were consistently outwitting them and the local authorities who were equipped with radios. In some ways, Tony was way ahead of his time and had created the social media of his day. Of course, there was an easier way. All you had to do was point yourself in the general direction of the party, look out for a Prodigy-scale light show and listen for the thumping beats. Later on it was even easier, as an illuminated Ferris wheel filled with glowstick-waving loons in the middle of the countryside tends to be visible for miles around.

MOBY: I mean, people have been dancing to rhythmic music and staring at lights for thousands of years. It's as if house music and rave culture tapped into this odd, ancient predilection on the part of humans to stay up all night dancing and staring into the fire, and just supercharged it with electricity and MDMA.

TINTIN CHAMBERS: I imagine that the global spread of dance music, from its acid house roots, was somewhat unstoppable ... The raves of 1989, such as Sunrise, and my own parties – Energy – amplified the spread, and certainly the press that we created did more than anything else to turbocharge the rave explosion into the mainstream.

TREVOR FUNG: I was always looking for that change. When it took off it was amazing. It was like thinking, 'Is this really happening in the UK?' What done it for me was when I played at Sunrise at Oxford and I was coming up at five o'clock on a beautiful sunny day with 20,000 people in front of me and two arctic trucks of speakers on either side. I'd already played at another gig earlier. I dropped a track and could feel the hands going up until it hit the back, which seemed like ages, like a Mexican Wave, and that feeling described the whole summer and how it had grown. Twenty thousand people in a field in Oxford, that was amazing. The sheer scale of it. You knew you were in the Summer of Love.

On 24 June 1989 Colston-Hayter held 'Sunrise: A Midsummer Night's Dream' at White Waltham Airfield near Maidenhead. Over a thousand vehicles converged on the site, causing a three-mile tailback. Over 11,000 ravers came to party and ironically most of them were flying, which made the *Sun* newspaper's headline the next day, 'Ecstasy Airport', fairly close to reality for once. It was time to put the boot in. The *Sun* showed pictures of thousands of youth raving at a disused aircraft hangar. Unfortunately for them this was probably the best advertisement that the scene at that time could ever have had. They didn't understand the basic premise of the whole party scene; people didn't dance together any more, they Danced Together! 'Thousands of kids dancing all night on mind-bending drugs,' they wrote. Millions of other kids read it and thought: 'I'll have some of that!'

Tony Colston-Hayter has been a professional gambler, plodding his way around casinos and always imagining that 'this time next year, Rodney, we'll be millionaires'. Had he not chased the money so much he could have been a bigger part of something special, a player on the international dance music scene instead of ending up as a footnote. He should have left the unlicensed parties to people who were actually enjoying it like Quentin 'Tintin' Chambers and Jeremy Taylor at Energy and just enjoyed himself. The money didn't buy him happiness or peace of mind. He thought he could turn rave into gold and throughout history there are many examples of folks thinking they can turn something into a pot of gold. To do that you need to be an alchemist (or a leprechaun), and if Tony had understood the culture he was trying to exploit he'd have known that there was already someone with the title of 'The Alchemist' – Alfredo.

TINTIN CHAMBERS: Energy came about by chance. I had been on holiday with my friend, Jeremy Taylor, who was the organiser of Gatecrasher Balls with Eddie Davenport. When we arrived back in London (sometime in the summer 1988), Jeremy's driver was not there to pick him up. When we got to his house (and office) the safe had been emptied and the bank account cleared out. Eddie had [allegedly] cleaned him out. Well, obviously JT was quite distraught. It was out of this that I persuaded him to join up with me to organise acid house parties. I was very much on the scene and had a limited vision, and JT had the organisational ability to actually get something going (I was not capable of organising a lift home at the time, especially as I never wanted to go home!) ... We put on a few unsuccessful warehouse parties and one average event at the Brixton Academy in '88, and in early '89 began to get a little more serious about what we were doing. We were lucky to fall in with a wonderful creative named Marc Holmes and, with my good friend at the time Anton Le Pirate, we hatched a plan to create Energy, with the vision of providing an otherworldly experience through production. We launched Energy on 26 May 1989 at Westway Film Studios with 6,000 inside and as many out climbing the walls.

For some the raves presented a golden opportunity to be creative. DJs were a big part of the show but the full rave experience needed design, engineers and technicians, a whole host of skills that would help each party be bigger and better than the one before. There wasn't a manual covering how to do these things, there wasn't even really a way to have a crash course. Getting into a tightly closed scene often took ingenuity, skill and determination. Luckily for all of us, one DJ had all of these qualities in abundance. He's gone on to be possibly the greatest dance music DJ ever, someone who continues to be at the very top of the techno tree and who continues to grow the scene that he witnessed from day one. Ladies and gentlemen, I give you Mr Carl Cox. But even the mighty Carl had to get on the first rung at some point, and there were several false starts before he arrived.

CARL COX: I think I was quite frustrated in the beginning, not to be able to present what I thought I could add. I thought I didn't get the exposure because I wasn't there [at Spectrum, The Trip and Shoom]. What I could see was people who were excited to hear new music. But unfortunately, I wasn't able to deliver that through the realms of what was there to begin with. So, I had to create my own path. I had to create something that was going on outside of Paul and Nicky and Danny. I was on the outside of all of that. It came through all the rave organisations like Sunrise and Energy. I was basically at the forefront of the scene as a ticket seller for the South Coast for any of these events. I said I was only selling tickets for these events if I got to play. I got to play because I got people along. I started off as a warm-up DJ but I used to rock the house every time I played, even though all these famous DJs were in front of me. Eventually my name got pushed further up the bill, from twelve o'clock to 3am or 4am when everyone is coming out of the club and ready for me to absolutely rock the place. It became something of a phenomenon for me, back when I did this party when I went on until ten in the morning. When I did the three-turntable mix everyone got up and said it was 'wonderful' and 'brilliant'. My girlfriend at the time gave out my card to all the promoters saying, 'If you want to book him, the name's "Carl Cox",' and that was it. I never looked back.

On 5 November Colston-Hayter held the Sunrise Guy Fawkes Party in a derelict gasworks. They sold 4,000 tickets in advance but many more turned up. The police tried to close it down and it ended up with riot police being called in and shutting off the music. This didn't stop the partygoers, who were getting round blockades by running across dual carriageways and scaling barbed-wire fences. Hopelessly outnumbered by 5am, the police withdrew. Colston-Hayter had courted publicity and now he'd got it – and boy did he get it. He had to lie low for a while, and during this break Wayne Anthony appeared on the scene with his first Genesis party at a warehouse in east London.

Genesis put a new effort into the production experience, making the event visually stimulating for the revellers as well as focusing on excellent DJs. On 24 December they gained access to the venue and threw a Christmas Eve bash for 900 people in Hackney. They returned to the same venue two days later for a Boxing Day Genesis. What was different this time was that they had the written consent of the owner. The success of two days earlier had become a talking point and over 2,000 people turned up, ready to dance. Clearly there was big business here. In the meantime, Sunrise were playing it safe and hiring venues for their parties. Sunrise IV took place at Heaven on 28 December under the misleading title of Boxing Day In Heaven, and they followed this up with Sunrise V at the Astoria two days later. Big business means big money and Sunrise decided to team up with Genesis for a New Year's Eve spectacular under the combined name of 'Sunset' at Leaside Road in Hackney, the venue that Genesis had already used on Christmas Eve and Boxing Day. Although the party was a success, big money also means big problems. Colston-Hayter was set upon by a gang of football fans (apparently West Ham) who demanded a share of the proceeds. He was never in it for the peace and love, but this marked a turning point for him and a turning point for the whole scene. The press had already dubbed him 'Mr Big' and the self-proclaimed 'Acid House King' was the focal point of the media, who vilified him as a purveyor of all things bad, and the key players in the scene, who saw him destroying the special thing they had built up.

NICKY HOLLOWAY: I always wanted to DJ at the raves but promoting was the day job. We would go to them after. I went to them all. We would go on after the Astoria. The thing is, no one owns a scene, people think they do, but they don't. You can't tell people where they can and can't go. We were trying to be a bit more exclusive. I felt the rave scene was getting too many rough people going. It was getting a bit narky. There was always this fear it was gonna kick off.

Raves were happening all over the UK and the police were on the lookout. It made sense to do these out in the open. Land could be hired relatively cheaply and, while these parties were still unlicensed, having the landowner in the mix was a big help. Rave organisers would pay the landowners handsomely and send them away for the weekend so there was no one to serve the injunction on if the police even found the party. If this had happened in the USA they would have sent in the National Guard. In the UK, the Pay Party Unit was set up under police Area Commander Ken Tappenden. No one could have done more than he did to try to stop the raves, but he also built up a relatively good relationship with the ravers. He would buy tickets to get the phone number and then once he knew the location try to race there to stop it before it started, as he realised that once the party was up and running it was better to let it keep going than to try to shut it down. Early on he felt that the party scene was here to stay and wanted to see if there was a way to make things work legally and safely. He tried everything, but the ravers were always just out of his reach. It's said that he had a phone call once from the Raindance crew, who told him that the reason they were one step ahead was that one of them was 'bonking' one of his secretaries. Apparently, that was true. In the towns the call to the police often came from the locals, so finding remote locations was the logical progression. The police were still as determined to stop everything, but the relatively inexperienced rural forces were often too late. They tried to pick out the coded messages on pirate radio and would also try to follow certain DJs and promoters, who would in turn lead them on a magical mystery tour before losing them and heading off to the real party location.

They had a checklist of things to look out for when trying to spot a potential rave. These included locks and chains on private land being cut, power generators being hired or transported onto rural land, tents being set up, convoys of cars on quieter roads and flattened hedgerows. This assumed that the rave crews went around flattening hedgerows, leaving broken locks visible and going around drawing attention to themselves – which they obviously didn't. What they were doing, however, was engaging in a massive game of cat-and-mouse with the authorities, and rave was coming out very much on top. The British police don't normally carry weapons, and in the 80s and 90s armed police were mostly limited to movies and airports. The local bobby's weaponry normally consisted of a bicycle, a notebook, a whistle and the authority and respect that the uniform brought with it. Suddenly they were faced with thousands of kids who couldn't give a monkey's uncle and, to make matters worse, they too had whistles! On one occasion, when faced with Tappenden and a hundred officers, fifty of the vehicle drivers threw their keys into the bushes and with cries of 'Oi! Oi!' ran off into the darkness towards the rave, trapping the police in their own roadblock. Napoleon himself couldn't have come up with a better strategy. There was nothing in the police manual about how to deal with this. The lunatics were running the asylum, and this was happening absolutely everywhere.

CARL COX: It was an alternative to what was happening in London. The Manchester scene had some amazing rave parties. I remember going to one event and Banana TV was there and I was one of the people they wanted to speak to. They wanted to know why I would come up all the way to Manchester. The sound system was immense but there weren't that many people. It was a bit too early for the Manchester crowd to have this type of event up there. The thing about parties up North is that they were really swayed by the northern soul scene, it had derived from that. You had to go up North to experience it. If you really wanted to know what it was like in Manchester, you had to go and see it for yourself. The rave scene for me, Birmingham, Wolverhampton, anyone up there was nuts for me and the music.

This was also the time when you were finding that some DJs were just head and shoulders above the rest. It wasn't just what they played and how they played it but who they played it to. This wasn't just playing the hits to a bunch of people on the piss/pull in a formulaic disco ('Ladies Free B4 11' etc.). Keeping thousands of people from different backgrounds entertained was now a skill that was being refined and refined and refined until you either had nowhere else to go or turned it into an art form. For all the seemingly haphazardness of the scene, each DJ was trying to stand out in what was becoming an increasingly competitive field (literally). The key was to win over the crowd from the beginning and make them see that the energy was going two ways – the DJ was vibing off the crowd and in turn lifting the crowd higher.

NICKY HOLLOWAY: That's tough because everyone had different strengths. I remember Alfredo had it because he was someone we hadn't heard before. I've seen Carl [Cox] pull it off and Paul [Oakenfold]. Some DJs, when they are up there, they have this presence. Carl does. That's it. Some are stars and some are just 'other' DJs.

One of the most iconic raves was the *Boy's Own* event in East Grinstead. It was a pivotal moment in the development of the UK's dance music scene and was spoken about with such reverence by those that were there that it became a benchmark for how to do things well.

TERRY FARLEY: For our famous party in East Grinstead we hired the land from a farmer and the police turned up about nine in the morning quite angry. They were walking around seeing what they could find, it was discreet but they knew what was going on. We didn't know this at the time, but we found out later, that someone doing a big M25 rave had one about ten miles away and that's where all the police were that night. I don't know whether they'd closed it down or just harassed it, but they just stumbled across us by chance when it was all too late. We were very lucky. It was the defining acid house party of the summer. It actually ended up being so good because of the 'Ted' rave going on down the road.

'Acid Ted' was used by the inner circle – Shoomers, the *Boy's Own* literat-E – to describe the 'weekend ravers'. Rather than the free-and-easy look and the comfortable but on-point styling that had helped shape the scene a few months before, the Ted's were easily recognisable with their smiley or acid slogan T-shirts, bandanas and dayglo, as they sweated and danced under the influence of their first E's. *Boy's Own* famously remarked, 'Better dead than Acid Ted', but they didn't mean it. These new converts were simply at the starting gate, the place where the 'veterans' had been only a few months earlier. They'd read about it in the press, heard about it on the radio, picked up the flyers (in the same 'trendy' shops where they bought those T-shirts) and bought the music. They then queued up to get in, paid their money (which kept the scene going) and danced all night. So what if they shouted 'Acieed' four months too late? So what if they hadn't had to get past Jenni Rampling? So what if the E's were better back in the day? So what if they'd never been to Amnesia? These were the foot soldiers, the dancefloor legions who would go on to populate the raves and the clubs and take dance music to the colleges, the universities, the suburbs and the towns. They'd go on to buy the albums and as veterans of the scene themselves fill the superclubs like Ministry of Sound and Cream and end up having the time of their lives at World Dance, Tribal Gathering and Big Love. They could say they were there – maybe not on day one but on day two, which is good enough. After all, you can't be a leader if you haven't got followers.

DAVE SWINDELLS: We felt that this was going to be great – I'd tried to go to raves before, driven around all night being stopped by the police, being shunted about with roadblocks and queues of traffic – the best part of that experience was watching them dancing in their cars, the whole car shaking, but we never found a rave. That night we went to a party that Anton Le Pirate had organised near East Grinstead, Adamski played live, and that was on the same night. Then we drove off hoping to find the *Boy's Own* party that we'd heard about. It was a struggle, up and down country lanes, we got lost but eventually we got there just before the dawn and saw this amazing location. I knew they had great DJs, Norman Jay, Dave Dorrell, Danny Rampling and Terry Farley, but I just thought, 'This is incredible.' I thought I'd never see a party as beautiful as this again.

TERRY FARLEY: I think when we talk about acid house being a chemistry set, you know, we mean all the parts come together and then they explode. It's like, 'How do you make a bomb?' This party had all the right components, the venue, the weather, was perfect. It was in a valley. You parked your car and then you walked to the valley and it was lit up as the *Boy's Own* crew was coming through. I went there to set up. We didn't do production. What are we gonna do? We knew there was a farm next door and so we got some hay bales, put them around, set it up. I went home about five o'clock, got changed and I came back and it looked fucking magical. There was a big lake and the thing was, when you walked down and it was dark, you couldn't see the lake. We're a couple of hundred yards away, and nothing, but it got to half-four in the morning and the sun started to come up, and finally people saw the lake. A flock of Canada geese even flew in and landed on the lake right in front of us and people started clapping. This girl asked me if I had planned the geese coming down! This is like Danny's aura moment. People were so into this. It was a defining moment.

By the end of 1989 the rave scene had started to disintegrate, fast. The acid house scene was splitting into two camps: ravers and clubbers. Clubbers were part of the growing dance music scene, which was already starting to create sub-genres and was infiltrating the clubs, discos and parties across the UK. By the early 90s you could go to any run-of-the-mill 'let's let our hair down as it's Saturday night' disco and people were more likely to be dancing to handbag than dancing around a handbag. Most of the club DJs stayed wedded to the club scene as well as some special, normally licensed, parties. The rave DJs were out there and were building up names that would propel them to mythical status. DJs like Carl Cox ('The People's Choice', 'The King', 'The Three Deck Wizard') and Sasha ('Son of God') organically built huge followings playing to tens of thousands of party people that meant that any promoter worth his or her salt would want them to play at their club, which suddenly brought them out of the cold and propelled them globally. The music they played was new, fresh and exciting, and people loved it. The pop charts seemed a million miles away from the rave scene, but if 'pop' means popular then this was the new pop music. Within a short period of time you would find your dancefloor heroes at the top end of the mainstream pop charts.

CARL COX: Before I released 'I Want You (Forever)' I used to mix the elements of that record live. Paul Oakenfold said, 'You know that record you put together, make a mix and send it to me.' I knew that when Paul started going on tour with U2 it was a different sound, but Paul knew my popularity at the time and said that he wanted to be a part of that. He booked time in north London at a recording studio, took samples, did it live and in one day that record was born. We put it down, and I asked Paul to come check it out. We said, 'Why don't we change that a little bit?' and then here was our track. In a day and a half, the track was done and it went number one on all club charts, everywhere. It went into the national charts and we had to make a video, create a band around the DJ. We got people to play and dance around the DJ. We went to Pineapple studios and we got a girl to sing the song 'I Want You (Forever)'. I was booked for *Top of the Pops* but my record was a sample-based record so I had to recreate the samples live, with live vocalists. The vocalist who was meant to do the show that day got sick, so we got another vocalist in who didn't really know the song to go live to the nation on *Top of the Pops*. I was one of the first DJs to make a hit record – it spent seven weeks in the charts.

Even the raves had different levels of expectation depending on who was promoting them. As the scene went nationwide you could divide raves into three distinct categories: organised, disorganised and shambolic. For some ravers, the more chaotic the better, but no matter where you did it or why you did it every raver who went out to dance in a field, a car park, a farm, a building site or even on a boat created shared experiences. Every raver had their story to tell.

IRVINE WELSH: '... being carried onto a rave boat after taking strong pills in my mate's car, waiting on them to let us board. The pills came on too quickly and hit us in the legs. We couldn't move them but were determined to get on that boat. We enlisted squads of ravers to carry us on. They then held us up until we could get the legs working to the beat. Felt like hours, but probably only took about fifteen minutes tops.

The police were busy raiding the parties and in some cases beating the ravers. The raids were seen as part of the night out and this was something the authorities could never understand. These kids didn't seem to fear the police or worry about the consequences. At a party in Sevenoaks a student called Paul Hartnoll was beaten by uniformed police. He'd eventually go on with his brother Phil to form the band Orbital, headline Tribal Gathering in 1995 and be the first dance act to take to the stage at Glastonbury. Never forgetting their rave roots, Orbital was named after the M25 orbital rave scene.

To 80s youth, the word 'rave' really meant an illegal or at least unlicensed party, normally in the countryside and normally for hundreds if not thousands of people. Unfortunately for the scene, the word 'rave' was used to describe any event with dance music. Suddenly club nights, legal and licensed, found the heavy hands on the law on them.

JAY STRONGMAN: My best acid house experience was, of all places, in Oxford. A friend of mine called Bob ran a rare groove club just outside Oxford for a couple of years until the police closed it down. Then he got the chance to do a club in Oxford city and it was literally just as the whole Middle England panic about acid house set in. Once he got the place booked, we were called in and the owners said if anything happens you are personally responsible. Then the local papers got hold of it and were like: 'Acid House comes to Oxford'. There were police dogs in the queue and people were being dragged out and searched, it was really heavy-handed and over the top, it was ridiculous. I don't know what they were expecting. I don't think it would happen any more, that sort of moral panic about acid house. There was a real sense of us in here, and them outside, it was amazing! I remember people going crazy. There was one particularly beautiful girl who was one of the best dancers I've ever seen, dancing so perfectly. It was one of those amazing nights … We ended up sitting in some all-night café in Oxford wolfing down egg and chips watching the sun come up. For me, it was my first great acid house moment. There were lots after. That was '88, right in the middle of that whole acid house thing – when it was on the front page of the *Sun*, something like 'Acid House is killing our kids'.

The most important of these were the so-called Blackburn Raves which ran from 1988 to 1990. Originally started as small parties for their friends by Tony Creft and Tommy Smith, their reputation started to attract in-the-know party people from further afield. Tommy Smith was famously 'high on hope' and the parties grew organically, which gave them a chance to work out how to get it right before they grew too big. Finally, it looked like rave had a plan. It wasn't long before cars were converging on Blackburn from Manchester, Leeds and Liverpool. Dance culture icons like Dave Beer of Back to Basics fame, 808 State, the Chemical Brothers and future superstar DJ Sasha were a regular part of the Blackburn rave crowd. These parties were pure quality, with the scale of a full-on rave but with the care of a private house party.

> **NANCY NOISE:** You're all just having a really great time, dancing all night, it's a scene. You are part of something. The raves were further out as well. I think there was a lot more openness, you'd make new friends, people would connect a lot more. It wouldn't take as long to meet someone, you made friends immediately every time you went out. Obviously, there was the Haçienda with Graeme Park and Mike Pickering. They were doing their thing earlier. But the ecstasy thing really kicked it all off.

As the fame spread, they tried to placate the locals. Rather than hide they tried to make the people of Lancashire understand just what rave meant to them. They were even involved in a TV debate where the producers clearly had no shortage in angry residents to choose from. Police raids were par for the course, but no sooner was one party shut down than another one sprang up. Police frustrations began to boil over and the raids became more aggressive. The last large Blackburn rave was held at Nelson near Burnley and had a good 10,000 ravers there when the police moved in. And it wasn't just the police who were frustrated. By now these raves weren't only for locals. Some people had driven a long way and weren't going without a fight – and remember these are supposed to be luv'd-up kids. It all kicked off when the police marched in with their riot shields at 7am. One police car was turned over and another one was torched.

JAY STRONGMAN: The thing that was different about rave was probably the scale. The first night at Dirtbox was probably fifty people, then maybe three hundred people. I would stand on the door and we would basically let people in as people left. Even the warehouse parties were like 1,200 people. The whole thing with the raves was that it went from 1,200 to 10,000. I think it was just people becoming more and more aware that you could make serious money from dance music. It went from being underground to being overground, from being a niche market to basically becoming pop music in some ways.

JAMIE CATTO: These were the first and formative experiences where they felt connected to their peers.

MARK MOORE: I loved it. I went there and people were like, 'Why are you going, why the hell?' People were making friends. Everyone was off their faces. Do you know who I used to bump into from the Pet Shop Boys? Chris. No one would know who he was. Chris Lowe.

DANNY RAMPLING: I didn't play at any of them. Now I regret it. I didn't play for those parties of hundreds of thousands of people. The only thing I did was Edmonton Roller Rink for 10,000 people.

Eventually the rave scene would become legal and licensed and it was then that the dance music festival was born. There was (and still is) a place for the original ravers, but the scene outgrew even these giant parties. Fighting the authorities had taken its toll, and promoters, artists and DJs wanted to focus on the music and the fun, the reason they'd got into it in the first place. Rather than the music and the feeling of freedom, drugs had been allowed to have too much of a presence. At most clubs you'd be followed by a whispered hiss of 'E? Whizz?'

JAY STRONGMAN: I don't think it [drugs] ruined it, it just changed them. I tried ecstasy a couple of times and it was a great feeling, but I didn't want to be in a perpetual state of heightened emotions. With speed I knew I was in control, wouldn't be too drunk, speaking too much … I was always slightly wary of things. It was weird because some people changed overnight and with some people it took a couple of years to get into it.

PAUL OAKENFOLD: I was playing a lot of illegal raves. You'd be carrying two boxes in a field, it was pitch-black and everyone is taking pills and you're thinking, 'How am I gonna get back to the car when everyone is so out of it?' and you don't want to lose your records.

CARL COX: At one point, the police had made up a special task force to track down acid house parties. And they basically utilised me as someone to follow on the weekend to see where I'd end up. I had to talk in code to anyone about where I was going, what I needed, when I would be there. I had a hire van

Above left: 'Loud Noise!' Lisa Loud's inspired DJ partnership with Nancy Noise influenced the first wave of acid house clubbers.

© Dave Swindells

Above right: Original Amnesiac Nancy Noise is still an ambassador for the true Balearic sound and spirit.

© Dave Swindells

Below: Losing yourself in the music. The intensity of the dancefloor at Nicky Holloway's Trip.

© Dave Swindells

Above left: Been there, seen it, done it, bought the T-shirt, took off the T-shirt and then did it all over again. Ibiza legends, Mike and Claire Manumission. © *Mike and Claire McKay / Philip Silcock*

Above right: A magical Summer of Love moment – the morning after the night before, and you're on top of a haystack in East Grinstead at the Boy's Own party. © *Dave Swindells*

Below: The foundations for clubbing and festivals had been firmly planted throughout the Second Summer of Love. 5am at World Dance in 1989 looks a lot like the mega events we enjoy today.

© *Dave Swindells*

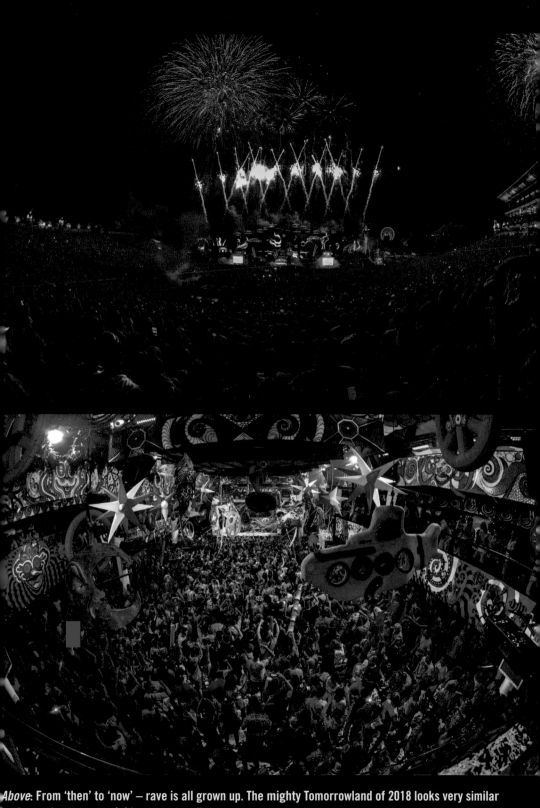

Above: From 'then' to 'now' — rave is all grown up. The mighty Tomorrowland of 2018 looks very similar to the outdoor events of thirty years earlier.   © Dan Reid

Below: It might be bigger but Elrow 2018 in Amnesia has a decidedly Future, Spectrum, Shoom, Land of Oz, Trip feel to it.   © Dan Reid

Above: Carl Cox, the King of Ibiza. 'Oh yes, oh yes.'

© Dan Rei...

Below: Carl Cox at Space taking his loyal subjects on an intergalactic journey

© Dan Rei...

Above: Like a cartoon superhero, mild-mannered Norman Cook transforms into Fatboy Slim and is ready to pounce.

Above left: The Godfather of House, Frankie Knuckles. A man whose influence still resonates across every dancefloor and whose smile still lights up every DJ booth.

© Dan Reid

Above right: A couple of university students whose cassette fell under the Boy's Own radar and, as the renamed Chemical Brothers, took their beats from the low-key but frenzied Sunday Social to headlining festivals all over the world.

© Dan Reid

Below: For newbie or veteran alike, the sunset in Ibiza continues to inspire and to unite. This is the magic ingredient that inspired the Ibiza Four to come back and change everything for everybody.

© Dan Reid

Above: 'We did it!': Paul Oakenfold, Alon Shulman and Carl Cox at Stonehenge in 2018. From an underground scene to invited guests at this Wonder of the World, dance music and club culture are all about creating those special moments that live with you forever.
© *Alan Shulman*

Below: 'Mind-blowing' electronic stimulation for the communication generation. Bringing together past, present and future at Stonehenge.
© *Alon Shulman / Photography: Dan Reid*

Inset: Stonehenge from above – sharing a smiley with the universe.
© *Alon Shulman / Drone photography: Craig Hellen & Simon Brown*

Sunset at Stonehenge with Paul Oakenfold in 2018. A fitting tribute to the energy and influence

called the Panda Hire Van, so whenever you saw the Panda Hire Van, you knew it was Carl Cox. The thing was, there was one party where nobody knew who the promoters were. They were all undercover police and the police booked the sound system off me, the lighting, the bar, everything. It was all from police funds. All the people you were talking to were undercover police. The party was called Space. The police needed to justify the amount of spending that they had to create a thing to capture all the acid house kingpins in one go. They caught us with nothing. No one had anything! They believed we were selling drugs. They came in, busted the party, kept us overnight in jail until Monday morning and in the same clothes we went to the court but it was thrown out as they didn't have sufficient evidence against us. That was the last we heard of the police.

Here is the thing. After I got caught by the police, which came to nothing, it did damage my career a bit in 1989, but not a lot. I can walk out with my head held high knowing I'm not what they say I am. You read the headlines and I was like, 'What!?' After that I was always contracted to be at anyone's event. Whatever it was, there had to be a contract there for me and I wouldn't go unless I got the money up front. It was turning into a proper business, with proper events, which meant the tickets were sold with permission [licence] granted. It made sense now. It meant that we had won the police and the government over. It meant we weren't gonna get busted.

DANNY RAMPLING: They were safer, they actually happened, they changed the whole face of the festival circuit. The rave scene was very pivotal until its demise with the criminality, the dark drugs, the gangs, all the dark energy that overshadowed the later part of the rave scene. The Criminal Justice Bill was introduced as a result of that. I was part of the scene and when they did it everything changed. We now brought the party to smaller clubs, it became about dressing up, that's where new 'Sexy' and 'Glam' nights came from, and all these other clubs started springing up. Those big events like Universe, they transformed the festival scene in the UK. The festival scene we have today all over the world is a reflection of what happened in that period.

CARL COX: I'm a guy that came from Shoreham. I used to play at house parties, in scout huts, I did weddings for a living. So being able to play with a sound system was a joy. When I got to play at all these illegal parties and being seen as someone that was at the pinnacle in making these parties work – I never thought that this would happen. I went from playing in the UK from two parties on a Wednesday, to one on a Thursday, to three times on a Friday, to two on a Saturday, to one on a Sunday. It was incredible. I basically took it all, as much as I could to get my name out there, to promote myself as much as I could, and continue to do that today but obviously on a much bigger scale. I never thought it was going to happen.

THE SECOND SUMMER OF LOVE

There were raves, there were clubs, there were warehouse parties, but there was also this special feeling, a unifying mindset that linked everyone and made this such a unique time. This movement wasn't about standing out – everyone was happy to be the same.

GRAEME PARK: With acid house, for the first time ever you see barristers dancing next to builders dancing next to nurses dancing next to teachers, next to football hooligans – everyone's taking this 'magic' pill. Everyone came together against a backdrop of recession and a fairly right-wing government and thought, 'We are just going to enjoy ourselves and blot out the nonsense.'

We now consider 1988 to be the Second Summer of Love, although we also acknowledge that for a few people their second Summer of Love was 1987, which would make '88 their third. At the time, the Summer of Love took place over the … er … summer. Some people's Summer of Love took place in Ibiza in '88 while others felt that it took place in the UK and if you were in Ibiza you missed it. Some people on the edges of it were proud to be part of it while some of the key players in the eye of the storm that was the Second Summer of Love were oblivious to it. At the same time, acid house wasn't about acid, although there was lots going around in the Summer of Love in '67. Nowadays, the consensus is that the Second Summer of Love refers to the whole of 1988. There is a popular school of thought that has the Second Summer Of Love running straight through until the end of 1989. Confused? Don't worry about it, you're in good company.

> **DANNY RAMPLING:** Well we knew it was the Summer of Love but where from I can't be sure. It was the Summer of Love because everyone came together in youth culture, it was a breakdown of social class, race, sexuality, taboos and there was something going on every night. A lot of people said that what was so good about acid house was it was far more inclusive than the 60s. There really was a lot of love going on.

> **NICK HALKES:** The energy and excitement that surrounded the scene in 1988 was absolutely infectious. Whether you were mainly interested in the music or the drugs or the parties or the fashion or any combination thereof it was an unfolding story that tens then hundreds then thousands of people found themselves keen to be part of.

DAVE SWINDELLS: It was a very special time because you could see this was the start of something exciting and had the potential to really change society for the better.

TINTIN CHAMBERS: Honestly, I can somehow remember all the parties I went to between '88 and '89. The experiences will live with me forever. It's impossible to pick a highlight.

TREVOR FUNG: 'It was the start of it, like JB, James Brown, was to funk. It's what everyone refers back to. All the new music coming out has elements of the tracks that were out in those days. It's a massive influence. A lot of people are trying to do the old thing, but you can't do it unless you were there. You can't feel it.

CYMON ECKEL: Acid house was the spearhead of a bigger cultural movement and awakening, it's when cool magazines, writers, artists and creators, even big corporations, realised the future of a country and the world lies in its youth.

The term 'Second Summer of Love' was actually coined by the Scottish urban shaman Fraser Clark, who had created the *Encyclopaedia Psychedelica* in the late 80s preaching a return to the values held by the original 60s hippies. Clark, who had created an intellectual space for people looking for more spirituality (remember at the time they were in the midst of Thatcher's Britain) founded the Zippie movement, which promoted the original Summer of Love guru's amended philosophy of 'Drop out, and drop in again'. Clark was fascinated by the freedom of the acid house scene and the subsequent rave culture and went on to throw some small underground parties of his own before launching Megatripolis. The club was held every Thursday for three years at Heaven, following on from Fabio and Grooverider's Rage night, and 4,000 people attended the free opening night on 21 October 1993.

The scene had already spread to the main towns in the UK, fuelled by what was happening in London and the sudden interest and influx in the house records coming over from the USA. Suddenly the entertainment capital of the USA wasn't Los Angeles and the musical capital definitely wasn't Nashville. For kids all across the UK everything that was great to them about America was coming out of Chicago, New York and Detroit.

BRANDON BLOCK: Acid house was the catalyst that created the music scene as it is today. Simple as that.

MR C: The Second Summer of Love in 1988 felt amazing. It was like no other period in dance music before it and that was due as much to the proliferation of ecstasy as it was the music. Of course, both electronic music and MDMA had been around for a few years but there seemed to be a convergence at just the same time that the youth of our fine nation were disenchanted with clubbing, which was quite violent in London in the 80s. We were also entering a recession under the iron grip of Thatcherism so this brand new music and new drug seemed to give people a hedonistic escape from the moral drudgery of life, as much as it gave a euphoric coming together of people. Racism signalled its way out as love and unity took its prime seat in the way the youth of London wanted to express itself. All of these different things are in my humble opinion what made the Summer of Love truly magical.

DAVE SWINDELLS: The Summer of Love was so special. It made me feel incredibly excited. In 1988 we thought this was going to be massive and so exciting and change people's lives – and it was. It did change people's lives. That's the really important thing. It was not just empty talk. It really did happen. It tied into a political change that was happening. There was a feeling that the world was changing for the better and we were also helping change things for the better.

TREVOR FUNG: The Summer of Love was the start of dance music worldwide. It created a massive industry. What more can you say?

It definitely wasn't just a London thing. There were DJs, admittedly just a handful, in other big cities who had discovered house and had tried to give it a presence at the clubs they played at. Liverpool was traditionally the place 'Up North' that, proud of its place in musical history, would give things a go. This time round the second city of dance music was Manchester and the place to be was the Haçienda.

The Haçienda was inspired by the big New York clubs like the Paradise Garage and was opened on 21 May 1982 by Factory Records. The plan was that this would be the superclub that would change clubbing in the North. An amazing venue with an amazing sound system, it was only missing one thing ...

clubbers. As slow burns go, this ambitious project was going at the speed of the Brexit negotiations and was just as fruitful. Imagine planning the best party in the world, throwing open the doors and no one turning up. Welcome to the Haçienda.

One of the DJ's, Mike Pickering, who would go on to form M People, kept showering the dancefloor with house. It had to catch on eventually. Didn't it? Mike had started the club night, Nude, in 1986 and was mixing house in with underground staples of soul and hip hop.

> **GRAEME PARK:** We had some of the Americans from Chicago and Detroit come over and do stuff for us. They weren't doing stuff down south really.

This had all the makings of a great night and then in 1987 ecstasy started to enter the mix, which was just what regulars like Shaun Ryder and Bez needed to bring the Haçienda's vision into their reality.

> **GRAEME PARK:** I remember Mike Pickering and I looking at each other at the Haçienda one night, off our heads. We thought, 'This is big,' and were hit with the realisation that this is going to run and run. If you had told us it was going to run until the next century, run so you could make your career out of it, I wouldn't have believed you. Yet here we are!

Hopefully when humanity eventually invents a time machine one of the interns in the lab will use a lunchbreak wisely and travel back to the Haçienda in '87 to witness and record the first time Bez hit the dancefloor on a Bumble (buzzin' on

Bumble Bees). Cleverly, Pickering didn't rest on his laurels and in the summer of '88 launched 'Hot' and was joined by DJ Jon DaSilva. DaSilva embraced the Summer of Love concept wholeheartedly, making A Guy Called Gerald's epic masterpiece 'Voodoo Ray' his anthem of that summer. One club and one DJ had created a whole scene that joined the UK's growing acid house network.

DANNY RAMPLING: I first went in '88. I was invited to play there by Mike Pickering. That was my first gig outside of London. Playing in a club outside London on that scale was pretty amazing. It was a core scene, similar to Amnesia. I was pretty nervous playing, there was a huge buzz. I was playing some Italian tracks that I had covered up the labels on but I told Mike Pickering what they were. I was welcomed. Everyone was on one. There was no North/South divide. I had a good affinity with Mike and the crowd but I didn't fully appreciate that I was at Haçienda and how special it was.

GRAEME PARK: There was a big community spirit at the Haçienda. The Gallagher brothers, Stone Roses, Mick Hucknall, Inspiral Carpets, lots of people who went on to make amazing non-dance music were all here, all part of the scene … you had so many record companies in London and they were all desperate to outbid each other for the next big record from America and that meant that every Friday the British Airways flights to Manchester, the British Railway trains from Euston and the M1 and M6 were full of record company people, all coming up to the Haçienda to hear what me and Mike were going to play. All the hotels were full of these record company types. They were really exciting times.

These London record types – and at this point there were still lots of labels of all sizes – inadvertently propelled one local DJ into global superstardom that would, in the future, include a residency at Twilo in New York. When the Haçienda closed down for several months in 1991 the record companies needed somewhere else to go to. Somewhere to try to hear the latest big records and to see how the dancefloor reacted. Shelley's in Stoke became the place to go and it was this that led to the resident – a young DJ called Alexander Coe, who preferred to go by the name Sasha – being offered remixes and opportunities that would have been unthinkable to him a few months earlier. Sasha's profile was already right up there, he was playing at raves in Blackburn and Birmingham, and Stoke was in the middle, so he had a strong and loyal local following.

Sasha is an expert at building a crowd, leaving them gagging for more. He honed these skills as a warm-up DJ, building his set to get the crowd ready for the main attraction to come on and play all the big tunes, that he had deliberately held back. Once you can rock a crowd without the big tunes you can take them to a whole other level when you hit them with the tracks they really want to hear. With the Haçienda out of commission, his big tunes and style of playing made him an instant star. His name on a flyer had an allure that was irresistible. In the early 90s he was billed on a flyer for a licensed club night where the promoter had his name, the date and the opening hours but had forgotten to put the venue. A few people were spreading the word and doing guest lists but the flyers were meant to be the main promotional tool and the mistake was only noticed once they'd all been distributed. Come opening time at the Café de Paris in central London, the word had spread to such an extent that the queue stretched right up the road and right back down again. That was the power of Sasha. Sasha would become a fixture at Shelley's Laserdome and then landed his iconic residency at Renaissance where he created Northern Exposure and formed a long-lasting partnership with John Digweed.

NICKY HOLLOWAY: I went up to Manchester a few times because Tony Wilson invited us up. I only went to the Haçienda a few times and it was rubbish, I think I didn't go on the right nights. I didn't think they were stealing our night at all, if you actually look at it. On the opening night of The Trip I had Mike Pickering and Graeme Park who were the Haçienda DJs – I was booking them! In Ibiza you had people from London and Manchester so when they came back from there they did their thing up North. The Manchester thing, I didn't really see much of it. I only did a couple of nights up there.

BRANDON BLOCK: The difference between playing up North and London for me was that people up North seem to make more of an effort when they attend the nights. There are not the same number of clubs as in London where club and bar culture has become the norm.

The Ibiza pleasure palace, Manumission, actually started in Manchester. Anyone could put on a club night, but Manchester was getting a reputation for in-fighting among security firms and various elements trying to get involved in the growing and lucrative club scene. The brothers who started Manumission had a simple solution: pretend that they had such deep pockets that nothing could touch them.

MIKE MANUMISSION: We used the pseudonym of Roger More, which was the name of a very famous person in NYC who wanted to revolutionise clubland but didn't want to put their name to it as it would unfairly taint the club's success. The backer was famous and rich beyond belief so there was no point in anyone trying to starve Manumission out with cheap beer nights. The club night's opening was advertised before we had a venue. The legend ensured we were given one. Plus, we bussed in 150 of the best gay crowd from London and Leeds so when the people of Manchester came to see Manumission fail they were blown away by the eye candy! And so it began. Manumission rose from nothing but an idea and ethos to being the number-one club in the UK according to *DJ Mag*.

GRAEME PARK: All the years I DJed at the Haçienda I actually lived in London. Ironically, I only moved to Manchester the week the Haçienda closed when my radio show became daily. Before that I used to fly up or get the train up.

Pete Tong had gathered up a whole bunch of Chicago house tracks and released a compilation onto a largely unsuspecting public who pretty soon would be 'Jacking' left, right and centre. The *House Sound of Chicago Vol. 1* (now there's optimism and business savvy for you) had dancefloor fillers from the likes of Chip E., Darryl Pandy, Farley 'Jackmaster' Funk and Fingers Inc. (consisting of Larry 'Mr Fingers' Heard, Ron Wilson and Robert Owens, who would create the anthemic 'Can You Feel It' and would tour the UK in 1988). The Americans were starting to come over and, as excited as we were to welcome our heroes, they were excited to be in Europe, which had given them so much electronic inspiration. They'd only really been exposed to the European scene through buying records or listening to the radio in the States and, for all the glamour associated with the USA, they weren't a well-travelled bunch. Frankie Knuckles had never been out of the country and got his first passport when he came to the UK in 1986.

Already a convert to house, Pete wanted to help spread the vibe. In April he joined fellow DJs Paul Oakenfold, Nicky Holloway and Johnny Walker at the Prestatyn Soul Weekender, which was a lot less glamorous than it sounds. They were now all well enough known that they felt they could play the dance music that they were playing in the clubs of London. The older DJs didn't really get it and hung up a banner reading 'No Acid House'. Within a few months this older generation would be playing catch-up and eventually the only field that they'd be shaking and dribbling in would not be full of ravers but the one they would end up being put out to pasture in. For them it had definitely 'all gone Pete Tong'.

What anyone in the scene could see and feel, but what seemed to pass by everyone else at this point, was that this Summer of Love was not a fad and that house music was (and is) something very special. There was a good reason why it would go on to be the cultural driving force for a generation who felt that this was their thing.

FATBOY SLIM: I think because it was run on the whole by people who genuinely loved what they were doing and weren't in it for money or fame. The clubs, record labels, magazines and musical output were controlled and curated simply for the joy of what was going on. This seems impossible in the Instagram generation.

Outsiders couldn't equate that kids didn't have to be able to read or even play music but could cobble something together in their bedroom, bang out a few copies to a few DJs, and lo and behold there was a hit. Or not. The great thing was that hit or miss didn't really matter – tunes weren't judged on sales but on audience reaction. DJs were given reaction sheets by the pluggers and their opinions and the opinions of the crowd mattered. These reaction sheets would make their way to record company board meetings who were looking for remixers, hit records and anything else that could keep them in a job. They'd be listening to a promo, nodding along and smiling at the appropriate moment, while inwardly they'd be scratching their heads and watching the Christmas bonus go up in smoke. This was all about optimism, not trying to sign some moody band and then hoping they wouldn't OD until they had enough material for a 'best of'. DJ reactions helped make the decision for them and gave them something to blame if it went wrong. It is because of audience reactions that we ended up with tracks like Lil Louis' 'French Kiss', but unfortunately it also resulted in Whigfield's 'Saturday Night' and the accompanying dance.

Ironically, the track that elevated the whole scene to the mainstream and that crossed over between the UK charts and the US underground scene was created as a bit of fun by somebody who fused an electronic acid house style and energy with a 70s retro disco feel, and whose major influence was one of the original heroes of the Summer of Love of '67, Sly and the Family Stone. Mark Moore had been playing house in clubs for a couple of years, waiting for everyone else to catch on. His band, S-Express, released their 'Theme From S'Express' in April 1988, which went to No. 1 in the UK charts, Top 10 in over a dozen other territories and No. 1 on the US dance chart.

MARK MOORE: It got to '86, we thought, 'Oh my God, it's going to change overnight,' but it didn't. What happened there was great timing. The underground movement was getting together, I met Danny Rampling, I'd been to Shoom, he then asked me to DJ at Shoom, things at Shoom were getting bigger and bigger, and I'd been part of Future slightly before that. Everyone was on the same wavelength. They had just come back from Ibiza and knew that I was playing house music. Shoom was going on and the scene was getting bigger and bigger. In March '88, I brought out '[Theme from] S'Express', suddenly radio stations were playing it. There weren't any spokespeople for the scene, but it looked like something was going to happen.

CARL COX: That was based on talented producers and DJs. By guys who believed in what they were doing. That was played at nearly every party, it was a hit, [but] it doesn't mean that it was made commercially; it was just good and something to believe in. Our strength in numbers was madness at that time. Anyone that was making that kind of music at that time crossed over. We were really changing things ourselves across the music industry as a whole. Rather than us follow the music industry they followed us.

MARK MOORE: Mostly, everyone thought it was great, because it was opening the scene up a bit but in a way that wasn't going to ruin it. People like Derrick May were saying, 'It's fantastic,' because they suddenly thought, 'This is it.' I remember Derrick May telling me, 'This stuff's gonna start something for us.' S-Express opened doors and these are doors that we are all going to be able to walk through. All those people from Detroit and Chicago weren't jealous, they were really happy. I met a lot of them in England as they started to come over. Globally it was slower. They didn't quite get it, but they wanted to get it. In Germany, they were like, 'How can we relate to this strange music?' I said, 'Well, you've got Kraftwerk, one of the greatest bands ever.' They went, 'Oh, they are not a band.' Then of course I went back six months later to promote the new single and everyone in Germany was saying they were an expert in dance music and house music, saying, 'We invented this. We had Kraftwerk.' So suddenly people went from not quite getting it to wanting to be part of the party and being an expert overnight.

JAY STRONGMAN: S-Express was really important. It was a great record. The way Mark had taken all these elements and put them together, it reflected the way Mark DJed. It ensured their success, at least financially. It was huge. It exploded for a lot of places who were aware what was going on. It made people aware that people from the scene were creating music as well as just playing American tunes.

JON PLEASED WIMMIN: S-Express were such a feel-good gang of club misfits and the fact they didn't take themselves too seriously was a real breath of fresh air at the time. The great mix of musical styles in their tracks was also very forward-thinking. Whenever The Pleased Wimmin saw Mark out (which was a lot) we would run up to him and screech the 'Higher, higher, up and away!' refrain at him. We still laugh about it now with him.

GRAEME PARK: Unlike punk rock, the acid house thing had a wider appeal and more global effect. You'd be watching television and people that you knew were raving on *Top of the Pops* and you thought, 'This is big.'

MARK MOORE: It was a journey, the train was the journey, it's taking you on a journey but at the same time it was a reference to the 60s and because I was a huge fan of psychedelia and the 60s and stuff like that I wanted this record to be a psychedelic pop record.

PETE HELLER: Any good music has a way of connecting, of expressing a feeling or an emotion. So good house/dance music has that and in terms of dance music in general a way of making you want to move. It's a fairly basic human desire, really, which connects us to our primitive selves. So good dance music does that. And great dance music moves you both emotionally and physically.

NICK HALKES: Great dance/electronic music makes me not only feel alive but truly glad to be alive also.

NANCY NOISE: I suppose we all just loved the music. Think of the amount of people that were going out clubbing, that's why so many records got into the charts, so many people were going out clubbing. There was lots of people going out dancing to them, they became real records.

MARK MOORE: I had a feeling Prince was listening to S-Express when I heard the B side of 'Alphabet Street': 'This is not music, this is a trip, no, it's not a drug, it's something more hip.' I thought, 'I reckon he's been listening to it,' and then I got a phone call from the record company and they said, 'Prince's people are on the phone, they want to speak to you.' There was this big build-up saying, 'Prince will be calling you in thirty minutes, then again in forty minutes.' He said he had been listening to my music, stuff that was influenced by my funky heroes of the past. He said he thought teaming up would be the best thing in the world and he said he had all these amazing things to remix: 'I'd like you to do a mix of the "Batdance", officially.' Once he heard my remix of 'Batdance', which ended up on his B side, 'Electric Chair' and 'The Future' came after. He was saying, 'I've got these things I think you're gonna love, it's really up your street.' And he sent them to me. I could see that Prince is trying to get on the dance thing, but it wasn't quite right. Then he tailed off, I think he realised it wasn't his forte.

Everyone was talking about the Second Summer of Love. Was it '87? It was for some. Was it '88? Yes – it was for everyone. This was when it all happened. People were either on one or not but they all came together to enjoy the summer. There would be other summers to follow where acid house was still a key element, but across dancefloors and in fields during the glorious summer months of '88 something truly magical happened.

DANNY RAMPLING: House music ... when it blew up in the UK and in London, the message was about one family, the message was hope, inclusion, faith, positivity and change. There was massive change under way, there was a huge shift under way and everyone felt it. When punk came along in the 70s, there was a movement going on there and there was an energy, a really good strong energy, things happening every night. Punk was inclusive, but it was all about drop-outs, there was all that anarchy, whereas this was about love, optimism, inclusion – and we were all having the time of our lives.

NICKY HOLLOWAY: I'd always heard the phrase Summer of Love when watching TV documentaries about hippies. I suppose when the whole house thing first started it felt like you belonged to a movement and there were a lot of things that made you think of Woodstock and hippies and all of that. It felt like it was our time. I suppose probably every thirty years it will come out. Things have to skip a generation to then come back being cool again.

CARL COX: They have to be part of something. Woodstock had this kind of title and this was like the modern-day Woodstock at the end of the day. If you saw people who were dancing to funk and soul and hip hop they had a certain dress, a style that they were wearing, most of it was black. Whereas techno and acid house was anything, pink shirts, smiley faces, glowing, happy. You just transformed everybody. If you weren't into this then there was something wrong with you, you didn't understand it. We didn't care about that at the end of the day because we were having fun.

RUSTY EGAN: I heard about the Summer of Love in '88. Wasn't the Summer of Love in '87? In 1988 my daughter was born. September '88 I was in a club and I heard Marshall Jefferson, 'Raise your hands if you understand,' and this guy came up to me and said, 'You realise the entire club is on one,' and gave me a pill. I'd just split from my wife, although I didn't realise it, I thought we were having a break to sort some problems out. Judge Jules was playing and that record spoke to me. I really understood it and it was a moment for me. Can you believe that I met my second wife on the dancefloor that night, her hands in the air. I met her and we connected. To me, that moment told me that the next generation was here now. My previous life of the 80s was over and I needed to start another club again. I got hold of this club called Wall Street, which was run by my friend Gerard. I used to take Jules there. At the close of the club Jules said he was doing another rave and I jumped in the car with him and ended up in Archway. We'd end up in all these places 'til nine, ten in the morning and I was like, 'I've found it.' Then I introduced Judge Jules to Mick Jones from The Clash and we did a song called 'Contact'. How's that for a Summer of Love?

NANCY NOISE: I think the Summer of Love phrase came around once Future had started. There was Shoom, Trip, Spectrum. Spectrum really kicked off from about April. We had crowds outside and this goes on all through the summer. Then there are things like when the Amnesiacs article came out, when Dave Swindells took photos of us lot and we were dressed quite hippie. It was a mixture of things that happened plus the clothes we were wearing. It was about love, sharing, people united.

PAUL OAKENFOLD: I can't remember when I first heard the phrase 'Second Summer of Love', I guess it means I was there!

DANNY RAMPLING: Being on that dancefloor in Amnesia and having that revelation, that inner sense of knowing that this is the way forward, and that really was where that feeling and that intention came from. In the front end of '88 I felt a boost in the energy and my own energy and zest for life. The intention was coming back to the dancefloor and the DJ.

MOBY: I think I've experienced a bunch of summers of love, as I was in San Francisco for the first Summer of Love in 1969 ... although I was three years old at the time. As I lived in NYC in the late 80s and early 90s I only visited the UK for the acid house Summer(s) of Love, so I was more of a tourist than a home-grown participant.

JAMIE CATTO: I think it's the memory and association of those first times they felt connected, not alienated – that's what the DJs did for the generation – the mixture of that inclusive tribal attitude and the heart-opening drugs.

BRANDON BLOCK: The Second Summer of Love made me fall even more in love with music, and in love with life.

CARL LOBEN: Acid house culture – or whatever you wanna call it – changed my life. I wasn't in London during its first wave, but even so my early experiences of raves were transformative. I went from what I suppose I'd call an 'indie kid' and political activist into being a dance music devotee who started DJing, promoting, writing about the culture and immersing myself in it as the 90s progressed. As the de facto soundtrack to the counter-culture, it wasn't just a part of life — a leisure pursuit, an interest, a hobby. It became life itself.

PETE HELLER: I just think it was something that needed to happen at that time. Once you were part of that, had experienced the power, energy and sense of togetherness, there really was no going back. In that sense it was completely transformational. It also spawned that whole culture of being able to have a go at something – run a club, start a label, sell T-shirts or whatever. It gave people another outlet, an alternative to the mainstream, which was fairly conservative and restrictive in lots of ways. And of course, when something is transformed, it can't return to the way it was. It's just not possible.

GRAEME PARK: I like to focus on what I'm doing, as long as I'm happy. I'm lucky and privileged to do what I do and I get on with it.

DANNY RAMPLING: I felt like I was standing on top of the world. No amount of money can buy that feeling. No amount of money. Absolutely incredible feeling when you have worked so tirelessly, and you're so committed to a vision and an ambition and a dream and that dream comes true and unfolds, there is nothing like it ... well, there are some things like the birth of children, but not much more.

JAY STRONGMAN: The first time I DJed in Greece I just played all the new stuff, acid stuff, '87, '88, and the crowd was going for it. The other DJ put on all stuff that I used to play and the crowd went crazy because that was all the stuff that they were used to. That's what they expected us to play. Some of the other stuff was weird. It was only when a bunch of English guys with their girlfriends came along that they got it. Italy loved it. Germany was weird because it was hard for them to get it at first.

As the Second Summer of Love became more than just a media headline and acid house became more than just another 'thing', what the scene needed was DJs and venues to embrace the music. Music was vital but then so were the places to do it in. People were really coming together, and doing the things you enjoyed with others who also enjoyed them was a big part of the buzz. Some of the 'night people' embracing this new culture didn't need to change their attitude or lifestyle, they carried on doing the same stuff but just a lot more of it.

IRVINE WELSH: More partying, drug-taking and shagging opportunities, I suppose ...

MARK MOORE: It became that way. Not all about it. But drugs went with the music. Everyone overdid it.

DANNY RAMPLING: We were still walking around a year later handing out flyers. I had an energy and I think people warmed to that. I remember walking around London giving out flyers to people for about the first six months of '88. We enjoyed doing it because we'd be out there meeting people. Even though the club was full, we'd still do it.

JON PLEASED WIMMIN: I wasn't really that into house at that point ... although I loved The Beloved, S-Express and KLF ... I initially came from a new wave/goth background, this then morphed into the high energy/Italo/Euro stuff and then eventually into house. I always loved Mark Moore and remember him DJing at a club called Sacrosanct along with another great DJ called Mark Lawrence, sadly no longer with us. I also adored Jeffrey Hinton and all the DJs at Daisy Chain at The Fridge in Brixton, which was a very important night in my musical development. I loved Danny's selection at Glam, the mix of European and US stuff with some Balearic gems thrown in.

You had your shining stars like Danny Rampling, your supernovas like Paul Oakenfold and even your dark stars like Mr C, but more were needed, and fast. Most DJs appeared on the radar of the promoters and other DJs, switching styles if they felt that acid house was for them. Always one step ahead, even before he had his Perfecto label up and running, Oakenfold decided to create his own DJs from scratch. They'd be free to play for anyone and didn't have to play for him, but he knew that he had the platform and in order to spread the scene he'd need DJs to be at the helm with him. His first target was Nancy Turner, the girl he'd met in Ibiza and who he'd asked to find out what Alfredo was playing.

NANCY NOISE: I went back to London after the summer and bought some of the records I'd heard. Paul came over to my flat because I had started hanging out with Paul lots more, we got on really well in 1987.

I moved back home but I got a job and through the job I got this flat. Paul came up one day and I had all these records lying around and I told him this was the stuff I had bought. A little bit of time passed and we were still just hanging out. Paul had brought Alfredo over to London. Paul was the same as everyone else, he wanted to carry on the party like everyone else. It wasn't so much, 'Oh, we are going to make money,' it was more we had gone crazy and fallen in love with Ibiza. We couldn't wait to get back to Ibiza. Then one night at The Soundshaft, where Paul played all night, there was a one-week gap, then the next week I DJed it with Paul from the beginning. Then Paul said, 'I'm calling this club the Future because it is the future,' and it was so true. This is the future of clubbing.

On that flyer it just says Paul Oakenfold and Nancy. I was working for this record company and Paul used to pick me up sometimes and they used to call me Miss Noise because I always used to come in and give my boss a track and say, 'I love this noise on it,' and they said, 'Why do you call it noise?' My boss used to call me Miss Noise and so one day when we were leaving he shouted out, 'Bye, Miss Noise.' Paul had heard it and we were in a van one day going to a party and he unravelled this poster and it said Paul Oakenfold and Nancy Noise. He gave me the name, which I don't really like, but I'm stuck with it forever. I didn't have plans on being a DJ but then Paul saw the records and him and Ian [St Paul] said, 'Do you fancy playing?' The first week I just took a carrier bag with me but I remember as the weeks went on I was saying to people, 'Tell Paul to come up, I'm running out of records.' I didn't have that many records, obviously I got into it eventually and bought more stuff but I nearly gave up. Paul saw something in me. He turned up one day in my flat with this double-deck thing. Obviously, I didn't have proper decks. He was like, 'You have that for a week.' I remember sitting on the floor and thinking about the records. Then the club started getting really busy and I remember saying to Paul, 'I can't handle this.' I remember when I first said I'd do it I just thought I'd be playing to the Ibiza crew and friends and I really, really freaked out. I went off to Ibiza in 1988 and said, 'I'm not sure if I'm gonna carry on,' and he was like, 'WHAT?' Then I came back and said I wanted to come back and play. Then I started record shopping.

Established DJs like Terry Farley had been taken by surprise. A big part of the scene and was developing so quickly, and suddenly missing out became a worry in itself. Even a couple of weeks could make a difference. Terry Farley missed out on going to Ibiza in '88 and wasn't going to do the same in '89.

TERRY FARLEY: I had already booked my 1988 summer holiday to Portugal with my girlfriend. I remember walking up and down the beach in Portugal with a Walkman on and thinking, 'What the fuck am I doing here, why the fuck am I not in Ibiza?' The idea that people would go out for a whole weekend, people didn't do that, even in '88. I go to Ibiza now two or three times a year and I think nothing of having two big nights. In 1988 that wasn't even on the cards. It wasn't that you couldn't afford it, but no one would even think about it. I think the flights went weekly. Basically the idea of going was just like 'no'. At the start of '89, Paul Oakenfold gave me some invites to the opening party of Amnesia. It was free to get in and free drinks all night. I went with Steve Hall. It was Boy George's birthday too. So it was a joint party between Amnesia and Boy George. We just had these passes and Paul said, 'It's really hard to get in.'

There was a problem on the plane going to Ibiza. The plane got left on the tarmac so we didn't arrive until about two in the morning and I had it in my head that it was that night. So we arrived at the hotel, got changed and we got a taxi and the driver kept saying, 'Amnesia's not open tonight' and we were like, 'Special invitation,' and they said, 'It's not open.' They drive us down the road and we could see the sign and we pulled in and it was all closed. The guy said, 'I tell you, it's tomorrow.' So, the opening was the first time I ever went to Amnesia. It was one of the finest nights of my life. I remember records, moments, leaving there, taking loads of pictures on a Polaroid camera. We had hired a car and this car was white and when we got to the car park every car in the car park was a white hire car. It got to about 5am and I had a jacket on, it was a nice jacket so I wanted to take it back to the car so I went out to find the car. I was walking around and there were free drinks but they also had people walking around with backpacks on and they had 'Coca Loca' in their bags, which was kind of an Ibiza cocktail but with MDMA in, and they were spraying it in people's mouths. When I left, I found the car, and remember breaking the window to unlock it. I hid my jacket under the seat with the camera and the pictures. Alfredo played the whole night – for twelve hours. We came out at 10am after the last record. Then we got back to the car and I realised I had broken into someone else's car and put my camera and my coat there, which is a real shame because those pictures would be gold dust now.

NICK HALKES: By the end of 1987 I was well aware that Ibiza felt like a must-visit destination for the summer of '88 and I decided I'd try my hand working there. As soon as uni finished I packed a rucksack full of records and headed out. I procured a DJ gig at a beach bar in Playa d'en Bossa almost immediately, which was great – it finished at 12.30 each night so I was then free to explore the island's nightlife . I ended up at Amnesia one night sitting next to a girl who had a hand-painted smiley T-shirt. A steady stream of people were approaching her asking where she got the shirt and she explained each time that she painted it herself. Realising that there was an opportunity here I got chatting to Ulysses, who ran the boutique in the club, and explained how the smiley was rising in popularity in the UK. He kindly offered to take me to a factory on the island that printed T-shirts and offered to purchase my first twenty shirts – black with a yellow smiley on the front (based on an amended version of the smiley used on the front cover of the Bomb the Bass 'Beat Dis' vinyl that I had brought out with me) and with 'Ibiza Happy Happy' written on the back. This initial run sold out swiftly and I spent many nights through that summer hopping on my moped after my beach-bar set and checking on stock levels and delivering T-shirts to the island's clubs. It was crazy the extent to which the smiley thing had exploded once I was firmly rooted back in the UK by the end of the year.

PAUL OAKENFOLD: The Second Summer of Love was about unity, the coming together of like-minded people. The story is us lot coming back from Ibiza and starting a club and people coming to the club, buying into it saying they wanted to be a part of it. There was no social media, no phones, no scene like this. Suddenly you'd be involved.

GRAEME PARK: It was incredible. I was very lucky that in the summer of '88 I had four weekly residencies that all ran throughout '88. Wednesday I was in Sheffield, Thursday in Leicester, Friday in Manchester and on Saturday I was at The Garage in Nottingham – it was a euphoric period, not just in my life but of all the people who used to come.

The exploits of the Ibiza Four, the coverage in the national press as well as *Boy's Own*, *The Face* and *i-D*, must have made Ibiza and in particular Amnesia seem like Shangri-La. It had been a nonstop assault on the senses since the end of the summer of '87 and now the summer of '88 was here. The summer that will forever be known as the Second Summer of Love.

ALFREDO: In 1988, the English, they start to be more.

NANCY NOISE: I found it really difficult. For some people, it was their first experience of Amnesia, but for me, as someone who had spent two whole summers in a club and then we'd gone back and started all these nights, it had changed. Obviously by then more people knew about it. When we went in '88 there were so many people saying, 'Hi, Nancy,' I was like, 'OMG, what have we done?' There were so many people from England. I found it quite difficult, but I was looking back at some video clips from about 1989 and I actually cried because it still looked so amazing. I think it's just at the time, even my little sister, when Spectrum got busy, she was like, 'People keep dancing like us and dressing like us.' It was a really weird feeling, when you're in the underground doing something and then it explodes. My other friends would say they wished they'd enjoyed Spectrum more because I felt like we'd lost our special thing. I kind of felt really strange.

DANNY RAMPLING: Going [to Ibiza] the following year, everyone had started to get to know each other better, everyone was connecting the dots. That second year of going there really gave me the sense that there's a whole core of the scene that knew each other.

AUTUMN

By the end of the summer of '88 acid house was every-where. The Amnesiacs returned from their long hot summer in Ibiza with vastly swelled numbers. They may have hoped to keep their 'discovery' to themselves, but the word was out and so were the party people. In a strange way time has stood still for them in Ibiza. The island already had its groove and those that had been before quickly settled back into the pattern that revolved around the dancefloor at Amnesia. The newbies quickly fell into line and all of them came back home after the summer ready for more of the same.

Sometimes a story paints such a vivid picture that you can visualise a moment in time to such an extent that it can become etched in a collective consciousness. You can almost feel what Neil Armstrong was thinking as he made his 'one giant leap'. For nearly a thousand years British kids have subconsciously put their hand up to their eye when hearing about Harold and the Battle of Hastings. Putting yourself in the shoes, hang on a minute, I mean standing barefoot in the footsteps of the indigenous people and seeing Columbus's ships majestically heading towards you makes you want to shout out and warn everyone around you. You can feel the icy blast of the bone-chilling wind as Captain Oates stepped out of the Antarctic tent on that freezing night, leaving his exhausted compatriots behind, immortalising that moment with his selfless parting comment: 'I am just going outside. I may be some time.' It turned out this act of immense bravery, done to save his friends and recorded in the diary of Captain Scott, was a futile gesture and even though we don't 100 per cent know what happened we can clearly see in our minds what we think it was like. Now imagine if Oates had taken a few paces and thought, 'Sod this, I'm freezing my knackers off out here, I'm going back in,' and upon opening up the tent had found his mates laughing and joking while cracking open a bottle of champagne. 'But mate, we only have four glasses,' would not have cut it, although it's a fair guess that Scott wouldn't have put Oates's reaction in his diary. It may have felt like a split second but that is all it takes for everything you expected to be as it was before to have moved on. This is what it was like for the Aciderati.

Returning from Ibiza at the end of that summer was like Carl Douglas's 'Kung Fu Fighting'. Everybody was at it. The UK was awash with all things acid. At club closing time the West End echoed to a chorus of 'Where's the party?' and over the summer your mum was as likely to have wished you to 'Have a nice rave, dear' as she was to tell you to wrap up warm in winter. Anything was possible, you just had to reach out for it. One minute you could be trying to get into a club, the next minute you'd have your light-bulb moment. The music was everywhere, and the fashion and acid house lingo had already engulfed the nation.

There was still a strong underground scene, with pirate radio and raves dictating the rapid growth of the culture. You could be dancing in a room/place/club/den/cave with the likes of Paul Rutherford from Frankie Goes To Hollywood, Kevin Rowland from Dexy's Midnight Runners, Rusty Egan from Visage, ABC's Martin Fry, Mark Moore from S-Express, Culture Club's Boy George and Soft Cell's Marc Almond to music that you were all discovering at the same time.

> **GRAEME PARK:** You can define acid house as the music that DJ Pierre and Marshall Jefferson came up with messing around with the 303 in Chicago or you can refer to it as a movement. It was the scene that democratised the whole thing. We could be playing at the Haçienda to 2,000 people but when it was full, it was full. People who couldn't get in went off and did their own nights – it led to other people becoming professional DJs. It was a different time then. Now you can start movements and trends pretty quickly with social media – often with big corporations behind it trying to give the impression that it is more organic than it actually is – but back then, back in the day, it was word of mouth. In the late 80s pubs generally closed at 11pm and clubs closed at 2am. At two people were like, 'I don't want to finish, I don't want to go home,' which led to afterparties in warehouses and fields.

You all danced the same, sweated the same and drank the same drink (water) and you were all on the same wavelength. You knew everyone in the place, everyone in the queue and you knew there were thousands of people just like you looking for somewhere they could go. You looked up towards the DJs who were playing music made by other DJs and realised that you could do this too.

The genie was most definitely out of the bottle.

Jenni Rampling had famously (and responsibly) had to put a plea out to the Shoomers to stop giving up their day jobs as people started to 'drop out' having felt that they had found their true purpose. Looking back, it seems bonkers that you could believe you were put on this planet to take an E, dance and hug people, but these were life-affirming times. Start a record company, be a manager, design stuff, produce music, create a fashion label, promote, run a club – you could do any of these things and, as everyone around you wanted to do the same sort of thing you did, you could work together. The founding fathers of house and techno from the USA were making visits to the UK and dance music was on TV and radio (pirate and mainstream). These legends from Detroit and Chicago turned out to be pretty normal people. A bit of an idea, some technology, persistence and belief had turned kids into gods. This underground scene was paradoxically also visible on every high street. You'd always been told that making things happen was 1 per cent inspiration and 99 per cent perspiration (probably from the same source that says that 74 per cent of statistics are made up) but now you could see that if you got it right, 100 per cent inspiration would result in 100 per cent perspiration. Anyone could be a someone and you didn't have to support the scene wholeheartedly to still be a part of it.

JAMIE CATTO: I was always the one in Faithless getting into trouble for musically criticising and being sardonic about dance music – 'music so bad it takes a class A drug to enjoy it' kind of thing ... as usual, foolishly biting the hand that's feeding me.

NICKY HOLLOWAY: You know it [ecstasy] can take the edge off. You can turn around and talk to a stranger and not worry if you get a knock back. If they walk away you don't care. It mixed up a lot of things. You have council estate boys knocking back with Kensington people. You get a content feeling, you feel at peace. When I played on it, I was less worried about what I was doing. I was better ... though sometimes it went wrong.

The Second Summer of Love was a frantic time but surprisingly calm. 1987 and 1988 had seen the inception, creation, emergence and spread of a new sound and a new way of expressing oneself, with music very much at the centre. Normally you'd expect to work hard to make something happen and then sit back and enjoy the fruits of your labours. The end of the Second Summer of Love was different. The control had passed from the instigators to everyone else. The influenced were becoming the influencers. Things went from frantic to frenzy.

CYMON ECKEL: To this day, nothing can beat that simple chemical and physical reaction, those raising hairs on your neck, that beat, that vision and the places you can go!

There was suddenly so much to do. Apart from the obvious clubbing, raving and dancing, you also needed to gather lots of flyers, try to find out some reliable intel as to where the party actually was, get some mates together, sort out some tickets, get sorted on some 'other' tickets. Around this you had to eat, sleep, work, study and generally try to keep it together. The acid house crowd started to congregate all over the place. It was fun to be with like-minded people who were experiencing what you were, were part of your tribe. One of the most recognisable Shoomers, Anton Le Pirate, is believed to have instigated the 'Happenings' which took place every Sunday daytime when up to 10,000 ravers, sorry, I mean members of the public, would turn up and just basically hang out. It had a great, non-threatening, chilled vibe. Some people were dancing to low-level sound they had with them but most were just sitting around in small groups, chatting and cementing the relationships and friendships that had been made in the clubs the night before. The word spread and by the end of the afternoons people were rocking up from places like Brighton and Southend. This could have gone on forever but some bright sparks starting printing up flyers for it so the police had no choice but to pull the plug.

TINTIN CHAMBERS: There must be hundreds of reasons that the culture didn't fizzle out. The movement had so much momentum both creatively and carried by the people partying. Many will tell you that the political environment had a part to play, no doubt, but I'm no sociologist. What I did witness myself was a notable breaking down of social barriers. Parties were integrated, which whilst in London was already normal, outside of London was not so. You would imagine technology has played its part, as the world has become more connected. Surely the biggest reason is that people were just having a fucking amazing time. Getting high, being silly, having lots of sex, listening to wonderful music, dancing all night and day, and just being free.

You didn't need to sing along, you didn't even need to go along, you just had to get along. It was in your car, your home, your Walkman and in your life. You heard it in clubs, pubs, café's, shops, and so did all your friends. You'd never been to Future or Shoom or Spectrum. You'd never met Nicky Holloway or Andrew Weatherall or Mr C. You couldn't pinpoint Ibiza on a map, let alone Chicago and Detroit. Your little sister was buying singles she'd seen on *Top of the Pops* by the likes of S-Express, Bomb the Bass and Yazz, while you were more in the know and going a bit more underground with tracks like 'The Jack That House Built' by Jack'N'Chill , 'I Need a Friend' by Farley Jackmaster Funk and 'Big Fun' by Inner City featuring Kevin Saunderson. You probably had a slightly older mate, a bit cooler, and he was introducing you to stuff that he'd discovered like Jaquarius's 'Love is Happiness', 808 State's 'Flow Coma' and Bam Bam's 'Where's Your Child?'. In the meantime, Bobby McFerrin was telling everyone 'Don't Worry, Be Happy'.

IRVINE WELSH: Dance music was always about fun, sex and community. But the DIY ethos of early acid house pulled people into dance music – industrial working class, punk sensibilities – who would previously have seen dance clubs as effete compared to rock 'n' roll gigs or pissing it up in the boozer. It made electronic dance music a mass rather than niche concern.

FATBOY SLIM: It opened my eyes and ears to a different spirit in music. I had loved the rebellion of punk, the urban edge of hip hop and the raw groove of funk but it seemed to encapsulate all of them but with a feeling of togetherness and collective escapism on the dancefloor I had never witnessed before.

Suddenly, clubbers could put on their own nights, play their own music and maybe make some money. It is not as simple as some people think. There isn't a magic formula, replicating a successful night is no guarantee of success and you can't go out and get a degree in rave-ology. What you could do was come up with a name and identity that would excite people, catch their attention with a flyer, make sure your DJs were hard at 'It' and collect a core crowd that would enjoy the night and spread the word. There was the advantage that ecstasy was now commonplace, and it intensified the experience, which in turn made people more accepting of music they hadn't heard before.

DANNY RAMPLING: The DJs became the stars.

Nevertheless, these nights didn't always work out. Some of them were great. Some of them were excellent. Very occasionally all the ingredients would once again align to deliver something exceptional.

CARL LOBEN: It was always premised on futurism. It utilised new technology, and didn't initially adhere to the outmoded model of rock 'n' roll – tortured performer and rapt audience. Acid house, by its very nature, was participatory. Everybody was the star.

GRAEME PARK: In the summer of '88 all clubs closed at 2am but there was always somewhere to go on to like a house party. In Nottingham people would head over to this park with massive sound systems in their cars, open the doors and carry on partying listening to tapes of DJs. Everything would carry on.

The Second Summer of Love exploded on 1 October 1988 sending dance music shrapnel in every direction. Not wasting a moment or missing a beat, that was the same day when a couple of DJs, Fabio and Grooverider, made Rage at Heaven their home. Monday at Heaven was the home of Spectrum, which was the club that would define the scene and then the entire industry. Rage was started by promoter Kevin Millins, who showed that this night was a serious addition to the scene when he brought in DJs Danny Rampling and Mark Moore to get the night off the ground. Music was at the heart of this night, with the two residents, Trevor Fung and Colin Faver, having free rein and introducing their crowd to some of the big American DJs who'd be brought over to DJ as guests, including Frankie Knuckles, David Morales, Kevin Saunderson and Derrick May.

Fabio and Grooverider, largely unproven on the club scene, got the chance to DJ in the upstairs bar. They didn't have any preconceptions about what they'd play and, not being particularly up on the acid house sound, they played records that they felt would go down well blended with the house music that they liked the sound of. To them, house was house and it was only later that they found out that the majority of what they played was in fact techno. One of their big tunes was Moby's 'Go', the B side to his first track which even he was amazed became such a global sensation, eventually doing over two million units.

> **MOBY:** … complete and utter bewilderment. My first single, 'Mobility', sold around five hundred copies and got played nowhere. I assumed that 'Go' would follow suit and slip quickly into twelve-inch obscurity, so I was baffled when DJs started playing it and it became such an odd, underground hit.

Fabio had been a real London clubber. He was at Crackers, where George Powers and Paul Anderson were the DJs and it was all about the dancing and the dancers. He was at Gossips with Tim Westwood listening to electro, and burning up the dancefloors at Spatz and the 100 Club. These little clubs were in the heart of the West End but operated for the dancers and so these were among the first places where the black and white crowd really mixed. He'd even got himself onto a pirate radio station, Faze1, playing funk. It was there that he heard about Spectrum and the crowds that Paul Oakenfold was pulling in each week. Seemed like the kind of crowd that would be up for an afterparty, so he went down to check it out. This was the moment when it all made sense to him. He took one look at Oakenfold, surrounded in smoke, like a deity with his adoring worshipers, and saw something that he wanted to be part of. Fabio was hooked, but it was more than the music. It was the feeling that the music gave you and the shared energy with the other dancers, different to what he was used to. He was used to DJs like Paul 'Trouble' Anderson, who played a track and raced round to the dancefloor to take his turn inside a circle of dancers waiting patiently for the chance to show what they could do. You know a DJ is great when he not only plays the kind of records that he would dance to but gets on down to them there and then. Anderson was a huge influence on the scene and on a whole host of future world-class DJs like Norman Jay, Danny Rampling and Terry Farley. At Spectrum there was no circle, everyone was dancing nonstop. Fabio was mesmerised watching Oakey play, lost in the music but aware of exactly what the crowd needed to lift them higher and higher.

The radio station in Brixton planned an afterparty at an after-hours place next door and one of the few DJs on the station playing house was asked to join in – he went by the name of Grooverider. The party started slowly, by 1am there was not one single person there. Just as they were about to pack it in, it happened. One solitary punter rocked up and then suddenly hundreds of people descended on the place – and one of the most iconic partnerships in dance music was born. They carried on throwing this party every week, filling the place from the people dancing outside clubs like The Trip. Their night had the big advantage of being an after-hours thing (that allegedly sometimes ended late afternoon the next day), meaning that other DJs and promoters like Paul Oakenfold and Trevor Fung could come and check them out. They were developing a crowd of their own and Fabio and Grooverider themselves began to have a following rather than their night, mainly because they hadn't gotten around to naming the thing.

Playing upstairs at Rage was amazing for them. They'd made it, they were in a proper club as DJs. Trevor Fung and Colin Faver were the main guys and one week they both happened to be away at the same time, leaving Fabio and Grooverider to take over the main floor. Eventually they would take over permanently. The techno they were playing, mainly German and Belgian, went down very well but when they started chopping in breakbeats it almost blew the roof off.

They had a dancefloor that was jumping like no other. Every time they played a breakbeat their friend, Danny Jungle, would start shouting 'jungle, jungle' and, like Gary Haisman's 'Acieed', the crowd picked this up and the breakbeat sound of Rage became known as 'Jungle'. No one had ever heard anything like it. The effect it had on the crowd was off the charts. You only have to look at the roll call of regulars who became future superstars like Kemistry, Storm and Goldie to realise how influential this club night was. Suddenly, jungle was a thing and then drum 'n' bass was a thing too – and all from Rage. Up until the mid-80s seismic shifts in cultural tastes normally took a clubbers' generation to come about (which was approximately seven years in duration).

Acid house changed all that and Rage was the first case in point. By the time it shut its doors for good in 1993, Fabio and Grooverider's Thursday night had masterminded the first two home-grown British dance music genres with jungle and drum 'n' bass, which joined the countless electronic music styles that were filling dancefloors all across the globe. On 11 September 1995 Rage was reborn for one night, this time at the Blue Note in Hoxton where under the Rage banner Fabio and Grooverider were joined by Kemistry, Storm and Doc Scott at the album launch of Goldie's *Timeless*. By this point the many offshoots of house, techno and every other kind of electronic music had spread across the world and a market was created to cater for this, but could this really be attributed to acid house? Would it not have just happened? No time for a 50/50, definitely not the point to 'ask the audience' (and get into a massive debate), this is a 'phone a friend' moment. It was time to ask an expert how important acid house was to the global spread of dance music. The thing is, especially with dance music, everyone is an 'expert'. Fortunately, the black book contains someone who has, since the early 90s, been at the heart of documenting every genre, sub-genre, nearly genre and not-a-genre alongside every emerging and established DJ and club. So how important was acid house in shaping the electronic music world we live in today?

> **CARL LOBEN:** Crucial. It brought together different strands of electronic music, gave it more of an identity and a culture, and captured the imaginations of tens of thousands of youth. In a way, the UK put a new twist on German and American-derived sounds and ramped up the populism factor.

Just for the record, the 'ask the audience' option gave the same answer.

> **TERRY FARLEY:** Stormzy is the grandson or even great-grandson of acid house. If it wasn't for acid house, Stormzy wouldn't be here. Speed garage comes from the Ministry of Sound, which was only open because of someone's love of house. If I spoke to Stormzy and said, 'What's your favourite acid house record?' he probably wouldn't know, but without acid house records, he wouldn't be here.

Considering what was actually going on across the UK and that lots of entertainment journalists were getting to see the euphoric action close-up in towns like London, Manchester, Leeds, Nottingham, Stoke and everywhere in between, plus the availability of publications like *i-D*, *Face* and *Boy's Own*, the tabloid press had been quite restrained. They hadn't been slow off the mark and they definitely knew all about it. In October '88 the *Sun* had been happily selling 'a groovy and cool Acid House T-shirt for £5.50' but now that it was November it was clearly time to put a stop to this 'terrible noise' once and for all. A national newspaper with that much power coming straight for you – what would their first move be? If you said, 'Research and write a piece giving the true facts about acid house,' then you have obviously never read a British tabloid and are unaware that 'Freddy Star Ate My Hamster'. If you said, 'Bring in a team of leading investigative journalists, get them undercover in the rave scene, find out what's going on, publish your exposé and hand the dossier to the police,' then you'd still be way off. If you said 'Withdraw their T-shirt offer, start a "Say No To Drugs" campaign using a round yellow badge with a frown as the logo,' you'd be nearly right. They did this and enlisted a host of celebs to come out against drugs including Shoomers Mark Moore, Boy George and Bananarama! To give the campaign added credibility they also brought in DJ, TV personality, charity marathon runner and all-round odd-bod Sir Jimmy Savile. Apparently he was on a mission to save youth from itself (or for himself, as we would find out after his death). For reasons best known to the *Sun*'s advertising agency, this masterplan didn't work.

Across the whole electronic scene, acid house is recognised as the point in time when dance music became unstoppable. Only something so momentous could have, in one fell swoop, pushed all other contenders aside and paved the way for dance music to take over the world. Dance music had become so ingrained in popular culture that you could see references to it everywhere and equally be pretty oblivious to it and still have shared experiences. But everyone wanted a taste of it and now that the DJs were stars they knew where to go.

CYMON ECKEL: How hard is it to leave the dancefloor when you're having that much fun!

Stella McCartney, now a leading designer and head of her own fashion house, could pretty much call on anyone she wanted to perform at her birthday party (even her college graduation show at Central Saint Martins was famously modelled by Kate Moss, Yasmin Le Bon and Naomi Campbell). Her dad was a Beatle, his song-writing partnership with John Lennon is the most successful in history, one of his songs, 'Yesterday', has been covered by over 2,200 artists … she knew he could get her a serious act or two for her eighteenth. A call from McCartney and the world of rock would have come running. But it was 1989. Time to load a sound system into a van with a couple of DJs and drive to a secluded rural location.

CARL COX: It was really surreal. Paul [Oakenfold] got the gig. Stella was asking about Paul Oakenfold – 'Daddy, could you get Paul to play?' Oakey said, 'I need Carl.' We all met on the farm and security were like, 'Who are you?' and we said, 'We're the DJs for Stella's.' We went in, Paul McCartney said it's fine. We put up the banners, the smoke machine, the turntables, the mixer, boom, away we go. I played a bit, Paul played a bit, we all had a great time. At the time the McCartneys had made a record. Linda and Paul were dancing to this record in front of us whilst we were playing it. I was back in the van when Paul McCartney tapped on the window and said, 'Let's have a pizza.' I remember it was the most delicious pizza I've ever had in my life. It was a margherita with oregano and I was hanging out with Paul and Stella. It was bizarre. Eventually they sent me a thank you for making their daughter's dream come true.

Dance music was everywhere and developing at such a fast pace that the original soldiers of the scene were starting to be heavily outnumbered by the next generation of clubbers. Apparently, a new clubbing generation emerges every two years, and the newbies had it on a plate. They didn't imagine that they could destroy what had become part of everyday life or that they would come under such heavy fire from the establishment. After all, they were young once too weren't they?

MARK MOORE: There's definitely a change. There's a whole new group of people. Some people came along for the ride. The ones who couldn't fit in, they had a hard time adapting because it wasn't just the clubs that had changed but the whole fabric of the world. Great Britain had changed. At first we thought it was a brilliant change, it was very positive, about creative change, revolution and making the planet a better place. But as we took more and more drugs, over the years, it became about standing in a field waving your arms about and forgetting all the changes we were gonna make to the social strata. Then people started to burn out a bit from overdoing it. Then with the government trying to clamp down on illegal parties, everything started to change. That's when the superclubs were born, we had to have legalised clubbing that carried on with permission. So it changed. I DJed at Gatecrasher and Ministry of Sound. All of that was brilliant. There became a kind of having to plug into the system. It was about leaving the old system behind and plugging in your own parties. From the mid-90s onwards, the general mood changed, there was a general dumbing-down in culture.

JAY STRONGMAN: The whole rave thing got a bit crazy. People had died and it put a lot of people off who thought that wasn't what they'd signed up for. I remember in Hamburg by '92 the guy I was DJing for switched to house and said the crowd would love my stuff. And I got up there and all they wanted was hard-core stuff. Everything I did I had to play plus-ten. I was playing all the garagey stuff and I had to play it all plus-ten. I thought, wow, Germans had really caught on to this. It had come full circle again.

Britain's youth had come together, musically, creatively, even chemically, but there was a strong feeling of unity that could only be a good thing. Football hooliganism was down, apparently partly due to E's, and society was becoming more accepting and more tolerant. This was nothing like punk, no spikey-haired tourist punks sitting around in Sloane Square, this was people like your kids. From the onset of the rave scene there had been an attempt to tighten laws surrounding what was deemed antisocial behaviour. On 27 January 1990 the Freedom To Party rally had taken place at Trafalgar Square 'in a peaceful protest against the new anti-party laws being introduced'. One week later 2,000 ravers gathered in Manchester and this was followed with (largely) peaceful protests around the country. The organisers handed out flyers stating, 'If the new law goes through there won't be another "Summer of Love" and there won't be any more raves, so stand up for your right to party. Show the media and the government our strength. Are you going to let them take away your right to party?' As the Brexit situation has shown us, other than the fear and violence instigated by the attempted return to a medieval poll tax in the 90s, protests don't seem to achieve much. The poll tax riots of March 1990 saw close to 200,000 people demonstrating, resulting in 213 injured, including 100 police officers, and 340 arrests. Even then, more than anything else it was the failure of the councils to be able to implement it that led to its scrapping. Clearly a protest by a bunch of people sucking oversized baby's pacifiers while shielding their eyes from the sunlight and demanding the right to dance around in fields while hugging each other didn't feature high on the PM's to-do list. The government should have listened.

Despite the media and the tough stance from the authorities there was the odd shining light for the rave scene. On 13 October 1990, The Eclipse opened in Coventry. Situated in a disused bingo hall, it was the first licensed all-night club in the UK. Within the licensing stipulations alcohol was not permitted to be sold, which didn't bother the 1,600-capacity audience. Promoters like Energy, Helter Skelter and Amnesia took advantage of the legal-rave status of the space and people travelled from all over to hear DJs like Carl Cox, Sasha,

Tintin and Mickey Finn, safe in the knowledge that the party wouldn't be shut down and that they could dance all night long surrounded by fellow ravers. No roadblocks, no convoys, no stress.

This wasn't anarchy, this was the future, it was something to embrace. For all its wildness, the scene was following its own rules – and where there are rules, no matter how laxly adhered to, there are possibilities. Every promoter and venue had its own way of doing things and its own methods of bringing the crowd they wanted in. The Zap Club in Brighton kicked off its new Thursday nights in January 1991 with resident Carl Cox and guests on rotation including Dave Angel, Sasha and Fabio for the princely sum of £5, but 'Persons with visible tattoos will not be admitted'. Even then, securing Carl as a resident was a coup and with a club the size of Zap and five squids on the door you can see that Carl was doing it for the love. If he played any UK venue now at five times that price the queue would be round the block and, for sure, most people's skin would look like a living, breathing, colouring book. Cheers, Beckham. This was also the same year that Carl, now the undisputed King of Ibiza, first played there and the island's love affair with Senor Cox started.

CARL COX: At first I went there just to go and listen to other DJs. I didn't get to play there until about '91. There was a promoter in the UK who used to run a club called Sterns on the South Coast. He decided he wanted to go to Ibiza and take the Sterns DJs with him. I was one of them. He wanted me to be a part of it. I played all these clubs there and totally rocked them! People on the island were like: 'Who is this DJ?' Eventually I

had the opportunity to play at Space in Ibiza for React
Records because I had a record out with them in 1996.
That's how I got to play in Ibiza.

Meanwhile, our early 90s ravers were having the time of their
lives. Everything seemed to be moving in the right direction.
By 1992 the police hadn't admitted it but realised they had
lost the battle against the raves; licensed premises welcomed
DJs and dance music, pirate stations were going for licences,
record labels and publications made dance music more
legitimate, clever promoters turned up to raves with lawyers
and barristers in tow, people signed contracts, everyone was
playing ball and we were about to turn a corner and ride off
into the sunset together. Or so we thought. Surely nothing
could go wrong. Nothing could take this back to a point where
the authorities would publicly lose control and then have to
come back at the rave scene as if they were smashing a miners'
picket. Surely we'd bide our time, win the public over, shake
hands with the authorities and be recognised as the essential
celebration of the human spirit that they would be proud to
say started in Britain. The only thing is, people wanted to
rave now and it would be a shame not to use up all those
glowsticks. Then along came something that would challenge
the authorities like never before. One word that would change
everything. Castlemorton.

Castlemorton was an illegal rave like no other before or since.
The biggest and best sound systems like Spiral Tribe, Bedlam
and DiY converged in the Malvern Hills in Worcestershire
on 22 May 1992 for what turned into a week-long party that
attracted about 40,000 people. These sound systems dominated
the London squat scene where there was no grey area. Once

in, the landlords and the authorities would try to get them out while the squatters tried to keep themselves in and the powers that be out. Parties were being thrown in buildings in which the revellers exercised rights that prevented them from being kicked out, and when the inevitable happened they would move on to the next property.

The area surrounding Malvern felt the full force of 40,000 people who came to dance but also needed to eat, sleep, relieve themselves, have sex and all the other things that us humans like to do. You wouldn't have wanted to live nearby and have a front garden. There were queues at all the local payphones, with dealers driving up from all over the UK. This was definitely no episode of *Countryfile*. The police were powerless to stop it and might as well have joined in for all the good they did. At least they would have had some fun before being severely bollocked when they rolled back into the station after a pointless waiting game. The press were all over it and made sure they photographed the wildest ravers and the most bewildered policemen. As the party started to wind down the police moved in and started to do what they could. Spiral Tribe ended up with thirteen of their crew arrested and the media had the photos it needed to show that dance music and the rave scene that promoted it had gone too far.

A slap on the wrist wasn't going to be enough here, and there was little incentive for the powers that be to reach any sort of compromise with a multimillion-pound largely cash business fuelled by illegal recreational drugs. Ken Tappenden retired in 1993 as a highly decorated officer after thirty-two years in the force. He had been such a part of the scene that it was said that some diehard ravers shed a little tear. After all, you can't play a game of cat-and-mouse without the cat. No longer 'feared', but respected by most of the dance community for his fairness in the face of the massive uphill struggle he faced, Ken is now, ironically, a toastmaster and master of ceremonies, and I'd like to think that even if he doesn't he is sometimes tempted to slip in the odd 'Booyaka'.

> **DAVE SWINDELLS:** I wish I'd been there, but I couldn't get up there. As soon as it happened and you heard about it you knew they were going to crack down big time. The raves had already upset people all across the Home Counties but this was like a rave times ten because it carried on for five or more days and you knew there was going to be a serious comeback. You knew it was going to impact on free parties and on raves, but it turned festivals into legal raves and raving went legal and indoors.

The powers that be had thought they could contain it, then they tried to control it and now they just wanted to cancel it. If young master Ravey wasn't going to play nice then Nanny Government was going to take all his toys away. The countdown to the Criminal Justice and Public Order Act of 1994 had begun.

The Bill covered a whole range of things but the one that stood out was Section 63, the part that was aimed at the free-party scene and gave the police the power to shut down any event that had music that was 'characterised by the emission of a succession of repetitive beats'. They made it next to impossible to legally put on a rave, as it gave the police the authority to stop a rave in the open air when a hundred or more people were attending, or where two or more people were making preparations for a rave. It also allowed any uniformed police officer who even believed that a person was on the way to a rave within a five-mile radius to direct them away from the area. The last truly successful outdoor event of the rave era was Universe's 'Big Love' in 1993, which pulled in 30,000 people, but even then sound restrictions forced the sound to be turned down during the Prodigy's set. These were miserable times. The writing was on the wall in '94, which didn't help as graffiti was also on the antisocial behaviour list. The risks in staging a quality event were very high and the police were confiscating sound systems. Many promoters fell foul, some remained hidden underground, some moved into mainstream clubs and some even went abroad. After Castlemorton, Spiral Tribe and Bedlam moved across Europe, squatting and partying as they went. Universe went to Germany and held a Tribal Gathering at Munich Airport. Acid house and the whole electronic culture was clearly about more than just music. It had become a way of life; much more than a party, it had become the cultural driving force for a whole generation.

> **IRVINE WELSH:** It did this because it had strong lifestyle rather than just recreational elements. People were leaving their towns and travelling – meeting like-minded sorts from all over the country ... and the world. Also the establishment popularised it by making a cunt of things as they always do; the tabloid headlines, the drug hysteria, the CJB [Criminal Justice Bill] – they made raving the go-to way to rebel for a whole generation.

Uncertainty was stifling creativity and while the world was partying away the UK's ravers once again took to the streets. Fifty thousand people marched to Trafalgar Square in July, and after the summer and with no progress 35,000 took to the streets on 9 October. The mood had changed, and the peaceful protesters were joined by a more militant group. In charge of the police was Chief Superintendent Richard Cullen and the police were expecting some marching, speaking, maybe even shouting. What they ended up with was full-scale rioting as the police fought running battles through the streets in what would become known as the Park Lane Riot. Matters went from bad to worse when more police were brought in to quell the disturbances, unaware of the nature of the protest and what it was all about. With hindsight it is easy to see how, in the confusion and with the adrenalin pumping, the placards reading 'Kill the Bill' may have been taken the wrong way by the police.

> **CARL COX:** They forgot that young people have a voice, that they need to be heard. Our right to party was our right to party. You shouldn't be able to take away what makes us happy in this country and people were getting really upset. But meanwhile, these parties were bringing people together. We needed them.

Any illusion that the Summer of Love could go on forever lay shattered on the pavements of Mayfair alongside the discarded whistles and broken placards. The illegal scene may have had its day but there was still a big demand for the culture.

> **DAVE SWINDELLS:** All-night drinking wouldn't have happened without acid house. There we were in the middle of the 1980s dreaming of being a global clubbing city with 2am licences – it was never going to happen.

Acid house made London the leading clubbing city in the world for at least a decade. It had been New York before that. In the early 80s it was all about New York, house changed that.

In 1995 underground club and rave promoters started to team up with established concert promoters to put on 'proper' events – not the 'running for your life down a country lane carrying a record box' kind of proper but in a 'we have a licence and all our paperwork is in order' kind of proper. The established promoters were able to keep the dance music culture buoyant, which was fortunate as 1995 was also the year that Leah Betts died after drinking seven litres of water in a ninety-minute period after taking an ecstasy tablet at home at her eighteenth birthday party. Not in a field or at a rave, not even at a club, but at home.

A national poster campaign with a photo of Leah and the tagline 'Sorted: Just one ecstasy tablet took Leah Betts' had a big impact on an entire generation of young people. An interesting aside to this sad tale is that the poster campaign was funded by advertising agencies linked to alcohol and energy-drinks companies, who had an interest in scaring clubbers away from E's and into drinking. Leah Betts's name is etched in a collective consciousness. Most people can name a celeb or two who overdosed and if you've been close to someone who died because of drink or drugs they will be in your mind. It is unusual to be able to name a stranger who died in their own home over twenty years ago. Of course, she was all over the media, but then so were many others, living and dead, whose names escape us.

A year and a half ago there was a terrorist attack on London

Bridge. A member of the public, a football fan, nicknamed the Lion of London Bridge, single-handedly took on three attackers armed with knives, launching into them with his battle cry of 'Fuck you, I'm Millwall'. He's been in every newspaper, on global TV stations, he's done interviews, it was eighteen months ago. What's his name? Exactly my point. Leah Betts resonates because even though it is not a dance music fatality and not linked to clubland the dance music history feels a responsibility and has kept her memory alive when it would have been easier to let the story drift away. That's because, despite her age, the place she died, and the fact that you've never met her, she is still 'one of us'.

There was a genuine attempt to understand what was driving youth and to appreciate their scene. Legal raves, the precursor of the modern-day festival, replaced the illegal raves. Underground promoter Universe teamed up with major festival and venue owner The Mean Fiddler to stage the Tribal Gathering '95 at Otmoor Park in Oxfordshire, a totally legal and fully licensed event for 25,000 people with The Prodigy, Orbital and Moby headlining. Different stages and tents catered for different genres of dance music, and looking at the different dance tribes coexisting was a eureka moment for the whole dance music community.

> **MOBY:** On the one hand I was in a very rough place. I was sunburned from being in Israel for three days, and I was at the beginning of a very complicated break-up with my then girlfriend. But on the other hand I was thrilled to be at this festival that was informed by the maturing dance scene, and also a really remarkable ethos of community and tribalism.

NICK HALKES: For some years there was nothing more vibrant, exciting and connective in youth culture than dance/electronic music. In that environment, of course, the scene was destined to expand at a rapid rate.

Promoters, artists, punters, all realised that they were part of something much bigger than just the scene dominated by music they liked. They were part of a united movement where you could style-surf and explore different sounds. You could dip in and out and the shared experience of coming together with kindred spirits was what it was all about. It worked, and a new formula was created that could cater for the rave crowd, appeal to a festival audience who liked repetitive beats and fall within the law. It brought home-grown and international acts to a wide audience while maintaining a carefree approach to musical diversity. It was now all about entertainment overload and Universe's event in '96 at Luton Hoo featured over a hundred artists including the Chemical Brothers, Black Grape, Leftfield, Goldie, LTJ Bukem, Laurent Garnier, Carl Cox, Danny Rampling, Richie Hawtin, Jeff Mills, Marshall Jefferson and an up-and-coming duo called Daft Punk.

The free-party scene was pretty much over in the UK. Fortunately, there was a purpose-built scene, a continuation of the original scene and with the same mentality behind it, in place so that the ravers didn't miss a beat. Life carried on. Dance music was big business and Big Brother was most definitely watching.

Something was definitely needed to draw the Second Summer of Love to a definite close on a positive note. The scene was strong. Clubs, music, festivals, DJs and events – it had never been stronger. This would be the perfect time to take the scene to the next level.

And so, as we 'whistled a happy tune', just when something special was needed the most, it happened. There was one last good old-fashioned freebie in 1994, hosted by one of the innovators of acid house, but it didn't take place in the UK. Paul Oakenfold had just done another *Essential Mix* for Pete Tong on Radio One. Pete had built up an incredible catalogue of mixes with DJs showcasing what they were known for. Oakey did something very different. Known by this point for his melodic trance style, he switched to a new style, psychedelic trance, and delivered what has become known as The Goa Mix. It is still voted as the best *Essential Mix* ever and helped Paul support a whole host of new trance acts with his Perfecto Fluoro label. Paul had got into this from his good friend and Spectrum co-promoter Ian St Paul. Ian had been in Ibiza with his cousin, Trevor Fung, when Paul had his Amnesia moment and once again his vision had delivered an underground scene into Oakey's lap. Amnesia, Spectrum, Psytrance, Goa – Ian St Paul must be one of the most unsung heroes of acid house and the dance music industry that followed. And that's just the way he likes it. Anyone who doesn't mind his DJ stopping a dancefloor in mid-flow and launching into a classical symphony without panicking and interfering with the DJs creative process would either have to be mad, thick-skinned enough not to care what a club full of people thought of him or have balls of steel. Fortunately for the dance music world, Ian St Paul has all three. *'Deu borem korum.'*

Perfecto had a massive year and they celebrated the success with a party at Ku in Ibiza, with Oakenfold alongside Sasha and John Digweed. It was the busiest party of the season. The same night, Paul threw the Perfecto Fluoro free party up in the mountains alongside Mike McGuire, Juno Reactor and Man

With No Name. The party was kept on the lowdown and held in the middle of nowhere. There were no roads and no signs. You were given a map and had to look out for stones by the side of the road that had been painted in fluorescent paint by the locals and would be picked up by the car's headlights. These locals were the young *sanyasi* kids, children of the original Ibiza hippies who had grown up between Goa and Ibiza. Their parents had renounced materialistic goals and dedicated their lives to following a spiritual path. But then everyone likes a good party, don't they? Everyone was dancing in the dirt and the dust was flying. This party was free in every sense of the word and for one last time everyone came together to enjoy a special moment. The spirituality of the music took the crowd to another level – remember, they had just enjoyed Oakenfold, Sasha and Digweed followed by an adrenalin-filled drive off-road up the mountains.

> **PAUL OAKENFOLD:** Man, that was ground-breaking. We had six to seven thousand people in the Ku Club for the Perfecto party and then we slipped off into the mountains and held the Perfecto Fluoro party. It was an iconic party.

It was fitting that as the sun came up, bathing the dancers in its warming glow, the word on everyone's lips was 'Perfecto'. It was the first time there had been a big free party by a big dance brand. This night has become part of the folklore in Ibiza's history. The clubs obviously were less pleased – free parties could cost them money – but there have been free parties since then, although normally as part of the promotion or marketing of an established night. Once again Oakenfold was the first, and in a sense he was giving back to the island and the dance music community that have given him so much.

WINTER

The scene had spread, and dance music was everywhere. DJs who had been engrossed in making things happen suddenly looked up and realised that they had created something special. It is amazing to see how much the scene changed the way one did things.

TREVOR FUNG: House music was driving a whole generation, it's still driving generations now with the same force, but all over the world.

People had traditionally gone clubbing with a few mates, maybe they'd pull, maybe not, and that was that. Suddenly you'd go to a club for the first time, maybe take some drugs, and walk out of there with hundreds of new mates. With the intense media spotlight most people tried to keep things low key, hoping to carry on unnoticed. As we've seen in recent times with the likes of Jimmy Savile, Harvey Weinstein and the monumental swindle that was (nearly) the Fyre Festival ('slice of cheese in a

Styrofoam box anyone?'), sometimes hiding in plain sight is a strategy that works best.

In 1990 England were all set to record their World Cup single, something to unite the nation behind our boys. Past efforts would involve the squad lined up on *Top of the Pops*, school-photo style but with a few perms and moustaches thrown in, singing or miming some terrible offering that you felt you had to buy. With something so important you can almost picture the Royal Composer running in his buckled shoes down the corridors of the Palace, quill pen and roll of parchment in hand as he bursts into the Queen's private study and excitedly blurts out, 'Ma'am, we have it,' before she groans, looks at the latest tone-deaf 'genius' and picks up the telephone to 007. That aside, no matter how terrible it was, and it was guaranteed to spend eternity sitting comfortably alongside masterpieces like 'The Cheeky Song (Touch My Bum)', it would get airplay everywhere, maybe even be sung out and about.

'World In Motion' was different. Recorded by Madchester's New Order, it had a rap from player John Barnes and lyrical contribution (plus some odd dancing 'round the back') from the actor Keith Allen, a regular Shoomer. There had to be a B side, of course, in this case one mixed by *Boy's Own* writer and pioneering DJ Andrew Weatherall. The A side was mixed by the Haçienda's Mike Pickering and Graeme Park, clearly a decision by New Order as it would take a very brave member of the establishment to bring on board the main Haçienda DJs in the middle of the 'rave crisis'. Obviously, it hit the No. 1 spot, which meant that every television channel, radio show, football fan (formerly terrace thugs before they'd embraced MDMA) and school kid was heartily proclaiming at full volume, 'It's E for England!' The same year as we were being encouraged to sing this at the top of our voices, police in full riot gear stormed a warehouse near Leeds where a rave called Love Decade was just reaching the 5am mark. A major stand-off and battle ensued that came to an end just after 8am when the police finally made it in. Eight hundred and thirty-six ravers were carted off in what is still the biggest mass arrest in British history, which is no mean logistical feat if you think that's over three times the total population of POW camp Colditz in 1944. The police ferried them away in pre-booked coaches and if the radio had been on they would have heard the nation's sporting battle cry: 'Express yourself / You can't be wrong / When something's good / It's never gone'.

Things had to become commercialised if they were to survive, but while this was going on all over the world and was bringing people together it retained a solid underground and non-commercial, experimental side to it.

> **NICK HALKES:** Acid house provided explosive energy to the front end of the global dance boom. However, what was needed to really take the scene worldwide was the commitment and contribution of many DJs, producers and dancers in many different countries.

> **PAUL OAKENFOLD:** I think it was a feeling that evolved over time because there were no international DJs at that time. I started getting asked to go to Greece, or various places in Australia. I remember thinking, 'I'm a radio DJ.' They were saying, 'You're an international travelling DJ,' and I thought, 'I am? – I am!' That's when I realised I was seeing the world through a box of records. Then I started doing remixes and the doors

opened with U2. I did a remix for them. They asked me to do it and then the remix became bigger than the original and then they asked me to open for them on a world tour and then everything changed.

The easiest place to see this change was in Ibiza. It is still a playground for the rich and famous and still attracting the cosmically in-tune 'right on' jet-set crowd, and the massive seasonal influx of clubbers and club operators changed the vibe completely. Holidaymakers can relax and have a carefree week in the sun, but for the locals who had to make sure they were fed, sheltered, secured and cared for, the summer became a time for hard work. The small tourism business had grown to become a full-on industry with fortunes to be made. Prices sky-rocketed, making the island less inclusive than it had been when everyone had partied as one. Alfredo left Amnesia in 1989 and by 1990 they'd added a roof so you couldn't dance under the stars.

NICKY HOLLOWAY: It's a bittersweet thing because the whole thing is different now. It's all about money. It's lost a bit of substance for me, but I still have a great time. There are just so many people that just buy their fame. You stick someone's name on a billboard that no one's heard of and you can be nobody and buy your fame.

DANNY RAMPLING: Sunset is a very special time. The sunset in Ibiza has become a very big, commercial thing in Ibiza and other places around the world, and commercial operators have made business around that.

NANCY NOISE: We used to hang out at Café del Mar and there was a sunset every night there with lovely music. I've seen sunsets in all different countries, sunset is a beautiful thing wherever you are. I just played a sunset set now when I was out there. It was beautiful being able to play music for it. Café del Mar was where we'd be, playing backgammon. Play during the day, party during the night.

Dance music had become so big that even people in the middle of it didn't necessarily realise just how much a part of it they were. It was such a part of daily life that rather than keep up with the latest style it was easier just to embrace the whole scene and then pick and choose the bits you liked and how you fitted in. You could call it what you liked. Suddenly the lines were so blurred that there was no right or wrong. People were finding links and connections in the music that weren't planned or thought of by the artists themselves. Like 'Lucy In The Sky With Diamonds' in the 60s, people really do see and hear what they want to. Anything from 'Make mine a large one' to 'I'll have an E please, Bob' was a hidden reference.

JAMIE CATTO: When we [Faithless] recorded 'Insomnia' and Maxi said, 'I can't get no sleep,' no one in the band, including Maxi, had made any connection to that line and clubbing – it was a very happy accident that it fit.

JON PLEASED WIMMIN: I don't really look at what I play as just house music, I like to call it dance music as I've always enjoyed mixing genres together and not really following the rules. You can't beat mixing in something totally unexpected and seeing the reaction from the crowd. To me, a whole set of the same kind of music with no curveballs is pretty tedious.

This was an internet-free world and downloading music was inconceivable, which meant that releasing records cost money. Studio time, engineers, white-label vinyl and promotion all cost money. You had to invest time and money to get your sound heard. It was unlike today, where you can knock out a tune and stick it online and then do another one and another one. Today it is often quantity over quality. Of course, it is inevitable that some amazing material will be produced. It isn't quite like sticking a bunch of chimps in rooms with typewriters and eventually ending up with some Shakespeare. But you had to have a very good ear and then of course you had to get your material into the right hands.

TERRY FARLEY: Andy Weatherall was playing a gig and he came into *Boy's Own*'s office. He gives Steve Hall a cassette that he said two students had given him. He said, 'It's really good, you should listen to it.' He listened to it and really liked it. It was slow, the first version of Dust Brothers' 'Song to the Siren'... We were getting in trouble from the Dust Brothers who were a hip hop band from America. We just looked at it, it was called 'Dust Brothers – Chemical Beats' and we said, 'Why don't you just be called Chemical Brothers?' and that was how it worked. They signed to Virgin when they really went big. The records that were released on that album are on their greatest hits ...

My favourite Junior Boy's Own record would have to be 'Muzik Xpress'. I pushed them into going into the studio, Rocky and Diesel. I was playing at Back to Basics that weekend and I was driving there and I played their record in the car about six times. By the sixth time I thought it was the best record I had ever heard. Then we said, 'We need a band name.' One of the few things I'm good at is making up band names. They were X-Press 2 (I didn't realise there was three of them at the time). So we thought we'd keep Express in the title, so we called the track 'Muzik Xpress' … We were having such a wonderful time, we were riding on the back of a stallion.

That was before all these kind of business opportunities that DJs have now. We were in the studio, we hired in a grand piano, not like a keyboard, we hired in a fucking grand piano! We were selling like 1,500 records and Virgin were spending £10,000 in the studio. Basically, we had signed quite a good deal with them and they kind of said, 'We are gonna leave it,' but we still had the deal and that was paying for our office. We had a song called 'Beating the Bones'. Steve Hall said to me: 'Why don't we start our own record label,' as our label didn't want to release it. I said, 'Yeah, OK.' We could release club tracks with no pressure. We thought, 'What are we going to call that label?' At that time, I had some Junior Gaultier clothes, Jean-Paul Gaultier's cheap range. I said, 'Why don't we call it Junior Boy's Own.' Junior Boy's Own really kicked off, that was their loss.

With so much great music being released and so many people wanting to hear it the logical next step was a legal place big enough to accommodate them. Ministry of Sound was that place, pumping dance music's hypnotic beat to a global audience who could enjoy the delights of a full on assault on the senses in a relatively safe and organised environment.

PAUL OAKENFOLD: Ministry of Sound changed the landscape of clubbing, the sound system was incredible, it was based on the iconic club Paradise Garage and you went just to dance. I was the first resident at MOS for several months. The sound system at Spectrum wasn't as good.

NANCY NOISE: We really just embraced the music. We loved it. Obviously when Ministry opened, it wasn't just acid house stuff.

BRANDON BLOCK: It transcended all generations, it has changed the face of music forever. I think there are a number of factors: technology, people's need for escape, and the community it created of like-minded people.

DANNY RAMPLING: I think we've transcended that. The popularity of it, you know, music, house and techno, it's popular music but it's not pop.

NICKY HOLLOWAY: Oakey was very important. Paul did the America thing first. He was the first before anyone else to try to crack America and he made it his home. Paul Oakenfold was the biggest DJ, after the ZOO TV tour with U2. It was brilliant for him. He learned so much from that. That's where he learned how to do rock 'n' roll stuff. He was the first to learn to be a star. It was great for him, that really put him on the map.

The London scene was a full-on acid house world. The generic word, house, had taken over as the umbrella title for the global scene but the spirit at the very core of the original idea, to break down barriers, was very much the way that everything was running. There were fantastic legal raves taking place in fields and in warehouses all across the UK throughout 1991 held by organisations like Fantazia and Raindance. By the mid-90s the core house and techno crowds had moved into the emerging superclubs and the rave scene moved forward in a distinct direction under the umbrella of rave with two main sounds, the oxymoron that is 'happy hardcore' and 'jungle'. Cries of 'Hardcore, you know the score', 'Wickid-ah, Wickid' and 'Booyaka, Booyaka' were everywhere. More than its recent predecessor, this new rave scene was perfect for pirate radio and made stars of both the DJs and the all-important MCs. The music was home-grown and there was plenty of it, you could cut a dubplate for £30 and get it to your favourite DJ. There were still 'traditional' rave promoters like Helter Skelter and Dreamscape, who still enjoyed full-capacity events, but as festivals became better organised, more comfortable and attracted the biggest acts including the new drum 'n' bass stars, these events soon became marginalised.

TINTIN CHAMBERS: No one can claim they started this culture and no one can really claim they were more important than the next person that carried the baton. The scene evolved, the music evolved and here we are looking back on the longest-lasting youth culture movement ever.

The single most important moment for live dance music happened in 1994. Dance music was and always will be DJ-led and the mainstream festival and concert promoters didn't see that the skill needed to create electronically was on the same level, both artistically and from an entertainment point of view, as a band with drums and guitars. Sure, they could rock a crowd from behind the safety of a DJ booth, but surely they couldn't keep it up on a stage with an audience who were serious music lovers. All those preconceptions changed in '94 when Orbital played Glastonbury. The first pure electronic dance act, born from the rave scene and the orbital motorway raves, delivered the goods with a spectacular show and performance of original music that the crowd wanted to hear and appreciated. By the following year when Orbital headlined Tribal Gathering, Glastonbury introduced a dance stage. Orbital were no longer seen as playing rave music – just music – and this performance went on and opened the international festival circuit to an endless diverse array of incredible live acts such as Aphex Twin, Plastikman, Moloko, Leftfield, Faithless, Moby, Juno Reactor, Fluke, Total Eclipse and Roni Size. Artists like Marshmello, Stormzy and DJ Snake keep on spreading the word and it is the crossover appeal of dance music into a mainstream world that allows a DJ like Martin Garrix to pull in over one billion streams of his music (on Spotify in 2017).

The club scene had totally opened up, driven by the clubbers themselves rather than having to enjoy what the owners wanted them to. The unofficial colour bar in clubs was gone. Straight danced with gay, black with white, old with young and no one batted an eye. Some of the greatest parties ever were happening in the biggest cities in the world and venues were more than happy, in fact in some cases honoured, to hand over their prime Saturday to an underground promoter for a weekly dance music club night. You could go to any town or city in the world and find something to do and people who'd want to do it with you. Acid house let people feel that there was more out there for them: careers in film, music, fashion, design and a host of creative industries seemed like a possibility. The next stage was to actually do it, and clubs were a perfect place to make contacts and get inspiration. Writers like Irvine Welsh, artists like Damien Hirst, fashionistas like Kate Moss, TV presenters like Davina McCall and actors like Idris Elba had the international club scene as part of their lives. One minute Davina's on the door and rocking the dancefloor at London's Iceni, next thing she's a presenter, starting her career with a show on MTV. The new way of clubbing, where everyone was welcome and anything could happen, resulted in more and more innovative parties where promoters worked harder to stand out, and the club nights were a way to channel the promoters and DJs creative energy through the clubbers.

One of the most talked-about nights was Kinky Gerlinky, a place where anything goes and where you could never be dressed up (or undressed) enough. The crowd was often compared to some of the wildest parties, the stuff of legends like Freddie Mercury's hedonistic birthday party at Pike's in Ibiza.

DAVE SWINDELLS: Kinky Gerlinky was ground-breaking because they were going back to the future.

The people who ran it had had enough. They were into fashion and were sick of people looking like they were just going down to the chip shop. They wanted people to dress up again. They started their club at Legends behind Savile Row and rapidly moved it on to a bigger venue before it found its home in Leicester Square. At the time everyone was dressing down – it was rave time. It was every sexual persuasion; every gender was there and people really travelled for it. It was a Monday night and they'd get 1,500 to 2,000 people who would come from as far away as Italy and South Africa, just for the night.

Not since the early 80s in Ibiza had there been such a mix of people, and if you were lucky enough and were considered to have made an effort you might get in as long as you got past the door whores, the 'greeters', who would put you down with comments like, 'This is Kinky Gerlinky not Kinky GerStinky,' or hold up a mirror to you and say, 'Would you want to party with that?' You could never get away with that today in this era of hashtags and social media but then it was all part of the experience. Like being chased around through the fields and not finding the rave, just getting to the front of the queue at Kinky Gerlinky only to be turned away was still an experience to tell your friends about. Once you were in you were transported to a world where anything goes. Remember, there were no camera phones and cameras were definitely not allowed, so people could really let go. The regulars were what made the night spectacular. They were part of the show, and they knew it. Standing head and shoulders above the rest (as only tall men in high heels can do) were The Pleased Wimmin.

DANNY RAMPLING: They were entertainers!

JON PLEASED WIMMIN: It's hard to imagine a club like Kinky Gerlinky now, it was so free and decadent, but the sheer size of it was mind-boggling really. I have fond memories of performing with the other Pleased Wimmin for KG on a cruise to Amsterdam, and also as support for people like Grace Jones and Dee-lite, along with the other 'Kinky Girls'.

MARK MOORE: I remember every time I walked in, especially when it moved to The Empire, walking down those stairs, The Pleased Wimmin would be lined up at the bottom, and they would screech, 'Hey, music lover,' around me. They would follow me around the dancefloor screeching. I'm still friends with those guys. I love Jon.

NANCY NOISE: Kinky Gerlinky – I've had so many good nights there. I loved it. It was fantastic.

DANNY RAMPLING: The Pleased Wimmin used to come to Pure Sexy and it transpired that Jon was an aspiring DJ. I thought, 'Why not come and play for the night?' He did, and he was great. And when we went away for the summer to Ibiza, between him and Smokin Jo they played every week for that summer. That platform at Pure Sexy really put the spotlight on him.

JON PLEASED WIMMIN: Danny and Jenni saw us dancing and performing at Kinky Gerlinky and asked us if we'd like to come and dance for them at their club nights Glam and their one-off big parties they were throwing with the likes of Tony Humphries and Larry Tee as guests.

MARK MOORE: That's why the gay clubs were so great, because you'd get interesting straight people who would come and have fun with no attitude. They weren't groping women and being sexist, they would come there because they knew they wouldn't be hassled ... and they'd probably meet a nice girl.

JON PLEASED WIMMIN: Every week at Glam I would talk to Danny about the music and harangue him to play certain things, he could tell I was a bit of a music obsessive and he asked me if I'd like to do the warm-up over the summer while he was in Ibiza. Of course, I jumped at the chance, even though I didn't have any decks at home or anything (it took about a year after that before my boyfriend kindly bought me some as a present). So I really learned how to use decks on the job. The great thing about Glam was that it was like a big family, so really I felt like I was just playing records at home.

Every club, from the most underground to the most mainstream, had dance music as its musical starting point. The rave culture and acid house style faded and a more dressed-up feel crept back onto the dancefloors. It was still great music but the acid house generation were that little bit older and the next lot saw the music as the clubland soundtrack rather than something new. Going out was everything, something special that was treasured, so of course you'd make a bit more effort no matter where you were and where you were going. Holiday time was no exception. Whereas the laid-back Ibiza spirit resulted in the original dressed-down 'I don't care' look of the Second Summer of Love, the island now hosted thousands and thousands of clubbers who were there to dance. The expectations were high, after all this was the fabled Balearic playground of the rich and famous, a place where anything was possible. The clubs that emerged in the early 90s didn't disappoint and every night had lots of great places to go and hear amazing DJs. One party was so special that it turned the Ibiza party experience on its head and its impact influenced the global club scene. No trip to Ibiza was complete without trying to get into Manumission.

> **MIKE & CLAIRE MANUMISSION:** We never counted ourselves as a superclub. Manumission was our personal party – albeit for 10,000 guests. Superclubs bought size, and commercialism. Hordes of English. Manumission was a playground without boundaries, bringing together scenes who would not normally share the same dancefloor.

The Manumission family ran this night, which has been described as a 'cabaret meets freak show meets burlesque meets house music' party. There was a big team making this happen, from designers and DJs to choreographers and performers, and at the centre of all this was Mike and Claire McKay – better known as Mike & Claire Manumission.

MIKE & CLAIRE MANUMISSION: Manumission was theatre for the masses. It transcended nationality, race, gender and sexuality. It opened all kinds of boundaries, including those that sometimes kept DJs confined to playing one type of music. We gave them a platform on which they could find a different kind of freedom.

The performances were something that have never been seen before, even surpassing New York's original Studio 54 craziness. The celeb count was high and included Roman Polanski, Valentino Rossi, Kate Moss, the Gallagher brothers, Tom Cruise and Nicole Kidman (in disguise), Brad Pitt, Howard Marks and Naomi Campbell.

ALFREDO: They created great freedom like you used to get in Amnesia. At the beginning of Manumission everyone had the same right to be anywhere in the club. They mixed all the people together again.

MIKE & CLAIRE MANUMISSION: When we first arrived ... we were shocked to see that Alfredo was playing in a back room of Pacha. The first thing we did was put him on as our main-room resident under the name 'The Legendary Alfredo'. Alfie played our sunrise in the main room of Manumission for ten years, and influenced many DJs with his Carry On sets. Our after-hours in Space! And then there was 'The Motel' ... We were going into our fifth summer of Manumission. It was the biggest weekly party in the world. We were all about constant reinvention. And we knew we needed a place for ourselves, the Manumission/Carry On DJs, the team of NYC strippers we had recently gathered and our island friends to hang out. A rickety ex-brothel on the wrong side of town was the only piece of Americana on the island and we wanted it. When the deal fell through with some German pimps who wanted to buy it we convinced the owner to give us the keys! Opening night, Carl Cox was in room fourteen – *sans* hot water! Everyone from Fatboy Slim, Pete Tong, Norman Jay, Danny Rampling, Roman Polanski, Jade Jagger, Kate Moss, Claudia Schiffer, Jamie Jones, the Happy Mondays, Primal Scream ... the list goes on. Johnny the Dwarf was on the door. The press were banned and you couldn't book a room, they were strictly for ourselves, our DJs and the strippers. Our back room, Manu, hosts in '98 were Howard Marks, Irvine Welsh, Fatboy Slim, Wall of Sound, Kris Needs, and Wheels of Steel from NYC, who also stayed with us at The Motel. Andrew Innes of Primal Scream said it was the most decadent place he had ever been to in his life, in the true sense. It was the last 'free' place on the island.

Manumission prided itself on the music, which was the soundscape to the show they created, and they focused on DJs who added more than music but still lived and breathed it, who understood what they were trying to create and who could feel what they felt ...

FATBOY SLIM: Young, sexy and free.

MIKE & CLAIRE MANUMISSION: We were the first to bring Norman [Cook] to Ibiza. Back then he was part of the UK big-beat scene. We brought them all out to play Manumission and Carry On and they would begin to incorporate the house music being played back then and the eclectic music being played by DJs like Alfredo into their own sets – and so created a new style of music. We always had a huge amount of fun with our DJs. If they didn't do the 36-hour experience with us they were seldom invited back. We felt like warriors on a mission and everyone was expected to play their part. Fatboy came on the ride many a time.

DANNY RAMPLING: I'll continue to go to Ibiza for the rest of my life. I love the island. Everything changes and you have to accept changes and we have all been part of creating that change in Ibiza. I've been very fortunate to experience the Ibiza back then, being there back in the day and through that period, when it was a lot more basic. Rustic. The Ibiza of today, the service is on a par with London.

Globally, dance music exploded. Clubbing had become the number-one going-out activity for young people. There was so much going on and so many places to go that you didn't worry about getting in and with underground club nights having listings platforms in publications like *Time Out,* you knew what you were in for before you got there. Flyers had become a recognised art form and with the promoters fed up with being hounded and the authorities fed up of doing the hounding a truce emerged that encouraged the emergence of a nightlife industry. This was helped by local authorities realising that granting licenses to premises made the illegal party and rave scene less of a draw, especially when they made sure that clubs had proper security and medics in place. Social barriers were still down, so you could easily talk to someone without them thinking you were chatting them up, even if you were. If you wanted to dance there were plenty of places for you to do it in. You could go to a basement under a pub for nights like The Good, The Bad And The Ugly, see the 'beautiful people' at nights like Quiet Storm and Pushka, get down at The Goodfoot or Leave My Wife Alone at the WAG, watch a master at work at Carl Cox's Ultimate Bass, or dance right through at nights like Trade and Love Ranch. You could have amazing experiences and create lifelong memories and deep and lifelong friendships anywhere in the world and know that somewhere, someone was having a similar special moment at the same time. Each moment shapes your story.

TERRY FARLEY: My greatest ever gig was playing at Yellow in Japan. I got asked to play there because someone pulled out and the agency said it was in two weeks' time. I said, 'That's my birthday weekend – where?' and they said, 'Yellow,' which is the last club that Larry Levan ever played in. We are talking the stuff of legends and I thought, 'I'm going.' I did around five hours in there and it wasn't full, it was half full, but every person in that room was really connected with the music. There was a little picture behind me of Larry Levan and it had a Frankie Knuckles one and they had both signed it. I really felt the weight of standing on the shoulders of giants, as they say, and I left that club at like six or seven in the morning and we drove to my hotel across the Rainbow Bridge and the sun was already way up. I remember sitting in the car thinking 'Wow!' I was really wide awake because of the time difference, it was this mad adrenalin buzz. It was incredible. I drove across that bridge and I was so happy and I remember thinking if every gig could be like this I would be the happiest man in the world.

MIKE & CLAIRE MANUMISSION: Howard Marks became a dear friend ... Flying British Airways with Howard, the giant puff of marijuana smoke as the cigarette light pinged on. The air hostess who served us all the champagne on the plane had been listening to the audio version of *Mr Nice* on the way to work and was (as with most air stewards back then) a regular at Manumission. She took the joint off Howard and had a puff herself behind the curtain! ... Howard reading a passage from the bible at our wedding. His voice booming like Richard Burton and a thousand and one beautiful nights spent together in Ibiza, Formentera, London.

TREVOR FUNG: I had done Love at the WAG in '88 and the next day I was flying over to Spain with CJ Macintosh and Derek B, it was the Summer of Love. We were doing a tour and went straight from the club to the airport. The flight was delayed and delayed. We were playing at this big club in Valencia called Big Ben. We got on the flight at about four in the afternoon after being there all day. We're really happy. An hour into the flight the captain says, 'Because of the bad weather, I'm sorry, the plane has to be rerouted to Madrid,' so we missed the night and all the DJs were with us, so we stayed in Madrid and went to Pacha. What else can you do? There were 10,000 people waiting for us in Valencia and we had no way of getting there. They had to refund the money and put on their local DJs. We just went out for the night … and I lost my bloody records on that flight as well, so that didn't really help [laughs] but it's a great story.

FATBOY SLIM: Watching a hugely popular and respected (unnamed) DJ so wrapped up in the tune he was playing and the crowd reaction that he went into the crowd to dance and enjoy it with his people. Sadly, he was so lost in the moment that by the time the tune ended he had forgotten that he was the DJ and was one of the people booing when the record ended and there was silence on the dancefloor.

BRANDON BLOCK: One day in the early 90s I was DJing in Space and was so immersed in the experience I started throwing my records out into the crowd, sharing the love. They asked for one more at the end, I didn't have any left – someone had to bring one back for me to play.

MR C: While Superfreq is obviously a continuing bastion of acid house, the closing of The End remains for me the greatest dance music show on earth. Over thirty hours of dancing by people who were dancing like it was their last ever dance, leaving the club in tears of sadness, tears of joy and a closeness, a sense of family that you rarely get to feel at parties in London today. Of course, Superfreq still has that, along with a few other events, but nothing will top those thirty hours ten years ago that saw the closing of The End for good.

PETE HELLER: There are a few greatest moments but I'll settle with the night I played at the Sunset Soiree party that Claudia Cusetta, Kim Benjamin and Giant Steps used to run at the Raleigh Hotel during the 1999 Miami Winter Music Conference. It was towards the end of the night and my last record was 'Big Love'. Right away it started to pour with rain, but people just stayed and danced right through the downpour before the sound technician insisted the music had to stop.

MOBY: Probably the time I was performing at a rave in Tokyo and I was attacked and wrestled to the ground by an ex-pat in a giant tree costume. The audience loved it.

DAVE SWINDELLS: Turning up at *Boy's Own* was literally kind of, 'Is this the real life? Is this just fantasy?' It was amazing. That was fantastic – it was what we had dreamed of – and the music was great even though I never did get into the dance tent. That was lovely, that was the most wonderful location. Even now, years later, that was the most fantastic rave location I've ever been to for sure.

TINTIN CHAMBERS: I'll leave the social commentary to others, but I'll give you an example of how it was for me in those early days: I remember walking down the road after a party one morning early in 1988. I was wearing my Fluoro Mambos, with my long hair and tinted glasses. Basically looking like a freak, but a happy one. I spotted someone on the other side of the road, unmistakably dressed in dungarees, smiling … He spotted me … I waved … he waved, and two people that had never met, spent the next week together, partying, playing records, sleeping occasionally. It was this shared experience, as somewhat of an outlier, that for me was irresistible.

The rave scene had shown that people liked to dance in big groups and that the DJs, who by now were stars that you knew by name and by sight, could pull big crowds. It made sense to cater for them with something big, fun, loud and licensed. Clubs that could blend in, Clark Kent style, with the local community and then, come night-time, whip off those glasses, tear open their shirts and emerge ready to fly into the sky. 'Faster than a speeding bullet! More powerful than a locomotive! Able to leap tall buildings at a single bound! Yes, it's Superclub – a strange visitor from another planet who came to Earth with sound systems and lighting far beyond those of normal clubs.' The superclubs changed the dynamic but still kept dance music's world domination alive. The Fridge in London, Haçienda in Manchester, Space in Ibiza and the Sound Factory and Tunnel in New York already had the superclub mentality. As the 90s progressed there were more and more amazing places to party. Clubs like Twilo in New York, Zouk in Singapore, the Bunker in Berlin, Cream at Nation in Liverpool, Gatecrasher One in Sheffield, Layo and Mr C's The End in London and Privilege in Ibiza catered for big audiences who were there to dance.

Superclubs turned DJs into super-DJs playing every night of the week to sell-out crowds all over the world. DJs like Martin Garrix, David Guetta, Hardwell, Steve Aoki, Carl Cox, Skrillex, deadmau5 and Armin Van Buuren keep the clubs and festivals full while the likes of Marshmello, Mark Ronson and Calvin Harris top the charts. Collaborations such as those between Nile Rodgers and Daft Punk fuse styles, unite the generations and prove that disco never died. But actually it did, albeit only briefly, and it took the germination of the seeds planted by the pioneers of acid house to breathe the life back into it.

ALFREDO: Some they are friends but between the ones who are in similar positions there is a lot of competition, not directly, but through managers and agents: 'I don't want to play before this one, I don't want to play after this one.'

DAVE SWINDELLS: House has remained a dominant force but has mutated to encompass rave, trance, hardcore, new beats, electro sounds and now EDM. Are they house or are they something else? They are dance music. At the same time, because of house and because of rave and because it kick-started opportunities for DJs and producers, especially in the UK, to marry the energy of dance music with all the other influences from reggae to breakbeats and produce a whole slew of new dance music – jungle, drum 'n' bass, UK garage, grime, dubstep – there is a direct lineage you can follow.

MR C: House music and the Summer of Love were vital to what we have going on today. The attitude of acceptance of all mankind increased the dating ritual of dance in an innocent way that made people want to express love. Hatred flew out of the window and this same attitude can be felt on dancefloors all over the world today. Back then in 1988 it was first hundreds of ravers, then thousands. Now millions of people dance every week in much the same way.

PAUL OAKENFOLD: The bigger the crowds I play to, the more energised I become and the more creative I get in the studio. The bigger you get, the better you need to get. The show I did on Saturday was to 55,000 people.

The acid house pioneers inherited an amazing heritage based on great music, technology and human emotions. The sound that inspired them was supposed to be the music of the future. What they did with it by wholeheartedly embracing a way to deliver this music was create a shift in the cultural norm to such an extent that no matter how much the music and culture evolves, it quickly settles back in. Everything is the new norm and moving forward doesn't mean leaving the past behind. Mainstream and underground at the same time, it is the contradictory nature of the culture that allows there to be no right or wrong and for everything and everyone to be accepted for what it is and what they are. With dance music there is no music of the future. Dance music is the sound of now.

MARK MOORE: Dance music is still considered underground. Mainly because the kids got lazy. They are happy to recreate something that was done thirty years ago. Which is fine, I'm not averse to that.

ALFREDO: It's the first kind of music that a new technology keeps it underground. Yeah, it's still evolving, the lyrics talk about love but in a more profound way.

MR C: As we see today, we continue to have new hardware, new software and better sound systems so the evolution and continuation of electronic dance music can only continue unabated indefinitely.

PAUL OAKENFOLD: Everything that happens in the scene starts through the DJs. Within the umbrella of the scene you have different DJs playing different music. There will always be an underground scene under the umbrella of electronic music because there's always new technology.

DANNY RAMPLING: The scene stays underground because generally it's faceless. It doesn't have stars at the forefront of it in the same way as hip hop and R'n'B does. There aren't those kind of stars on it. There's often a DJ playing the music and there's a singer, rapper or a guest artist on it. That's it.

DAVE SWINDELLS: I'm excited by what the future might bring and where the new music might come from. You could travel round the world on different dancefloors – whatever you want you can find it – and you don't have to look that hard.

MOBY: One of the most compelling aspects to the acid house Summer of Love is still what drives people's enthusiasm for club and rave culture; surprise. That moment when you hear a perfect track on a perfect night with perfect people and you're truly surprised at this microcosm of perfection in a dysfunctional world.

TERRY FARLEY: I think it's people's passion that kept it alive. The scene is still alive now. There's eighteen-year-olds and sixty-year-olds dancing to house music and every generation in between. I think it's just people's passion. The older generations – it was the best years of their lives. If you went to Atlanta, you'd find sixty-year-old black guys going to hip hop revivals. Dance music isn't a fad, it's a trend, it's a culture. Once you go from fashion into culture then they last forever. Jazz is culture, reggae is culture. We are in a culture now. People can still be into things. Now, you can be a sixty-year-old guy who has no interest in going to a nightclub but will still listen to Pete Tong and will still download the latest Carl Cox mix. We have gone from a fashion to a culture with foundations. Dance music is as serious as rock music.

By the time America came on board dance music was already dominant. Although created in the USA, it would take a DJ who had been inspired by his experience at Shoom to really propel dance music into the American mainstream and reintroduce them to their own home-grown sound. David Guetta's remix for the Black Eyed Peas dominated the charts and this new, more commercial style really established electronic dance music. The American market took it to the next level with electronic music festivals that attracted a quarter of a million people and created a whole new market for the superstar DJs, live acts and producers, who can command in excess of a million dollars for a festival appearance. The rave scene had been growing steadily but the stigma of the word rave held it back. After a couple of rebrands, techno and then electronica, which stuck around for a while, it re-emerged as EDM.

Outside of the dance community itself, no one seemed bothered by the term EDM and with some Vegas money behind it the scene took off and took over. Money talks. Suddenly a DJ was a tangible, credible artist. Everyone wanted to associate with one. DJs appeared at fashion-week catwalk front rows alongside stars like Elton John (famous popstar), David Beckham (famous sports star) and Paris Hilton (famous for something or other). Paul Oakenfold had shown that a major rock band like U2 could tour the world's biggest stadiums with only a DJ as a support. On 10 May 2003, DJ Tiësto went one stage further when he played an epic eight-hour solo DJ set in a Dutch football stadium to tens of thousands of people who had all come just to see him. This was the first stand-alone DJ concert in a stadium, showing that a DJ could be as big a ticket-selling draw as any band. With the electronic music culture the audience want and expect to hear new music alongside music they are familiar with played in a creative way, as opposed to the stadium rock crowd who like familiarity and let out an almost audible groan when the rock star in question tells the audience that he's going to play a few songs from the new album. Concert promoters could do the maths. One guy and a few boxes of records playing for eight hours versus a full band with all the technical and backstage requirements that went with them playing for two hours. Step aside, big brother, it's our time now!

GRAEME PARK: It's big business now. You can't watch any TV channel without a commercial that has a house music soundtrack. With the USA finally coming on board with the whole EDM thing in Vegas, it's big business. That's great and I'm proud to have been one of those pioneers at the beginning.

CARL COX: I think it's really important to understand the past in order to appreciate the future. When you think about the last twenty-five years, none of this would have happened if it wasn't for what we did in the past. They probably weren't even old enough to understand. It's not their fault, but still it's something important to be able to move forward by looking back. Anything that's happened has been as a result of the past. The music we were playing twenty-five years ago in some small pub, the music was unbelievable. So, it's important to look back where the music comes from. We can only show them a bit of what it was like for us musically. We are in a brilliant position because at the end of the day, we are the creators of what is happening right now. Today you could be a promoter and then you think, 'Who should I book?' that's all you have to do. Whereas we had to fight to begin with, then get our voice across to the people to let them know the party is going on and if it's going on at a certain point, we had a window to get people there in order to enjoy themselves. Now you have all this amazing technology that goes worldwide with apps for everything. There is no mystery. It's changed a lot but it all stems back to why we started to begin with that got us to where we are now.

TREVOR FUNG: To think that to this day it's still going! It's created a massive industry. I'm really proud. I'm really happy.

MIKE & CLAIRE MANUMISSION: Music has always been an integral part of our lives ... Dance music took us out of our homes at a young age and brought many of us together. Including the two of us. What better place to get to know people than a dancefloor!

DAVE SWINDELLS: I often think that if you go out and know what the club is going to deliver, what's the point of going out? You go out to have an adventure. We were lucky enough to have lots of adventures. You want clubs to change your life.

I think if you went up to anyone in 1988 and said that they would create something by playing records that would take them from Streatham High Street to Las Vegas they would just laugh at you. Paul Oakenfold, however, would be more likely to say something along the lines of, 'Of course it will, and I'll take you with me. Where do I sign?'

PAUL OAKENFOLD: I think we have respect for one another. We remember when there was no money. We came through it. I was a qualified chef and there was no money in it, it was the love and the passion of the music that we would do it for.

ANOTHER MOMENT IN TIME

Thag had never been happier. Every night his beats resonated around the stones and were enjoyed by more and more tribes. Sometimes he'd spend hours hitting his favourite hand-held stone against one of the large rocks, sometimes he'd experiment with new beats, sometimes he'd just move and sway as others created their own distinct sounds to the ever-growing crowds. Each new group of visitors added their own distinct flavour and took something new away with them. The elders had decided that people could dance whenever and however they wanted to and with whoever they liked. Across the world, known and unknown, civilisations were springing up, and cultural unity centred around music and dance were a shared core value. Like future musical styles and cultural movements, the shared love and freedom that music evokes would spring up simultaneously. Thag's wish had come true – the party really was never-

ending. He knew that this place would always have music and wondered if he would be remembered by the music-makers in the future after he was long gone. He picked up his striking rock, stepped towards the stones and let his first beats ring out …

… The first beat rings out and the onlookers all stand in front of the stones. Our music-maker is looking towards the setting sun as he lets the beats work their magic on the assembled group …

He adjusts his headphones …

It is 2018 and Paul Oakenfold, one of the original Ibiza Four, has stepped up to the sacred stones at Stonehenge. In front of him is a custom-built DJ booth connected by cables over 100ft long to the generators that powered the system that was there for one night only.

This really happened and it's worth telling the story here to show just how far dance music has come and that there really are now no limits. Standing at Stonehenge is a far cry from a fitness centre in Southwark, a pile of haystacks in East Grinstead, a shebeen in Earl's Court or the unlicensed after-hours of The Project in Streatham.

Stonehenge is a wonder of the world in every sense and has been a culturally significant site for over 5,000 years. It continues to excite and fascinate, with every individual visitor having a personal connection to this marvel of engineering and spirituality. Stonehenge was produced by a culture that left no written records and this has helped create the many myths that surround its construction and purpose. The standing stones weigh about 25 tons and are aligned to the sunset of the winter solstice and the opposing sunrise of the summer solstice; they have mystified us since their original reason for being was forgotten. Standing proud on the barren Wiltshire landscape, Stonehenge continues to draw people from all over the world, keen to experience its magnificence.

The philosopher Edmund Burke wrote 'Stonehenge, neither for disposition nor ornament, has anything admirable; but those huge rude masses of stone, set end on end, and piled high on each other, turn the mind on the immense force necessary for such a work.'

Having changed 'ownership' several times over the last few thousand years, today Stonehenge is owned by the Crown, managed by English Heritage and is a UNESCO World Heritage Site. Over the centuries the stones have drawn people from far and wide – these thought-provoking pieces stand as a testament to our ancestors and to the spirit of human endeavour and as such have been a magnet to creative people across the centuries. Countless people from rock 'n' roll legends and underground music-makers to poets and film-makers have tried to perform at Stonehenge. Most failed, some came close and some even managed to do their thing – one effort even ended in a full-on 'battle' – but none were able to accomplish an officially sanctioned and approved performance. Until now ...

Dance music has come a long way, baby. It has grown from something found in underground clubs in Detroit and Chicago and out-of-the-way spaces in London and Manchester via the pleasure palaces of Ibiza to a dominant musical and cultural force, influencing every aspect of daily life. It earned its respectability the hard way, and the seeds sown during the Second Summer of Love when acid house exploded onto the scene needed help to flower and flourish.

In early 2018, Paul Oakenfold and I started talking about supporting English Heritage to raise funds for the monuments that tell the story of England while showcasing how welcoming we still want to be to our global cousins in the aftermath of the frustratingly misguided Brexit decision. This led to the planting of an idea for a full set at Stonehenge. Using the ancient stones as a canvas, Universe would produce something exquisite while Paul wrapped the experience in a blanket of sound. Of course, this would normally be one of those ideas that would remain just that. Dance music, particularly in the UK, is still closely linked with the unlicensed rave and warehouse parties that helped shape the scene. It seemed impossible that this could get off the ground and that, if this could happen, that an electronic music DJ would be given the nod from the authorities. After all, dance music and the authorities had rarely seen eye to eye. However, a chance meeting and conversation with the powers that be seemed to go well and with nothing to lose an official approach was made.

It became apparent early on that English Heritage understood the concept, where dance music had come from and, more importantly, how culturally significant it had become. It seemed that everyone was on the same page and that this could possibly work. Suddenly 'Universe proudly presents Paul Oakenfold Live At Stonehenge' looked like a reality.

The 'Where?', the 'Who?' and the 'Why?' were in place – all that had to be figured out was the 'How?' It's worth looking at this in a bit of detail. Every event has its challenges and when you see what this involved you have to bow in utmost respect to the original warehouse and rave promoters who pulled off the impossible, and in a time before mobile phones and access to our online information superhighway making everything available at the push of a button. Then it was all about word of mouth and communication. Sneakernet not internet.

What sounds straightforward – turn up to Stonehenge, play music and go home – was never going to be that simple. It became very tricky when they were made aware of just how important the ground on the whole site is archaeologically, and how many restrictions and guidelines there are surrounding what can and can't be done at Stonehenge, which even has its own Act of Parliament protecting it. It has no power, no easy production access, all elements need to be approved by the curatorial team, it is adjacent to the Royal Artillery's firing range, enjoys over a million visitors per year and is open to the public until the early evening, with no chance of having any kit visible that could hamper the visitor experience. It's also within sight of a major road, near to the town of Salisbury (which was going through major security issues after the Russian nerve-agent crisis), a sacred site for the Druids among many others, and the kind of place that had the potential to make global headlines for all the wrong reasons.

They were given special permission to go to the site the night before for a low-key run-through. The plan was to be at Stonehenge the night before and set up after the last visitor left, put everything in position, map the stones for the visuals, do a sound-check and dismantle it all by 2am. They could then get everything in place quickly on 'Show Day' as the plan had evolved for Paul to choreograph his music to the sunset, so timing became key. Paul sat in Ibiza over that summer and watched over thirty sunsets with a bag full of music on his shoulder trying to work out how to capture the moment – you can only be the first once and there'd be no chance to go back and do it again. Among his set would be music from Vangelis, Ennio Morricone, U2, Hans Zimmer, Andrea Bocelli, Empire of the Sun and William Orbit. Rumours had started to spread around the industry that Stonehenge might be 'on' and suddenly everyone wanted to know if something was happening and when. Everything started to come together. Paul was happy with the music, the long-term weather forecast looked good, guests were confirming, all permissions were granted and when Carl Cox confirmed that he would love to fly over and do a full back-to-back set with Paul in front of Stonehenge straight after Paul's historic world-first performance, it seemed they were home and dry.

Then they were told that some VIPs needed access to the stones the night they planned to rehearse and that they would only be able to start setting up at 7pm, which would give them less than thirty minutes before sunset to run over a hundred feet of cables and get the generators and lighting in so they could practise and see that the show would work. These VIPs couldn't know what was going to happen there as one of the conditions was that the date had to be kept very secret. If the date was released then the plug would have to be pulled. There was the real possibility that if the date leaked out tens of thousands of people could descend on Stonehenge. They also learned that on the day itself, Thursday, 13 September, they'd only have forty-five minutes instead of the agreed hour to set up and start playing before the sun actually set, and they knew that they needed an extra fifteen minutes to make it work. In the end the run-through went well but not well enough. The DJ booth was too heavy to carry (nothing can be dragged across the ground) so it was built, but didn't get close to the stones or tested with the kit. They missed the sunset and working at full speed without breaks it took over three hours to do what they would need to do in about thirty minutes twenty-four hours later.

Universe is known for legendary events with ground-breaking

production, special locations and entertainment overload, but delivering this looked like it could be one step too far. It was 2am when they realised what was needed if this was going to work – either the sun would need to set an hour later or they'd need more hands. The production manager, Oli, is a magician but opted for the second choice and, despite the hour, managed to confirm an extra team of local crew who would be able to be with them by late afternoon the next day. Again, this crew couldn't know where they were going or what they were going to be doing. There was an unusual calm among the seasoned veterans – of course, as youngsters they'd probably been part of a convey trying to make it as close to Stonehenge as possible. Today no one was looking over their shoulder or having to work under cover of darkness. There wasn't a Ken Tappenden to worry about.

The excitement was in the air as they made their way to Stonehenge the next day. Paul spent most of the day preparing and suddenly it was all happening. The crew worked like they were possessed, the curators were happy, the media had kept quiet, the sun was shining and there were no clouds, the generators worked, Carl Cox was there, the guests were on target and the DJ booth had been carried right up to the stones. It was on!

The guests arrived and walked towards Stonehenge listening to the soundscape that Paul had created. Fittingly, he started his set with an acapella of U2's 'Love Is All We Have Left'. Among the audience were pioneers of the dance music scene including Nancy Noise, Carl Cox, Tintin Chambers, Mark Moore, Terry Farley and Danny Rampling. As they approached you could see the look of wonder on their faces. They were expecting to be a short distance away from the stones, but the best had been kept until last. They'd been kindly granted very special permission so that they could experience the sunset from within the stone circle itself – an incredibly rare privilege reserved for the great and the good. I don't think you'd have heard the words 'mind-blowing' so many times or seen smiles so big. Later on, when Carl joined Paul for their surprise B2B set, those smiles turned to a mixture of full-on grins mixed with jaw-dropping disbelief. Job done!

> **PAUL OAKENFOLD:** We pulled off an amazing show. It's never been done before and it may never be done again. I am so lucky to be able to share my music from such an iconic site. The energy here is like nowhere else on Earth. Everyone that came will remember this for the rest of their lives.

> **SEAN GRIFFITHS (*MIXMAG*):** No one knows why they put these stones here. This is probably why ... It's probably written somewhere!

> **ANDY SERKIS (ACTOR/DIRECTOR):** It feels extra-ordinary to be here and then to hear Paul and Carl kick off with their music. It's surreal, it's humbling, it's just like, 'When are you going to get the chance to do something like this?'

> **EDDY TEMPLE-MORRIS (RADIO DJ):** This is absolutely mind-blowing. It's emotional. I had a moment earlier, when Paul Oakenfold dropped 'Blade Runner' and the sun was going down and I'm in the Stonehenge circle ... this is a moment, this is a hell of a moment we're sharing.

DANNY RAMPLING: I feel so blessed to be here. Incredible. Remarkable. This close to the stones, this ancient monument shrouded in mystery, and how far dance music culture has progressed. We couldn't imagine this twenty years ago but this is where we're at!

NICK HALKES: One of the great things about dance and electronic music is that it gives you the possibility of having amazing experiences literally anywhere. But this is something else.

CARL COX: We are all like-minded people and the music helps bring us together. To have a DJ booth to perform from here is amazing.

MARK MOORE: This is the most magical moment. I've been wanting to come to Stonehenge for a long, long time and finally I get to come and it looks like this! It's mind-blowing! Stonehenge is the cat's miaow!

CARL LOBEN (WRITING IN _DJ MAG_): There was an extra otherworldly feel to the proceedings. When Carl Cox finished on Paul Rutherford's Balearic classic 'Get Real', it was another proper 'moment' for some of the acid house originals in attendance.

TERRY FARLEY: What an experience. Amazing to be here and be part of this. Out of this world ... I was watching something recently on Channel 4, a documentary, and there's a moment where Carl Cox was playing at Space and I thought how wonderful it must be to stand there and think, 'Fuck, I've done something here.' I was thinking, 'I've never had that moment.' We have won awards for the best record label and I've never thought of myself in that way. But I don't think there's ever been a moment. There never was THAT moment. So, that moment when I saw Carl Cox, that was the first time that I thought that and I thought, 'Wow, I've co-achieved a lot of stuff.' It is 'we' – I've always liked collaborating, I don't like doing parties on my own, always had partners. I felt like I was part of something when Oakenfold asked me to be resident.

TINTIN CHAMBERS: I've stood in a lot of green fields seeing music and energy come together but this is as good as it gets.

NANCY NOISE: I said to Paul that his music choice was unbelievable and I nearly broke down in tears … Ennio Morricone, 'Blade Runner', William Orbit, 'Nessun Dorma' … I kind of held it together … and with the lights and the visuals … very, very special.

PAUL OAKENFOLD: I feel … how do I feel? Mixed emotions. Lucky, privileged, a wonderful experience. It's never been like this ever so there's only so much you can say. I haven't taken it all in, ask me in a few hours. It's one of those.

It was definitely 'one of those'. It was emotional with so much love in the air and a moment of dance music history. Here we were, standing in a field, possibly the most significant greenfield site in the world, with a sound system, and being welcomed with open arms. This is that moment to use the phrase 'full circle' to bring everything together and tie it to Stonehenge, but that would imply that we were back where we started. We aren't. We are so much further along. Now electronic dance culture is understood, accepted and listened to – and that's just the way we want it. The media coverage was huge. Television, print, online and radio, were all fully supportive. From *Mixmag* and *DJ* to *Rolling Stone*, the BBC and CNN, who put it out through all their territories, everyone got behind it and got it! You couldn't ask for a better example of how much support and understanding for dance music there really is, or better proof that dance music really has conquered the world.

There, I said it. Dance Music Has Conquered The World!

Dance music has always been about pushing boundaries and opening doors and this special event has helped elevate the whole dance music culture that we are all part of. This was all about being able to experience the magic at the sacred stones and connect directly to the ancient peoples whose essence remains all around Salisbury Plain. But it was much more than that, it was the beginning of the next stage of the electronic journey. With dance music we are only limited by our imaginations.

Dance music is now the soundtrack to everything we do – it is the soundtrack of now and of tomorrow.

As Alfredo says, 'It is the rhythm of your heart.'

It hasn't been an easy journey but it's been a fun one. Today's established and emerging artists have a rich history to draw on and a wealth of experience to tap into. They haven't been handed it on a plate but they don't have to struggle like the pioneers did to get where they want to be. Lucky them.

From small beginnings and with the vision of a handful of pioneers in Chicago, New York, London, Ibiza and Detroit, the dance music few became a global army, met by a grateful public who threw the gates open to the conquerors and welcomed them with open arms. Dance music conquered the world and embraced its captives. Everyone was welcome to join up, no one would be put to the sword. As they listened to the DJs the DJs listened to them, and they shaped a scene together that continues to grow and evolve.

The thing about dance music and its rich history is that you don't have to look back in order to go forward. You don't need to understand what went on at the Paradise Garage, Future, Shoom, Spectrum, The Trip, Shelley's, Warehouse, RIP, Energy, Space, The Loft, Haçienda or Amnesia to broaden your mind and be part of the electronic family tree. Just know that when the latest DJ plays the latest tune in the latest venue to a 21st-century-born crowd who might be enjoying their first night out ever, and raises his or her hand in the air and smiles, they are subconsciously and unknowingly giving a salute to the people and places that made the scene possible, made it what it is. And from somewhere not too far away, possibly over their shoulder or perhaps in a parallel universe, the great Frankie Knuckles is smiling back at them.

Winning over our hearts and minds is one thing – now it's all about keeping us dancing.

'The Only Way Is Up, Baby!'

APPENDIX A

OUR GUIDES

ALFREDO – The Alchemist. Without Alfredo there probably wouldn't have been a Second Summer of Love. His lengthy DJ sets inspired the Ibiza Four who had their call to arms in 1987 under his spell on the open-air dancefloor at Amnesia. It is almost as if he then sent his disciples out to spread his message of openness and love to the world. Alfredo still weaves his unique magic and continues to inspire on dancefloors in Ibiza and across the globe.

BRANDON BLOCK – The Jester. Brandon started his DJing career in his local pub just before the acid house explosion and went on to see the scene as it emerged from behind the booth at his residencies including Up Yer Ronson in Leeds, Scream in Plymouth, FUBAR at Nicky Holloway's Milk Bar, his Sunday Session on the Space terrace in Ibiza, and Club For Life in London. His antics in Ibiza, often with fellow DJ Alex P, are the stuff of legend, and he became a big part of 90s Ibiza's hedonistic story.

CARL COX – The King. From the earliest days of the rave scene, when he was known as the 'Three Deck Wizard' and 'The People's Choice', to the festivals, clubs and digital playgrounds of today, Carl was and still is the king of the dancefloor. He continues to push the boundaries musically and his sets are consistently the most downloaded and listened to across all electronic genres and across all platforms. Ruling his dancefloor subjects with warmth and generosity, he wears a double crown as he is also the undisputed King of Ibiza. Carl has climbed the dance music ladder from the very bottom to the very top and from where he stands on the highest rung looking down he has no equal. He can be having fun touring Australia with his 'Mobile Disco', playing on his own stage at Burning Man, headlining a festival or playing in a small basement; he doesn't care as long as he can share his music. 'Oh Yes, Oh Yes!'

CARL LOBEN – The Commentator. There isn't much about dance music that Carl doesn't know. His insights into the global club scene, every aspect of DJ culture and where dance music is going are second to none and he shares his passion, knowledge and expertise with us as a journalist, lecturer, radio presenter and DJ. Carl has been one of the leading cultural observers of the global electronic music scene since the early 90s and is editor-in-chief of *DJ Mag*.

CYMON ECKEL – The Voice. Cymon was a founder of *Boy's Own* and during the Second Summer of Love focused on keeping the fanzine relevant and authentic. At the same time he was at the very centre of all the *Boy's Own* activities, including organising and promoting the parties, the club nights, merchandise, the label and dealing with the letters in response to *Boy's Own*'s very own canine reporter, Millwall the dog, whose main role was to harass different football clubs' supporters. Cymon ('pronounced Cymon') is a pivotal part of the story of the acid house scene.

DANNY RAMPLING – The Pioneer. Not only was Danny present at the creation of the scene, he was its very heart and soul. After having his epiphany on the dancefloor of Amnesia in Ibiza in '87, Danny went on to create Shoom, the club that gave us the smiley face and the 'Danny Dance', and introduced Alfredo's Balearic style of free-thinking to dancefloors all over the world. The significance of Danny's visionary approach and the importance of this to the way we club and dance today cannot be underestimated.

DAVE SWINDELLS – The Observer. Dave documented the whole scene from behind the lens of his camera. The club and nightlife editor for *Time Out* for over twenty years, Dave promoted an underground scene through a readily available publication, with even the smallest underground club night being able to reach a wide audience. Every musical style was catered for and Dave would be out and about 'reviewing' clubs like Shoom, where he captured an exuberant Gary Haisman dancing in his *Boy's Own* T-shirt with his hands in the air, as well as attending the raves and warehouse parties like the famous *Boy's Own* party, where he took the famous haystack shot. His lens was the world's window to the Second Summer of Love.

FATBOY SLIM – The Funk Soul Brother. Above the trademark Hawaiian shirt is one of the most recognisable faces across all the dance music genres. The face of Norman Cook and his alter ego, Fatboy Slim. On either side of that face are his ears, and those ears are among the most finely tuned instruments in the business. Those ears, coupled with his deep musical knowledge, boundless energy and unlimited enthusiasm, have helped make Norman one of the greatest producers, crossover pop stars and DJs to emerge from the scene. His own songs like 'Praise You' and 'Right Here, Right Now' defined a generation and his head-nodding remixes for the likes of Cornershop, Beastie Boys, Jungle Brothers, Eric B. & Rakim, X-Press 2, Rebel MC, Groove Armada, Wildchild and A Tribe Called Quest are as good as they come.

GRAEME PARK – The Northern Crusader. No one helped spread acid house across the North more than Graeme. Aside from his countless DJ bookings around the country and across the globe, during the acid house explosion Graeme held weekly residencies in Sheffield, Leicester, Nottingham and Manchester. His residencies at the Haçienda lasted ten years and his first one there was from 1988 to '92 when he and Mike Pickering turned the place into one of the greatest venues in the world. From his DJ sets in clubs and his radio show to performing live alongside a full orchestra at the Royal Albert Hall, Graeme continues to educate and entertain us.

IRVINE WELSH – The Wordsmith. No one has documented the highs and lows of being part of youth culture in the 80s and 90s better than Irvine. We are lucky that someone with his skilful penmanship and depth of feeling and honesty for what was going on was actually there and experiencing it for himself. The style of his books, including *The Acid House*, *Ecstasy: Three Tales of Chemical Romance* and *Trainspotting*, spoke to a generation influenced by rave culture. The soundtrack to the *Trainspotting* movie caught their imagination and resonated with a global audience who only a few years earlier, like Irvine, had been part of the emerging rave scene.

JAMIE CATTO – The Cosmic Healer. Jamie's take on the Second Summer of Love is not the typical rave experience for the simple fact that Jamie wasn't a raver and wasn't really in to dance music – 'the best stuff is great, but it's not my genre of choice'. Jamie was and is all about opening up the heart and mind through channelling natural energy, individually, collectively and creatively; this comes across with his *1 Giant Leap* albums where he collaborates with some of the finest musicians in the world. Before this he was the co-founder of the multi award-winning Faithless, which would become one of the biggest acts on the dance music circuit and give us electronic music anthems including 'Insomnia', 'God is a DJ' and 'Salva Mea'.

JAY STRONGMAN – Daddy Cool. Jay was the most influential DJ in the UK in the early 80s, playing at the most influential clubs and parties. He was one of the few DJs who could always pull a crowd. With Jay and his record boxes behind the controls you knew you were in for a good time. Jay rode the acid house wave as a bystander to the underground scene, not being in the inner circle of the Ibiza-influenced movement or part of their new club scene, but still delivering the new sounds to an international club crowd at the venues populated by the movers and shakers, style leaders and opinion formers that ran in parallel and often in tandem to it.

JON PLEASED WIMMIN – Mr Blonde. Jon Cooper, better known to his legions of fans as Jon Pleased Wimmin or Jon Pleased or Jon of the Pleased Wimmin depending when you first heard about him, was 'discovered' as a DJ by Danny Rampling before becoming one of the most sought-after DJs on the UK and international scene. As a DJ and club face, Jon has been an observer at some of the greatest parties from the 90s onwards, including Dave Beer's Back to Basics, Pushca, Miss Moneypenny's, Cream and Renaissance. His flamboyant cross-dressing is not an act, it is Jon expressing himself as he wants to, which is what the true spirit of acid house was all about.

MARK MOORE – The Superfly Guy. Some people are lucky to be in the right place at the right time. Some people put themselves in the right place with hard work. From the start of his career Mark instantly became one of the most influential DJs. He was able to transcend the trendy club scene where he was a celebrated headliner and the acid house scene where he was an in-demand guest. DJ, producer and recording artist, his band S-Express was the first crossover pop group to emerge from the acid house scene.

MIKE & CLAIRE MANUMISSION – The Free Spirits. The Ibiza we know today owes everything to their iconic Manumission parties that came from Manchester and went on to rule the Balearic Islands, bringing glamour, sophistication, decadence, eroticism and naughtiness to the club scene. They set the bar so high that it is still out of most promoters' reach. Their parties were really shows, an assault on the senses, where the décor, the performers and the creative spirit along with the music propelled the Manumission ethos globally. Mike & Claire were the stars and their understanding of the burlesque and cabaret artforms are showcased at their international five-star costume extravaganzas.

MOBY – The Thinker. Arguably one of the most important figures in electronic dance music (EDM), Moby helped bring dance music into the mainstream on both sides of the Atlantic when his album *Play* went on to sell in excess of 10 million copies, with each track from the album being licensed for TV shows and TV advertising. Always experimental in his approach, his breakthrough literally came on the back of his first single as Moby entitled 'Mobility'. The B side, 'Go', was massive. Underground, overground, no matter which way you looked at it, the track was something special and has gone on to sell more than two million copies. He's worked with a wide range of artists including David Bowie, New Order, Public Enemy and Daft Punk, and continues to excite with each new project.

MR C – The Geezer. From the start of acid house Mr C, aka Richard West, has been at the forefront of the action. The fast-talking MC and DJ at the original Clink Street parties went on to own The End club and was at the epicentre of the tech house sound where he fused house and techno. He stormed the charts as the frontman of The Shamen with the controversial 'Ebeneezer Goode', while releasing underground tracks under a variety of names. He criss-crosses the globe with his Superfreq parties, making sure that the USA, in particular, can experience 'the sound of the underground'.

NANCY NOISE – The Balearic Queen. Without Nancy acid house would not have been what it became. From the first nights at Amnesia with the Ibiza Four to her residencies at clubs like Future and her collaborations with Paul Oakenfold, Graeme Park, Terry Farley and Lisa Loud (the First Lady of House and her partner in Loud Noise), Nancy Noise was a pioneer. She was into the scene before it was a scene and was the most passionate of all the Amnesiacs. She wasn't a DJ and hadn't planned on being one, she just understands how to enjoy the spirit and energy which transformed her life. More than any other DJ, she became wedded to the Balearic style of playing and continues to bring her love of music to the dancefloors.

NICK HALKES – The Insider. Nick is music industry through and through. He understands the dynamic between label and artist, having seen the business from both sides as well as orchestrating a host of dance music-related activities. If you bought a smiley T-shirt in Ibiza in '88, chances are it came from Nick. Remember 'The Bouncer' with the immortal line 'You're name's not down, you're not coming in'? by 'Kicks Like a Mule'? Nick Halkes again. The founder of two leading labels, XL Recordings and Positiva, Nick currently manages a roster of electronic music artists including the Prodigy's Liam Howlett and the Stanton Warriors.

NICKY HOLLOWAY – The Ringmaster. What Nicky didn't know about promoting wasn't worth knowing. As a promoter and DJ he saw the scene from both sides of the DJ booth and was already very well established before his eyes were opened at Amnesia in '87. His Special Branch parties were a scene all of their own. It was Nicky who invited his 'apprentice', Danny Rampling, to join him on that special adventure in Ibiza that gave rise to the Ibiza Four. Nicky's vision and experience gave us The Trip, which put acid house slap-bang into the public eye. One of the 'founding fathers', he was also close enough at the birth of acid jazz to cut the cord.

PAUL OAKENFOLD – The Guvnor. Paul is electronic music's greatest ambassador. Not many people can claim to have been instrumental in the birth of a genre of music but Paul has stood in that delivery room three times (so far). Having kick-started acid house from the UK, and then single-handedly championed a style that would become known as trance (which would lead to his phenomenal *Essential Mix*, The Goa Mix) Paul went on to spearhead the EDM scene from the USA. His iconic birthday celebrations in Ibiza would result in him launching Spectrum, the club that became the blueprint for modern club culture and propelled him to quickly becoming the first global DJ superstar when he supported U2 and then, alongside his record label Perfecto, one of the most important ambassadors for the entire dance music scene. Paul continues to be at the forefront of the scene as a DJ, songwriter, recording artist, talent spotter, innovator, producer, remixer and label boss.

PETE HELLER – Mr Big Love. Pete has been a mainstay of the electronic music scene from the early days at Shoom, where he was a resident DJ. Pete quickly found that he had an ear and a knack for production and alongside his own tracks has remixed artists like the Chemical Brothers and Moby's 'South Side', which charted high in the US billboard charts and was Moby's most successful US single. Having met the *Boy's Own* crew at Shoom, Pete became known for his many studio collaborations with Terry Farley, including producing 'All Together Now' for The Farm, which they did with Suggs from Madnesses. They also still often DJ together, where Farley & Heller bring a dynamic selection of quality beats, rhythms and tunes to the dancefloor.

RUSTY EGAN – The Instigator. The original Blitz Kid and a consummate mover and shaker, you can't imagine London nightlife without him. DJ, artist, promoter, producer, drummer, A&R, pop star, introducer, remixer, club owner – Rusty has been cutting a dash ever since he exploded onto the scene. New wave, punk, New Romantic, electronica – Rusty was there. He knows how to introduce important new acts, and the bands he was in as a drummer including the Rich Kids, Skids and Visage were no exception. Musically, Rusty has always been at the forefront of future sounds, introducing Kraftwerk, the Yellow Magic Orchestra and Ultravox to the British club scene and spearheading the 80s electronic and synthpop movement with Visage. Nightlife and club culture wouldn't be the same without him.

TERRY FARLEY – The Rock. One of the greats of acid house, Terry is what it is all about. Terry got it. A football-mad, street-fashion-loving soul boy whose *Boy's Own* thing alongside residences at Shoom, Spectrum and Land of Oz helped define the scene, Terry was present at every key moment and his love of the scene and his wonder at being part of something so special propelled the whole culture forward. Terry is as solid as they come, loyal to his friends, respectful of the legacy created by his heroes, appreciative of his many fans and supporters, and with no time for anyone negative. As a DJ he plays globally and as a producer, often collaborating with Pete Heller, his official remix magic is found everywhere from the deepest underground artist to the 'King of Pop', Michael Jackson. His *Boy's Own* fanzine immortalised dance culture as it was happening and his label, Junior Boy's Own, gave us acts like the Chemical Brothers, Underworld, Roach Motel, Fire Island and X-Press 2.

TINTIN CHAMBERS – The Optimist. In 1988 Quentin 'Tintin' Chambers (and it's not such an unusual name – before Fatboy was Norman he was also a Quentin) saw something pure and reached out to it. As an aspiring DJ, he hooked up with old friend Jeremy Taylor and acid house character Anton Le Pirate to form Energy, which would start holding their epic outdoor raves in 1989. The Energy raves were fantastic, done properly and put the ravers first. They set the benchmark that everyone would need to follow. The best 'Turbo' sound system, the brightest lights and phenomenal DJ line-ups including Carl Cox, Mr C, Paul Oakenfold (once billed as 'Oakenfield'), Jazzy M, Fabio and Joey Beltram. Watched closely by the police's Pay Party Unit, he was famously once chased by 'undercover' officers driving a Citroen 2CV, wearing dungarees and with a smiley sticker in the window.

TREVOR FUNG – The Catalyst. Sometimes being in the right place at the right time is all it takes. Sometimes you need a little nudge. Trevor Fung gave the nudge that resulted in the Second Summer of Love and the subsequent worldwide dance music explosion. It was Trevor, already an established club DJ, who gave Oakenfold his first DJ gig, and Trevor who showed the Ibiza Four around Ibiza. Along with his cousin, Ian St Paul, they brought them to Amnesia and introduced them to the mind-expanding magic of listening to Alfredo under the stars. Back in the UK, he was a big part of the acid house scene, playing at every major night. Deservedly recognised as the important pioneer that he is, Trevor continues to make dancefloors jump.

APPENDIX B

A PLAYLIST TO GET YOU IN THE SECOND SUMMER OF LOVE MOOD ...

A Guy Called Gerald – 'Voodoo Ray'

Elkin & Nelson – 'Jibaro'

Phuture – 'Acid Tracks'

The Night Writers – 'Let the Music (Use You)'

Lil Louis – 'French Kiss'

Larry Heard – 'Can You Feel It?'

Marshall Jefferson – 'Move Your Body'

Joe Smooth – 'Promised Land'

Rhythim is Rhythim – 'Strings of Life'

Mr Fingers – 'Acid Attack'

D Mob – 'We Call It Acieed'

Pierre's Pfantasy Club – 'Dream Girl'

Farley Jackmaster Funk – 'I Need a Friend'

Frankie Knuckles – 'Your Love'

Royal House – 'Can You Party? (Can You Feel It?)'

Adonis – 'No Way Back'

Paul Rutherford – 'Get Real'

Inner City – 'Good Life'

ACKNOWLEDGEMENTS

I have to start by acknowledging why writing this book has been such an enjoyable journey. It is because of the love and support from my wife, Samantha, and our children, Felix, Lara and new arrival Serena – who was born just in time to make the publishing deadline. This book is dedicated to them with all my heart.

I'm very fortunate to be motivated by my parents, Neville and Emma, who continue to guide and encourage me and to enjoy this love with my sister, Lauren, and my brother, Lee, who have shared more than a few dancefloors with me.

Thank you to those who went above and beyond to provide me with exclusive interviews and insights: Terry Farley, Nancy Noise, Mike and Claire McKay aka Mike and Claire Manumission, Carl Cox, Norman Cook aka Fatboy Slim, Richard West aka Mr C, Moby, Nicky Holloway, Paul Oakenfold, Carl Loben, Danny Rampling, Alfredo, Mark Moore, Pete Heller, Trevor Fung, Tintin Chambers, Jon Cooper aka Jon Pleased Wimmin, Irvine Welsh,

Graeme Park, Cymon Eckel and Brandon Block. You are all part of something so special and continue to champion new music to new generations of clubbers. I feel honoured and privileged to have shared this rollercoaster ride with you.

Paul Oakenfold and Danny Rampling – thank you for painting such a vivid picture and sharing your innermost thoughts and feelings. Looking forward to our next adventures.

They say a picture is worth a thousand words and I am very grateful for the pictorial support with this book from Dave Swindells, Dan Reid, Mike and Clare, Phil Silcock, Craig Hellen and Simon Brown. I must also thank Ellie Jacobs for helping transcribe the interviews and Carl Loben for getting me started.

The words and pictures came together under the watchful eye of James Hodgkinson, my editor at John Blake, and the team there, including the fantastic Lisa Hoare and Katie Greenaway. Great job! I am so thankful for all your hard work, the guidance and the deadline extensions!

Thanks for helping make Sunset at Stonehenge into such a phenomenal success: Oli Bartlam, Robert Barbieri, Anton Nelson, Dan Tait, Paul Dakeyne, Jay Cunningham, Luke Purser, Zoe Sobol, Fraser Boyes, Tim Binns, Tom Parkinson, Julien James Davis, Eddy Temple Morris and the Universe crew. Reaching out to 'Thag' with a cosmic high-five.

Without the Second Summer of Love, I'd be telling a different story. So, my final thanks must go to the hundreds of original Amnesiacs, Shoomers, Futurists, Spectrumites, Land of Ozers, and Tripsters who created a Summer of Love that inspired thousands, then hundreds of thousands and then millions and then hundreds of millions. Look what you started!

INDEX